Teaching Mathematics in Diverse Classrooms for Grades K–4

PRACTICAL STRATEGIES AND ACTIVITIES THAT PROMOTE UNDERSTANDING AND PROBLEM-SOLVING ABILITY

Volume 1

Benny F. Tucker
UNION UNIVERSITY

Ann H. Singleton
UNION UNIVERSITY

Terry L. Weaver
UNION UNIVERSITY

PEARSON

Boston   Columbus   Indianapolis   New York   San Francisco   Upper Saddle River
Amsterdam   Cape Town   Dubai   London   Madrid   Milan   Munich   Paris   Montréal   Toronto
Delhi   Mexico City   São Paulo   Sydney   Hong Kong   Seoul   Singapore   Taipei   Tokyo

Executive Editor and Publisher: Stephen D. Dragin
Editorial Assistant: Kate Wiley
Marketing Manager: Joanna Sabella
Production Editor: Paula Carroll
Editorial Production Service: Element LLC
Manufacturing Buyer: Megan Cochran
Electronic Composition: Element LLC
Cover Designer: Jennifer Hart

Previous editions were published under the title *Teaching Mathematics to All Children: Designing and Adapting Instruction to Meet the Needs of Diverse Learners* © 2006, 2002.

Many of the designations by manufacturers and sellers to distinguish their products are claimed as trademarks. Where those designations appear in this book, and the publisher was aware of a trademark claim, the designations have been printed in initial caps or all caps.

Library of Congress Cataloging-in-Publication Data
CIP data not ready at press time but is on file.

10 9 8 7 6 5 4 3 2 1

www.pearsonhighered.com

ISBN 10: 0-13-290728-3
ISBN 13: 978-0-13-290728-6

brief contents

contents

3 BEGINNINGS:
Mathematics Learning in Early Childhood   25

4 WHOLE NUMBERS AND NUMERATION:
Naming and Writing Quantity   42

5 ADDING AND SUBTRACTING WHOLE NUMBERS:
Combining and Separating Quantities   65

8   DECIMALS:
Working with Base-Ten Units Smaller Than One   172

9   MEASUREMENT:
Assigning a Number to a Quantity   189

about the authors

Benny F. Tucker earned his Ph.D. at the University of Illinois in 1975. He has authored or co-authored more than 50 books, on topics ranging from teaching methods for elementary school mathematics to the use of instructional activities in the mathematics classroom. He has authored or co-authored more than 20 articles in professional journals and has made more than 30 presentations at professional conferences.

Ann Haltom Singleton is Associate Dean of the School of Education at Union University in Jackson Tennessee. She earned her Ed.D. in Special Education from the University of Memphis. Her research areas include leadership development and mathematics instruction, especially in inclusive settings. She has contributed to numerous articles and has made over 30 national presentations. She was recognized as the Union University 2003 Faculty of the Year.

Terry L. Weaver honed his teaching skills in the Miami-Dade County School System. He received his Ph.D. in Special Education from George Peabody College for Teachers at Vanderbilt University. Dr. Weaver then shared his teaching skills at Carson-Newman College and Union University where he continues to teach. Dr. Weaver has served as an item writer for and participated in the revalidation of the Praxis II Specialty Area Test in SE (Core Knowledge). He is a co-author of *Teaching Mathematics to All Children: Designing and Adapting Instruction to Meet the Needs of Diverse Learners*, has presented on differentiated instruction and assessment, universal design, inclusion, and adapting instruction for diverse learners, and recently lead the revision of a chapter on mathematics in Vaughn's and Bos's *Strategies for Teaching Students with Learning and Behavior Problems*.

preface

Why This Book?

The diversity of students in K–4 classrooms is extensive. The children in a typical class-room are diverse in gender, diverse in race and ethnicity, and diverse in religion and culture. They are diverse in ability, diverse in interests, and diverse in preferred learning styles. And they are diverse in family background, and diverse with respect to resources in the home such as books and technology. In the face of such diversity, how can the teacher expect to plan for effective instruction?

Although teachers must certainly be aware of student diversity and the need to accommodate that diversity, it is perhaps more important for K–4 teachers to be aware of the ways in which their students are alike. For example, almost universally, children are kinesthetic learners. It is natural for them to be active and move around. They love class-room activities that allow (even require) them to be energetic and animated. Children are also naturally inquisitive. They are interested in what, why, and how. It is the nature of children to be curious about things. They like to talk to one another, to exchange ideas, and to discuss the things that they are experiencing and learning. Children are concrete learners. They enjoy handling things, seeing how things are related. They like to understand.

In this text, we provide an approach to the planning and teaching of K–4 mathematics that is based on the nature of children. We believe that the teaching suggestions in this text will help teachers be more effective as they plan and teach *mathematics in diverse classrooms, grades K–4.*

Structure of the Book

The book begins with two introductory chapters that provide a basic understanding of instructional activities and lesson planning. Then there are nine chapters devoted to teaching the content that most commonly appears in K–4 mathematics textbooks. We do not attempt to provide comprehensive coverage of every topic that might appear in a K–4 textbook. Rather, our intent is to emphasize a way of teaching effectively that will result in learning, understanding, retention of important concepts and skills, and an ability to apply those concepts and skills to solve problems. Important to that way of teaching is effective planning. Therefore, we have made planning for effective teaching an important part of this text.

Emphasis on Concept and Skill Development

On the basis of findings of educational research that support a more thorough development of concepts and skills as well as our personal experiences, we have chosen to emphasize more effective development of mathematical concepts and skills. As a result of that emphasis, virtually all activities suggested in the chapters are developmental activities (activities that develop specific concepts and skills). Because we made a conscious choice not to include practice activities in those chapters, we have devoted a section of the instructor's manual to activities and games that can be used for effective practice after the concepts and skills have been developed.

Basic Philosophy

We believe that successful teaching results in understanding, and that understanding provides the most sound basis for skill development and better retention of what is learned. The best way to help students understand mathematical ideas is to lead them to connect those ideas to other ideas that they already understand. For elementary school children, understanding of mathematical concepts and skills depends on the development of appropriate mental imagery for those concepts and skills. And we believe that *all children* should be given the opportunity to develop that kind of understanding of mathematics.

Acknowledgments

This book evolved from informal conversations with many colleagues about how teachers could plan to teach more effectively, from preservice and in-service teachers who responded to our ideas before they were fully formed, and from reactions of children who demonstrated that the more fully evolved teaching methods really worked. And, of course, invaluable assistance was provided by these professionals, whose reviews of the preliminary manuscript helped to direct the text into its final form: Rebecca Gehrke, Arizona State University; Karen Lafferty, Morehead State University; and Kevin Stanger, Brigham Young University, Idaho. Finally, we wish to thank the preservice and in-service undergraduate and graduate students who provided suggestions for clarification of this text.

Benny F. Tucker
Ann H. Singleton
Terry L. Weaver

one

INSTRUCTIONAL ACTIVITIES

The Building Blocks for Effective Instruction

What Are the Students Learning?

A common pitfall for teachers who use an activity-based program of instruction is to focus on the procedures of the activity and to judge its instructional value primarily on how fun it is, on how much the students like it, or on how "neat" it is. Certainly, we want learning to be fun. We want our students to like learning, and we want to do things with them that are "really fun." However, really fun isn't enough. The primary criterion for judging an instructional activity should be: *What are the students learning during the activity?* It follows, then, that the first step in selection of an instructional activity must be identification of the learning objective, and determining the nature of the objective. The kind of activity that should be used depends on whether the objective is for students to learn something new, to become proficient with something that they have already learned, or to be able to use what they have already learned to solve problems, or whether the objective is for the teacher to find out what level of mastery the student has achieved. For our purposes in this book, we will classify activities into four types:

1. Developmental (for new learning)
2. Practice (for development of proficiency with material already learned)

1

3. Application (for problem solving using concepts and skills already learned)
4. Assessment (for demonstration of level of learning)

Developmental Activities

Developmental activities are activities that teach something new. If students have to already know the target concept or skill in order to do the activity, then the activity is not developmental. There are two distinct levels of developmental activities: exploratory and consolidating.

Exploratory Developmental Activities

The purpose of *exploratory developmental activities* is to provide a core of experiences that will form the basis for generalization of concepts or skills. Sometimes the student's previous life experiences are an adequate basis for the needed generalizations. But more frequently, it is necessary to create opportunities for students (at least some of them) to have the needed experiences. This necessity arises out of the obvious fact that before student experiences can be used by the teacher to develop a new idea, the students must have had those experiences.

Consolidating Developmental Activities

The purpose of *consolidating developmental activities* is to help students to identify patterns and recognize relationships, to hypothesize and test those relationships, to clarify concepts, to develop procedures, and to learn terminology and notation with which to communicate about those patterns, relationships, concepts, and procedures.

Practice Activities

Practice activities are activities that help students to become proficient in the use of concepts and skills that have already been developed. Whereas the emphasis of developmental activities is to develop comprehension or understanding, the emphasis of practice activities is to develop skill. As a general rule, students do not learn new things from practice. However, through practice, they may very well become more proficient with what they have already learned. Appropriate practice may also help to add more permanence to that learning. As is true with developmental activities, there are two distinct types of practice activities: think time and speed drill.

Think-Time Practice Activities

Think-time practice activities place the emphasis on accuracy. The student has adequate time to think carefully about concepts and connections, and plenty of time to think carefully through each step of a procedure. The student may even be allowed time to look up things that need clarification. Students are told, "There is no hurry, but be sure you are right."

Speed-Drill Practice Activities

Speed-drill practice activities place the emphasis on quick answers. Some teachers believe that speed drill can contribute to memorization and to the ability to habituate procedures. Other teachers point out that, under speed-drill conditions, answers come from only the students who already have quick recall of the facts or those who can already quickly apply the procedure. These are, of course, precisely the students who do not need this practice. On the other hand, those who cannot respond quickly are encouraged to make a wild guess or simply say "I don't know" and then stop thinking about it.

We must seriously consider whether the overall effect of speed drill is negative rather than positive. Indeed, with very few exceptions, very little is accomplished with speed-drill practice that would not be accomplished more effectively with appropriate think-time practice. Speed-drill practice activities will, therefore, receive limited attention in this book.

Application Activities

Application activities are activities that help students learn to use concepts and skills in settings that are different from the settings in which those concepts and skills were learned. Application activities allow students to use the concepts and skills that they understand and are proficient with to solve a variety of problems. Application activities can be categorized into two groups: classroom applications and real-world problems.

Classroom Applications

Classroom applications include instructional activities that require students to build on already-learned concepts and skills by using them to develop new ones. Since an activity may involve application of old ideas to develop new ones, it follows that a single activity could be application with respect to one topic and also developmental with respect to another topic. Classroom applications also include contrived examples, such as textbook problems, that require students to use recently learned concepts and skills. A thin line separates this kind of classroom application from practice. The difference is that practice typically requires students to use the new concept or skill more or less as they used it when it was being learned. On the other hand, contrived examples used as classroom application typically require students to use the new concept or skill in ways that are, to some degree, different from the ways the concept or skill was used when it was being learned.

Real-World Problems

Real-world problems are problems like those that students will encounter outside the classroom. To devise a real-world problem that applies a particular concept or skill, the teacher must first determine how that concept or skill is used outside the classroom (that is, in the real world). The next step is to create an activity that will require the student to use the concept or skill in exactly that way.

Assessment Activities

Varied Assessment Methods

Assessment activities require students to demonstrate, in an observable way, their depth of learning of concepts and skills. Assessment nearly always consists of having students complete a task or several tasks that are indicators of their learning. For example, the teacher might ask students to complete a chapter test or to do homework consisting of a set of exercises, or the teacher might simply ask a student to answer a straightforward question. Unfortunately, assessment is often superficial because the assessment task is incomplete.

The old story about six blind men describing an elephant illustrates such an incomplete assessment. One blind man felt the side of the elephant and concluded that an elephant is like a wall. A second blind man felt the elephant's leg and decided that an elephant is like a tree. A third blind man felt the elephant's trunk and believed that an elephant is like a large squirming snake. A fourth blind man felt the elephant's tusk and decided that an elephant is like a large sword. A fifth blind man felt the elephant's ear and believed that an elephant is like a fan. The sixth and last blind man felt the elephant's tail and concluded that an elephant is like a rope.

Of course, all the blind men were correct but each of their descriptions was based on a biased perspective. Their descriptions of the elephant were correct but incomplete. Similarly, our assessment of student learning is often incomplete because, like the blind men, we rely on limited information. Instead of basing our assessment on a single assessment task, we can get a more complete, a more reliable, a more useful assessment of student learning if we get our information from a variety of sources.

People normally think of assessment as a formal process like giving a test or quiz, usually after the teacher has completed instruction. Such assessment can determine whether the students have learned the material that was taught. It can determine what material was not learned. And, it can even determine how effective the teacher was. This assessment information can inform the planning of future lessons. However, there is another approach to assessment that has many additional benefits.

Monitoring and Assessment

A typical lesson would include a variety of instructional activities. For example, a short practice activity may be used to review previously learned material. A series of developmental activities may be used to teach a new concept or skill. There might be an application activity that illustrates how the new material can be used. Each of these different parts of the lesson is an opportunity for the teacher to *monitor student understanding* and *gather assessment information.*

The significant characteristic that allows traditional instructional activities to produce assessment information is that *the teacher is paying attention.* The teacher must carefully monitor the students during every instructional activity. The teacher must take note of who knows and who does not know, as well as what the students know and what they do not know. The teacher must be aware of the contexts in which each student can and cannot do what is required. This information will provide a clear understanding of the student's level of learning. If the teacher is observing and gathering information (monitoring), then *every developmental, practice, or application activity can also be an assessment activity.*

Monitoring student learning should be an essential and integral part of every instructional activity. By continually monitoring the students' work, the teacher is able to make adjustments during the lesson for those students who are having difficulties. For example, the teacher might realize that other examples are needed, or he might refer back to prior knowledge that is the basis for the new lesson. Another possibility is the teacher might assign a practice activity, allowing students to work with partners while he works with individuals who are having difficulty.

An Example of Varied Assessment Methods.

Suppose, for example, that a teacher needs to test whether a particular child understands how to add a column of three or more numbers. The child's ability could be assessed in a variety of ways. The teacher could send students to the board to work examples. While they are working, the teacher would assess the students' ability to solve the problems correctly. However, this procedure can be embarrassing to students who are having difficulty. The teacher can eliminate the embarrassment by using one or both of the following procedures. The teacher might simply give the child a short test consisting of several column-addition examples. On the other hand, the teacher might give the child a few varied examples of addition of three or more numbers and ask the child to explain and demonstrate how to complete the additions. The first two assessment methods are objective. The teacher is concerned about whether the answers are correct. These methods are quick and to the point. The third method is subjective. The teacher is not concerned primarily about whether the answers are correct, but rather about whether the child understands and can use the procedure. This assessment process takes more teacher time and requires teacher value judgments about the student's understanding.

Either of two other methods might be used instead. The teacher might design a project for the student to complete that will require the student to add three or more multidigit numbers. Or, the teacher might move around the room as students are working with partners on practice exercises and observe the work of that particular student on the addition exercises. In both of these methods, the student is unaware that the assessment is taking place. The first of these two methods is an example of performance assessment. The addition takes place in a setting that is more "natural." However, the knowledge being assessed is integrated into a task that involves more than just addition. Therefore, if the student is unable to complete the project satisfactorily, it is not always clear which of the integrated concepts and skills was the problem. The second of these two methods is probably the simplest, requiring no test, no interview, and no project. Rather, the teacher merely remains alert to what is already going on in the classroom. However, a teacher assessing by observation as described here will need a clear, easily used procedure for keeping track of who knows what and who does not.

We have described five different ways to assess the learning of addition of three or more multidigit numbers. Any of these five assessment methods may be appropriate, depending on what information the teacher wishes to discover.

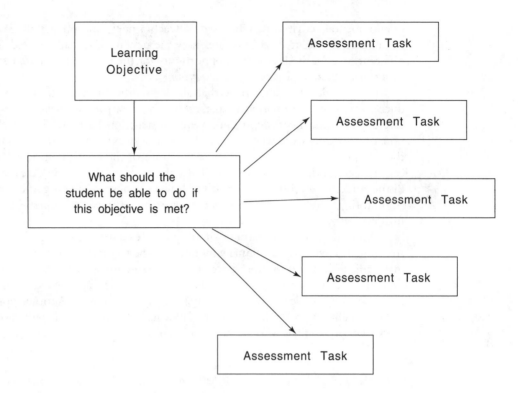

Level of Involvement

A key factor in the selection of instructional activities is the level of student involvement that will occur during the activity. The teacher always has a limited amount of time to teach, and the student always has a limited amount of time to learn. It is reasonable, then, to want to maximize the student's involvement in learning.

If the teacher teaches for 10 minutes but the student pays attention for only 2 minutes, that is a 20% level of involvement. We would certainly hope for better. If 6 students are playing a game where the players take turns and are not required to participate in any way when it is not their turn, that is 16.7% involvement. That is not good. If the teacher has an activity that requires virtually 100% involvement of 1 student while 23 other students wait, that is 4.2% involvement, a deplorable level of involvement.

Children and young people do not like to be left waiting with nothing to do; they want to be mentally stimulated. Russian psychologist Mihaly Csikszentmihalyi has studied this phenomenon. He uses the term *flow* to describe the brain when it is so involved in an activity that time becomes irrelevant to the person. To achieve flow, the activity must be challenging but not so challenging that a student becomes so frustrated that she gives up. Teachers must monitor students carefully to control students' foundering during these kinds of experiences if the activity is to create flow in a classroom. If teachers do not control students' foundering or if teachers allow "dead time," time when students are not involved, those students will find something to do, and more often than not, the teacher will dislike what they find to do. Indeed, behavior problems are often a direct result of the teacher's employing learning activities with a low level of student involvement that do not evoke flow.

Perhaps a word of caution would be appropriate here. Increasing the level of involvement *will* improve and maintain attention. However, it is essential that the teacher keep in mind that student involvement in useless activity has little value. What we should always be seeking is a high level of involvement in activities that are *purposeful*—activities that will help move the child toward achievement of the learning objectives.

It is impossible to achieve 100% involvement for any group of students and virtually impossible to reach that goal with a single student. But invariably teachers can improve the level of student involvement—first, by being aware of its importance, and, second, by constantly searching for ways to adjust procedures to increase the level of student involvement. All the activities included in this book are effective for learning, but they vary in expected level of student involvement. Level of involvement is not the only consideration, but it is an important one. Therefore, as you consider the activities presented, apply the level-of-involvement test. Is the level of involvement high? Is it high enough for your situation?

Flexible Use of Activities and Materials

In order to develop an activity-based system of instruction, the teacher must identify content topics and then develop a variety of instructional activities for those topics. Activities for each topic should include developmental activities, practice activities, application activities, and assessment activities. Pencil-and-paper activities, physically active activities, whole-class activities, small-group activities, or individual or partner activities should be included. The teacher's work can be reduced substantially if the teacher considers the ways that those activities can be used flexibly. Since virtually any effective instructional activity or game can be adapted and used in other content areas and at other levels, a game or an activity that works well with one content topic should be adapted for use with a variety of content topics. When a teacher has found a particularly nice set of materials or has spent time and effort to develop such a set of materials, it is always useful to consider the many ways that those materials might be used. In this way, a single set of materials can be adapted to meet a variety of instructional needs.

Exercises and Activities

1. Suppose you are preparing to teach first-grade children to add two- and three-digit numbers with regrouping (renaming, carrying). Describe an exploratory developmental activity that will give the children preliminary experience with regrouping outside of the context of addition. To build mental imagery for the regrouping process, use bundled sticks in the activity.

    For example, the number represented here:

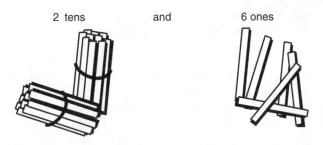

2 tens   and   6 ones

is the same as the number represented here:

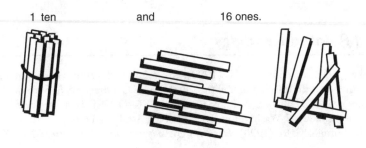

1 ten   and   16 ones.

2. Suppose you are preparing to teach a measurement lesson to third-graders on the customary units of length (inches, feet, and yards). Before teaching the lesson, you want to establish the need for standard units. Describe an exploratory developmental activity that will give the children an understanding of why we need standard units of length.

3. Consider the following instructional activity for teaching how to find the area of rectangles. Decide whether the activity is a developmental activity or a practice activity. Explain your reasons.

   Display, on the walls of the classroom, about 20 rectangles cut from colored construction paper. Write the length and width in inches on each rectangle. Have the children work with partners. Each pair of partners should choose and find the areas of 2 rectangles.

4. It has been said that whenever teachers evaluate the work of their students, they are also evaluating the work of their students' teacher. Explain what you think this statement means. If this statement is true, why is it important to include assessment activities in your lessons?

5. "Standard 6 in *Professional Standards for Teaching Mathematics*, (NCTM, 1994)

6. Choose any lesson from a commercially published elementary school mathematics textbook. Analyze the lesson plan that is presented in the teacher's guide. With respect to its contribution to learning of the stated lesson objective, identify and label each part of the suggested lesson plan as developmental, practice, application, or assessment.

7. This game is a practice activity for *hard basic addition facts*:

   Prepare a set of 24 cards, each showing a hard basic addition fact with the answer missing. Give the cards to two children and have them play this game: After the cards are shuffled, the dealer gives each player 4 cards, facedown. When the dealer says "Start," the players race to arrange their cards in order, from smallest answer to largest answer. If the first player to finish is correct, that player gets 1 point. If the other player challenges the result, the first player must prove the answers. The players repeat the process until all the cards have been played. The player who scored the most points is the winner.

   Adapt this game for the topic *area of triangles*.

8. This activity is a developmental activity for teaching triangles:

   Display about five triangles, all with different shapes. Explain that these shapes are all triangles. Ask the children to tell you what is the same for all triangles. (Answers may vary. For example, the children may point out that all the triangles have three sides. Or, they may say that all the triangles have straight sides. Or, they may notice that all the triangles are closed figures.) If they indicate that all the triangles have three sides, agree with them that all triangles have three sides, then draw a counterexample like the one on the right. Ask if this is a triangle. Ask why not. Repeat this process with counterexamples that do not have other required characteristics of triangles.

   Adapt this activity for teaching *rectangles*.

9. Find an article that describes a learning activity or game. Analyze the activity or game and decide whether it is developmental, practice, application, or assessment.

References and Related Readings

Baker, J. M., & Zigmond, N. (1990). Are regular education classes equipped to accommodate students with learning disabilities? *Exceptional Children, 56,* 515–526.

Bransford, J. D., Brown, A. L., & Cocking, R. R. (1999). *How people learn: Brain, mind, experience, and school.* Washington, DC: National Academy Press.

Csikszentmihalyi, M. (1990). *Flow: The psychology of optimal experience.* New York: Harper and Row.

National Council of Teachers of Mathematics. (1989). *Curriculum and evaluation standards for school mathematics.* Reston, VA: Author.

National Council of Teachers of Mathematics. (1991). *Professional standards for teaching mathematics.* Reston, VA: Author.

National Council of Teachers of Mathematics. (2000). *Principles and standards for school mathematics.* Reston, VA: Author.

Websites

www.ed.gov/pubs/EarlyMath/index.html
A site targeted at parents. Good parental involvement ideas.

www.ed.gov/pubs/parents/Math/index.html
What parents can do at home.

www.sedl.org/pubs/classroom-compass/
Instructional ideas in math.

http://mathforum.org/mathed/assessment.html
Links to articles.

www.nap.edu/catalog.php?recrod_id=2336
Measuring what counts.

www.learner.org/exhibits/dailymath/
Applications of math in daily life.

LESSON DESIGN

Creating Lessons That Meet the Needs of a Diverse Classroom

CHAPTER OUTLINE

Combining Activities into a Lesson

What Is a Lesson?

A *lesson* is a related set of instructional and learning activities organized in a coherent manner. It is generally organized in parts, each of which is designed to accomplish some part of the process needed to meet the learning objectives. For our purposes, we will organize our lessons into five parts. Although other components may also be included, most lessons would include lesson opener, development, monitoring learning, practice, and lesson closure.

Lesson Opener.   The lesson opener should provide context for the concept or skill being developed. It draws the attention of the student and smoothly leads into the lesson.

Development.   This part of the lesson provides the experiences that help students to learn the new concept or skill. Development should smoothly build on what they already know. Students progress from not knowing to knowing the new material. Development leads to their being able to do the independent practice exercises.

10

Monitoring Learning.　Ideally, this part of the lesson is not separated from the other parts of the lesson. When learning is constantly monitored, the teacher will be aware of who understands and who does not, of when teaching is being understood and when it is not, of what needs to be retaught, and of what needs to be taught differently. Some teachers mistakenly think they are monitoring learning by walking around the classroom making sure students are on task. Monitoring learning involves teachers stopping and listening to student dialogue and even inserting themselves into conversations.

Practice.　Practice provides reinforcement of what has been learned in the development part of the lesson and should not begin until the teacher is sure that understanding of the concept or skill has been accomplished. If the students do not yet understand, then more development is needed before the practice.

Closure.　The closure of the lesson allows the students to think about what was learned during the lesson and to reflect on the importance of this new information. Often, during closure, students are asked to verbalize their understanding of the concept or skill presented and are given the opportunity to demonstrate their learning by solving one more problem from the current lesson.

A Traditional Lesson Plan

We begin by examining a plan for a mathematics lesson that was developed by following the kind of suggestions that are typically provided in the teacher's guide. This lesson plan is very traditional. It calls for the teacher to teach the textbook pages in the way that most teachers would teach them. The lesson plan is actually a fairly good one.

LESSON OBJECTIVE

The student will recognize symmetric shapes and lines of symmetry.

Lesson Opener

State the following: "We have already learned to recognize congruent figures. Today we will learn to identify figures that are symmetric."

Development

Begin by showing half of each of the following shapes: circle, heart, star. Have students identify the shapes by looking at the half shapes:

Next, direct students' attention to the example here. Ask them how they could check to be sure that the two halves of the triangle are congruent. Point out that if the triangle were folded along the dotted line, the two halves of the triangle would match exactly. They would be congruent.

Tell the students that when a shape can be folded in half like this so that the two halves match exactly, then the shape is *symmetric*. We call the line along which the shape was folded the *line of symmetry*.

Tell the students that some shapes have more than one line of symmetry. Direct their attention to the shape on the right. This shape could be folded in two ways so that the two halves match exactly. This shape has *two* lines of symmetry.

Monitoring Learning

Lead students through the *Check Understanding* examples in the student book. On the basis of student responses to those examples, identify the students who have difficulty understanding.

Practice

Assign the *Reteaching Worksheet* to those who would benefit from reteaching. Assign the practice exercises from the student book to the rest of the students.

Closure

As math time is ending, remind the children:

1. A *symmetric* shape is one that can be folded so that the two halves match exactly.
2. The fold line for symmetric shapes is called the *line of symmetry*.

The Nature of Standard Traditional Lessons

Traditional lessons that follow suggestions from the teacher's edition are usually good lessons. Traditional lessons normally have two common characteristics. First, they are designed to teach the textbook pages. Second, they are aimed at the average child. In general, they serve their purpose well. The difficulty, of course, is that very few students fit that "average mold." Such lessons typically do not take into consideration the diverse learning preferences of most children.

Adapting Lessons for Diverse Learning Needs

Rather than attempt to provide separate adaptations of these lessons for every child's learning needs, we will adapt the lessons by expanding the types of activity that appeal to most learning-style preferences and that provide for most learning needs. It is understood, of course, that even after these suggested changes are made, additional adaptations may very well be needed to provide for some children. Traditional lesson plans will be adapted in the following five ways.

First, the developmental part of the lessons will be expanded. This is the most important thing that can be done to make lessons more effective—if we equate effectiveness with students' learning of concepts and skills. More thorough development of concepts and skills can be accomplished in several ways. Understanding must develop out of personal experiences with real things. Those experiences should be designed to allow the children to "see" important relationships and procedures. The nature of what we help them see should provide them with useful mental imagery for the concepts and skills being learned.

Understanding must be developed by helping the children see and understand how what is being learned is related to other things they already know (Carpenter, 1986; Ginsburg, 1989). These interrelationships should have an almost-constant emphasis. Whenever a teacher is trying to help a child understand something new, a common approach should be "Let's think about what we already know that can help us here." This will tap into the child's previous learning and encourage many more natural interconnections that enhance memory and recall.

In the development of concepts, a wide variety of examples and nonexamples should be examined. For every example of the concept, the children should discuss why it is an example. For every nonexample that is identified, the children should discuss why it is not an example. The why and why-not questions keep a constant focus on the essential characteristics of the concepts being learned.

The children should continually search for patterns and learn to generalize concepts and procedures from those patterns. Their ability to test those generalizations by trying them out to verify whether or not the generalization is correct helps develop students' confidence.

An excellent developmental teaching method is one called the **laboratory approach**, in which the students are led through a series of steps:

1. **Explore (or experiment).** In this step, the student explores the topic under the guidance of the teacher, using a physical or pictorial model. Usually, the student is led to use the model to find a variety of results (answers). If the process is modeled effectively, the student will believe that the results are correct. Because he can see where the answer came from, common sense will tell the student whether the answer is correct.

2. **Keep an organized record of results.** The teacher leads the student to record the results achieved with the model. The recording is done in a way that will facilitate recognition of the patterns that the teacher wants the student to notice.

3. **Identify patterns.** The patterns should be stated in the language of the student: "Every time we did this, the answer turned out to be . . . ." The patterns will suggest ways to get the result (answer) without using the model.

4. **Hypothesize (or generalize) how to get results without the model.** "We can get the answer by . . . ."
5. **Test the hypothesis (the generalization).** Complete an example using the hypothesized procedure. Then redo the example using the model to verify that the result is correct.

This instructional process, which is an **inductive** process, is utterly convincing to students, for they have discovered a way to get answers that are believable. They can literally see where those answers come from and they have seen the procedure working.

There is, however, one real danger in the use of inductive teaching. The results are derived from experience with a series of examples. If the examples are not sufficiently varied, it may be possible to find a pattern that is consistent for the examples used but not consistent for all examples. It is possible for patterns drawn from special cases to lead to procedures that are true of those special cases but not true in general. For example, suppose you used a model to discover that:

$$\frac{1}{3} + \frac{1}{5} = \frac{8}{15}, \quad \frac{1}{3} + \frac{1}{6} = \frac{9}{18}, \quad \frac{1}{2} + \frac{1}{3} = \frac{5}{6}, \quad \frac{1}{4} + \frac{1}{3} = \frac{7}{12}, \quad \text{and} \quad \frac{1}{5} + \frac{1}{2} = \frac{7}{10}$$

The children might see that, in every case, the numerator of the answer is the *sum of the denominators* of the fractions being added, and the denominator is the *product of the denominators* of the fractions being added. Although this "rule" is true whenever you are adding unit fractions, it is not true when you are adding other kinds of fractions. During instruction, then, the teacher should avoid making generalizations based on special cases, because children tend to apply those generalizations in settings for which they are not appropriate.

More thorough development of concepts and skills accomplishes several important things. Development results in more complete understanding, a common result when interconnections with other things that students know are emphasized. Because of those interconnections, retention of what is learned is better. Because of improved retention, much less time needs to be spent on review and practice. Due to the interconnections and better understanding, students are better able to apply what they have learned to solve problems.

The second way to adopt lessons is to provide more visual input. In most lessons, there is more than enough auditory information; however, students nearly always need more visual information. For example, procedures are described, but students need to have them demonstrated. Teachers tell students rules and directions, but students need to see them written down and demonstrated. Teachers tell students what a rectangle is, but they need to be shown. Teachers explain how to borrow in subtraction, but students need to see a 10 being traded for 10 ones.

Third, the lessons will be adapted to include more kinesthetic activity. Children are not passive creatures. Motion is an integral part of what they are. They fidget, wiggle, and squirm. They like to interact actively with things. They like to try things and do things. Teachers can wear themselves out trying to make children sit still. Lessons that place a high premium on sitting still and listening go against the nature of children. Kinesthetic learning activities, on the other hand, encourage children to move. They use the child's natural tendency toward movement for learning. Fewer behavior problems result because the child is able to do what is natural without getting into trouble. Because the child is involved both physically and cognitively in the learning activity, attention problems are reduced. It should be noted that kinesthetic learning activities are particularly effective for students with attention deficit disorder (ADD) or attention-deficit/hyperactivity disorder (ADHD).

Fourth, the lessons will be adapted to encourage more communication from and among the students. The classroom should be viewed as a community of learning. All members of that community should be a part of an intellectual exchange about mathematics (Baroody, 1996). Together, they should explore ideas, gather information, look for

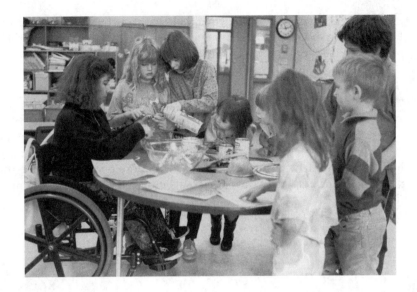

patterns, generalize concepts and procedures, and try out those generalizations and adjust them on the basis of their experiences. Unfortunately, teachers may not feel confident in discussing mathematics in this way. Many teachers come to the mathematics classroom with little experience in articulating their understanding. Some strategies to facilitate communication from and among students include (1) asking a student to explain or summarize another student's response, (2) asking a student to give an alternative way of solving a problem, (3) asking a student how a problem is similar to a previous type of problem, (4) asking a student how a problem is different from a previous type of problem, (5) asking a student how a problem demonstrates a key concept, and (6) asking a student how understanding the problems solved during a lesson can be used in everyday life. All of this requires constant communication within the learning community. One benefit of increased communication is a deeper sense of involvement on the students' part. Learning activities should be planned that encourage—and even require—communication from and among the students, as well as from the students to the parents (Escalante & Dirmann, 1990).

Fifth, the lessons will be adapted to make monitoring of learning more continuous throughout the lesson. Too often, learning is monitored only after the lesson has been taught. An after-the-fact check on learning can inform the teacher whether or not the lesson has been effective. However, if the lesson has failed with the whole class, or even with individual children, the teacher must wait until next time to clarify unclear ideas, correct skills that are full of errors, or straighten out misconceptions. By then, those unclear ideas, error-filled skills, and misconceptions will have been practiced and will be more difficult to undo. Rather, the teacher must monitor learning while it is happening. In the midst of the lesson, understanding must constantly be checked so the teacher has a strong sense of what is understood and what is not, of what the students can do and what they cannot, and of who is learning and who is not. The teacher should know when the teaching is being effective and when it is not, when another teaching example is needed, when a different approach is needed, when students are interested and when they are not, and when instruction is working and when it needs to be changed.

In summary, lesson planning that is more likely to be appropriate for all students in a diverse classroom includes accomplishing the following:

Expanded development using
    increased visual imagery
    increased kinesthetic activity
    increased student communication while
Continually monitoring learning and gathering assessment information

Adapting a lesson in this way makes it appropriate for a diverse group of children. However, you should also bear in mind that further adaptations may still be necessary to provide for the specific needs of some children.

A Lesson Adapted for Diverse Learners

On the following pages is a lesson plan adapted from the traditional lesson plan on symmetry that we have already seen. As you consider this adapted plan, note how much more time is devoted to development. Also note how visual input has been increased, how kinesthetic activity has been added, how more opportunities for student communication are included, and how learning is monitored during all the major activities of the lesson.

LESSON OBJECTIVE

The student will recognize symmetric shapes and lines of symmetry.

Lesson Opener

Cut symmetric figures in half along their lines of symmetry and pass out the picture halves to the children:

Explain that you have cut some pictures in half and that each person has half a picture. Have each student find the other student who has the matching half of the picture. Ask the students what they can say about the two halves of a picture when the halves are an exact match. [Remind them if necessary of previous learning. They are congruent.] **Monitor understanding**. Identify students who do not understand or who are having difficulty. Provide assistance to these students.

State the following: "We already know what congruent figures are. Today we will learn to identify symmetric figures."

Development

Prepare eight sheets of tracing paper with large letters on them. Prepare two copies of each of the letters *F, O, S,* and *Y*. Show the letters to the students:

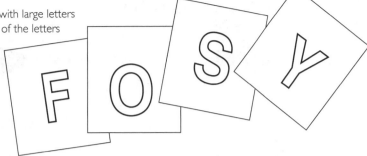

Ask which of the letters could be cut into halves so that the two halves would be an exact match. Allow children to come to the front and cut the sheets.

Ask how we could check to make sure before cutting. [We could fold the paper.] Fold the *Y* to see if the two parts will be an exact match. Have children come to the front to see if they can fold the other letters to get an exact match.

Group the students with partners. Hand out to each pair of partners a shape that has been cut from paper. Some shapes should be symmetric and others should not be symmetric:

In order to differentiate for students who are not ready for the level of difficulty of the above shapes, the teacher could choose to start with the following shapes.

Tell the students to work with their partners to try to fold the shape so that the two parts are an exact match. When everyone is finished, have them show what they found out. **Monitor learning**. Identify students who are having difficulty and provide assistance.

Tell the students that when a shape can be folded in half like this so that the two halves match exactly, the shape is **symmetric**. Write "symmetric" on the chalkboard. Tell the students that the line along which the shape is folded is the **line of symmetry**. Write "line of symmetry" on the board.

Have everyone with a symmetric shape hold it up for the class to see. Have those with shapes that are not symmetric hold them up for the class to see. **Monitor learning**. Identify students who do not understand and, at the first opportunity, provide assistance.

Next, direct students' attention to the following example. Point out that if the triangle were folded along the dotted line, the two halves of the triangle would match exactly. The shape is *symmetric*. The dotted line is the *line of symmetry*.

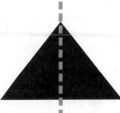

Tell the students that some shapes have more than one line of symmetry. Direct their attention to the second shape on the page. This shape could be folded in two ways so that the two halves match exactly. This shape has two lines of symmetry.

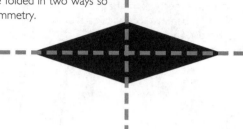

Hold up a square. Tell the students that a square also has several lines of symmetry. Have a student come to the front and fold the square to show one line of symmetry. Have another student try to fold the square to show a different line of symmetry. Continue until all four lines of symmetry have been found.

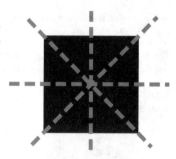

Show the students a shape like the one pictured at the right. Have students come forward and fold the shape to find lines of symmetry. Ask how many lines of symmetry the shape has. [three]

Use the third example on the student page to demonstrate how to use scissors to cut a symmetric shape from a folded sheet of paper. Have two students come to the front and cut out other symmetric shapes.

Lead students through the *Check Understanding* examples in the student book. **Monitor learning**. On the basis of student responses to the *Check Understanding* examples, identify those students who are having difficulty understanding.

Practice

Group the students with partners. Have them work with their partners to complete the practice examples in the student book. **Monitor learning**. Pay extra attention to the students who have been having difficulty and their partners. If their difficulties continue, provide help or reteaching.

Closure

As math time is ending, ask what kind of shapes we have learned about today. [Symmetric shapes.] Ask how we can tell if a shape is symmetric. [Symmetric shapes can be folded so that the two halves match exactly.] Ask what we call the fold line in a symmetric shape. [The fold line is the line of symmetry.]

Follow-Up

Tell the children to explain to their parents what a symmetric shape is. Have them, with the help of their parents, make a list of symmetric things that they see at home.

Adapting Another Lesson

Now we will adapt another lesson, this time a lesson on regrouping in addition. Again, we will begin with a traditional plan that follows suggestions like those found in a teacher's guide. As was true of the previous lesson, this is not a bad lesson. But notice that there is very little time spent developing understanding of the concepts and skills of the lesson.

LESSON OBJECTIVE

The student will add a two-digit number to a one-digit number and regroup ones to tens.

Lesson Opener

Choose students to give answers to the following facts: 2 + 5, 6 + 7, 4 + 6, 5 + 7, 8 + 5, and 5 + 4. Ask why 2 + 5 and 5 + 4 are different from the other facts. State the following: "Sometimes when you add, you have fewer than 10 ones and sometimes you have 10 or more ones. Today we will learn to regroup ones to tens."

Development

Begin by having a child read the following sentence: *If I join these two groups, I can make another group of ten.* Have the children point out the numbers 25 and 7. Ask, "How many ones are in the first number? How many ones are in the second number? How many ones are there altogether? Are there enough ones to circle 10? How many tens are there altogether? How many ones are left?"

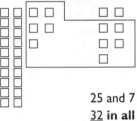

25 and 7

32 in all

Have the children write 32 in the answer blank.

Monitoring Learning

Lead students through the *Check Understanding* examples in the student book. On the basis of student responses, identify those students who have difficulty understanding.

Practice

Assign the *Reteaching Worksheet* to those who would benefit from reteaching. Assign the practice exercises from the student book to the rest of the students.

Closure

As math time is ending, remind the children that when they have 10 or more ones after adding, they must group 10 ones to make another ten.

Adapting the Lesson for a Diverse Group of Students. As you consider the adaptations to this lesson plan, notice the increase in the quantity of developmental instruction. Notice also the shift in instructional emphasis from teaching the pages of the student book toward an emphasis on teaching the concept. As before, we will increase visual input, kinesthetic activity, student communication, and monitoring of learning.

LESSON OBJECTIVE

The student will add a two-digit number to a one-digit number and regroup ones to tens.

Lesson Opener

Write 25 on the board. Have a child come forward to represent that number by using base-10 blocks. Have the student place the blocks in a box. Ask other students, "How many ones are in the box?" "How many tens?" Tell them to watch carefully. Drop 2 more ones into the box, one at a time. "Now what number is in the box? How many tens? How many ones?" Complete the addition sentence 25 + 2 = 27 on the board. Have a child look in the box to check the answer. Repeat the process with 32 + 4, and then with 46 + 3, except write the addition in vertical form.

$$\begin{array}{r} 32 \\ + 4 \\ \hline 36 \end{array} \qquad \begin{array}{r} 46 \\ + 3 \\ \hline 49 \end{array}$$

Repeat the process with 28 + 5. After the 5 ones have been added to the box, ask how many tens are in the box and record the 2 tens in the answer. Next, ask how many ones are in the box and record the 13 ones after the 2 tens.

$$\begin{array}{r} 28 \\ + 5 \\ \hline 213 \end{array}$$

Ask the children if that answer looks right. Ask what is wrong. (The student or you will answer: *It looks like we have 2 hundreds, 1 ten, and 3 ones.*) Point out that there is room to write only one digit in each place. So if you have 10 or more ones, that is too many to write. **Monitor learning**. Use these examples as an opportunity to be sure that all the children understand how to represent numbers with the base-10 blocks. Take note of those having difficulty and provide extra help.

State the following: "Today we will learn that when we have too many ones to write, we trade 10 ones for a ten."

Development

Begin by writing 43 on the board and labeling the tens and ones. Have a child come to the front and choose the base-10 blocks to represent that number. Pick up 1 of the tens. Ask how many ones you could trade the ten for. Have a child come forward to make the trade. After the trade is completed, ask, "How many tens are there now?" "How many ones?" Record this new result. Point out that this is still the same amount but is just shown in two ways. Repeat the process, starting out with 64 and trading a ten for 10 ones.

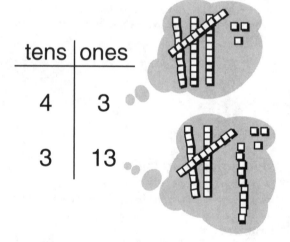

tens	ones
4	3
3	13

Monitor learning. Observe carefully to be sure that all the children understand that after the trade, they still have the same amount. You may need to show both forms of the number side by side so that the children can see that they are the same amount.

Next, reverse the process. Start with 5 tens and 18 ones. Trade 10 ones for a ten and record the number in its new form. How many tens are there altogether? How many ones are left? Repeat with 3 tens and 13 ones and then with 4 tens and 12 ones.

tens	ones
5	18
6	8

Write 28 + 5 on the board and remind the children that this is the example that they looked at earlier. Remind them that when they added 5 to 28, they ended up with 2 tens and 13 ones. Record this example on the board, labeling the tens and ones.

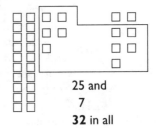

tens	ones
2	8
+	5
~~2~~ 3	~~13~~ 3

Point out that they now know how to make a trade to get an answer that can be written in standard form. Using base-10 blocks, a child to trade 10 ones for a ten and record this result. Repeat the process with 46 + 5 and with 39 + 6. **Monitor learning**. Observe carefully to be sure that all the children understand.

Lead the children through the following example. Point out that the picture is showing base-10 blocks like the ones that they have been using. Also point out that they are to draw a ring around the ones that they would trade.

25 and
7
32 in all

Monitor learning. Observe carefully to be sure that all the children understand how to "ring" 10 ones and how to record their answers.

Practice

Assign the practice exercises from the student book. **Monitor learning**. Observe the children to identify those who are having difficulties. Provide individual assistance to them. If children with lower ability have trouble with the pictured base-10 blocks, allow them to use real base-10 blocks.

Closure

As math time is ending, ask if someone can tell the class what we learned today.

Follow-Up

Write 34 + 8 on the board and have the children copy the problem. Have them take this problem home and explain to their parents how to get the answer.

The Planning Process and "Official" Lesson Plans

When adapting the preceding two lesson plans and when adapting lesson plans in later chapters, we use a format that includes certain lesson components. We understand, however, that teachers are often required to complete lesson plans by using a required format that may include components that are different from those used in this text. Teachers may be required to have lesson plans available for a substitute teacher to use when the regular teacher is absent. The plans may play a role in the teacher evaluation process. In either case, a consistent format is useful and, of course, teachers should comply with the lesson plan requirements.

We emphasize making five adaptations that will increase the thoroughness of the developmental part of the lesson: expand the development of concepts and skills, increase the use of visual imagery, include more kinesthetic activity, encourage (even require) more student communication, and provide for continual monitoring of learning. We believe that these five things are important when lessons are being planned or when lessons are being adapted to make them more effective for diverse students. It is this planning *process* that is important rather than any particular lesson format. However, for consistency—so that the reader can easily see how we have emphasized these five adaptations—we will use the same lesson format throughout the text.

The Planning Process and Teaching Notes

It should also be noted that the adapted lesson plans are very long and detailed. Again, we believe that the planning process should be very detailed. Thorough planning includes planning every teaching example so that the child is able to recognize the patterns that can be generalized into the concepts and skills that are being taught. Thorough planning includes anticipation of questions that might arise and what responses are appropriate. Thorough planning includes deciding what materials are needed and exactly how they will be used. Thorough planning includes determining what you will ask, what you will ask students to do, and what you will look for so that you will know who is learning what and how well he or she is learning it. Thorough planning includes all these things and more; so, when a teacher writes down what he or she has thoroughly planned to do, the teacher will have a very long and detailed lesson plan.

A teacher who attempts to teach from such a plan will often get lost in the detail and end up focusing on the written lesson plan instead of on the students. When the focus of the teacher is not on the students, many undesirable results may occur, ranging from unawareness that students do not understand to serious student behavior problems. Therefore, after a lesson has been thoroughly planned, the teacher might translate the plan into brief teaching notes that are sufficient to guide the lesson but are not so detailed that they will distract the teacher's attention from the students. Or the teacher could use the power of word processing (e.g., bold type, spacing, italics, or enlarged font) to modify the lesson plan and make that plan a more teachable tool.

Exercises and Activities

1. Read the discussion of "Standard 3: Knowing Students as Learners of Mathematics" on pages 144–150 of *Professional Standards for Teaching Mathematics*, published by the NCTM in 1991. Compare and contrast the recommendations in this chapter with those included in the discussion of this standard.

2. Choose a lesson from any published elementary school mathematics program.
   a. Identify the developmental part of the lesson. Describe how to expand the developmental part of the lesson.
   b. Identify procedures that the authors suggest that provide information to the students visually. Describe ways that additional visual input could be provided.
   c. Identify the ways that the children are involved. Describe how you could involve the children in more kinesthetic activity.
   d. Describe how you could provide more opportunities for the children to communicate among themselves and to the teacher about the concepts or skills being learned.
   e. Identify the parts of the lesson in which the teacher should monitor learning. In each case, what should the teacher be looking for?

3. Choose a lesson from any published elementary school mathematics program. Adapt the lesson by expanding the developmental part of the lesson, providing for more visual input, adding more kinesthetic activity, increasing opportunities for student communication, and calling for continual monitoring of learning.

4. Read Assumption 1 on page 17 of *Curriculum and Evaluation Standards for School Mathematics*, published in 1989 by the NCTM. How does this assumption relate to the recommendation in this chapter that the developmental part of lessons be expanded?

5. Read the discussion of "Standard 2: Mathematics as Communication," on pages 26–28 of *Curriculum and Evaluation Standards for School Mathematics*, published by the NCTM in 1989. How does this standard relate to the recommendation in this chapter that the lessons should include more communication from and among children?

References and Related Readings

Baroody, A. J. (1996). An investigative approach to the mathematics instruction of children classified as learning disabled. In D. K. Reid, W. P. Hresko, & H. L. Swanson (Eds.), *Cognitive approaches to learning disabilities* (pp. 545–615). Austin, TX: PRO-ED.

Carpenter, T. P. (1986). Conceptual knowledge as a foundation for procedural knowledge: Implications from research in the initial learning of arithmetic. In J. Hiebert (Ed.), *Conceptual and procedural knowledge: The case of mathematics* (pp. 113–132). Hillsdale, NJ: Erlbaum.

Escalante, J., & Dirmann, J. (1990). *The Jaime Escalante Math Program*. Washington, DC: National Education Association.

Ginsburg, H. P. (1989). *Children's arithmetic* (2nd ed.). Austin, TX: PRO-ED.

National Council of Teachers of Mathematics. (1989). *Curriculum and evaluation standards for school mathematics*. Reston, VA: Author.

National Council of Teachers of Mathematics. (1991). *Professional standards for teaching mathematics*. Reston, VA: Author.

National Council of Teachers of Mathematics. (2000). *Principles and standards for school mathematics*. Reston, VA: Author.

Whitin, P., & Whitin, D. J. (2002). Promoting communication in the mathematics classroom. *Teaching Children Mathematics, 9,* 205–211.

Websites

http://www.corestandards.org/the-standards/mathematics
The Common Core State Standards for Mathematics.

www.idonline.org/indepth/adhd
Links to resources on ADHD.

www.nctm.org/standards/
Principles and standards for school mathematics.

http://nctm.org/about/
About NCTM.

www.mcrel.org/compendium/SubjectTopics.asp?subjectID=1
Math standards and topics.

www.nwrel.org/psc/bestofnw/singleprac.asp?id=74&phrase=mathematics
Report on an exemplary school program that used a visual, hands-on approach.

http://teachers.net/lessons/
Lesson plans from teachers.

www.proteacher.com/100000.shtml
Lesson plans for content areas.

three

BEGINNINGS

Mathematics Learning in Early Childhood

CHAPTER OUTLINE

A Common Misconception

People who have not studied child development often think that very young children do not have previously learned concepts and skills on which to build. But, in fact, the opposite of this is true (Baroody, 1987; Court, 1920). Prekindergarten and kindergarten children are nearing the end of a period of extremely rapid intellectual growth. They are normally excellent problem solvers. They are very intuitive, in that they use their past experiences to make sense of new experiences. They are concrete thinkers, basing new ideas on their physical experiences.

About Young Children

Because young children learn new things in context rather than in isolation, it is generally agreed that the best approach to the teaching of early childhood mathematics is to keep the mathematical ideas in natural contexts. For example, if the child is learning about one-to-one matching, then one-to-one matching should be examined in the contexts where the child will see one-to-one matching naturally. The child might place one plate on the table for each person in the family—one for mommy, one for daddy, and one for me. The child might then place one napkin at each plate, and so on. Or, in another context, the child might experience one-to-one matching by placing one toy with each of five dolls.

A common phenomenon is a situation in which a child does some task in an orderly way and with apparent purpose to produce a result that makes absolutely no sense to the

teacher. For example, suppose a child is given an assortment of geometric shapes and asked which shapes go together. (The teacher obviously expects the child to choose the circular shapes, or the square shapes, or perhaps the shapes with some other common attribute.) The child might choose a large triangle and a small square. Although the teacher does not believe those two shapes go together, the child might choose them because, as they were presented, these two shapes together reminded the child of a tree:

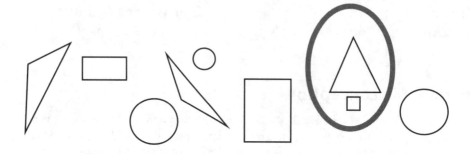

When shown a set of large and small red and blue circles and squares and told to pick out the ones that are alike, another young child might select the large red square, then select the large blue square, then select the large blue circle, then select the small blue circle:

Most teachers might not understand the criteria that children use to select the shapes. However, among young children, criteria for classification often do not remain constant. For example, after the first shape was chosen, this child may have chosen a shape that was like the last one selected. The first shape was a large square (a large red square), so another large square was selected (a large blue square). The second shape was a large blue shape so another large blue shape was selected (a large blue circle). The third shape was a blue circle, so another blue circle was selected (a small blue circle). The child was selecting shapes with the same characteristics, but the common characteristics were constantly changing.

In both of these cases, many teachers would be tempted to conclude that the child has simply given a wrong answer. However, when you are working with a young child, it is almost always more productive to assume that the answer is correct and then try to determine what question the child has answered. The teacher needs to work hard to "get inside the child's head" to understand how the child is thinking. One way to do this is to encourage the child to talk about the choices that have been made (Baroody, 1996). When the teacher understands why the child thinks those shapes go together, it is relatively easy for the teacher to rephrase the question to channel the child's thinking toward the geometric attributes of shapes. When the teacher understands how young children think, then it is easier to communicate ideas clearly and effectively.

There are three things to remember, then, that will help the teacher of young children be more successful in the teaching of mathematics:

1. Develop new ideas within contexts that are familiar to the children, building on their own experiences.
2. Encourage the children to communicate about mathematics in their own words.
3. Get "inside the heads" of the children. Learn how they think. Learn to think as they do.

Teaching Classification

Concept development is based on *classification*, so helping children develop this skill is an important responsibility of a teacher of young children. When children are learning to classify, their thinking should be focused first on this question: What are characteristics of the included objects? Later, the focus should shift to a second question: Why were other objects not included? We will examine one classification example, considering each of these two questions.

Suppose we are thinking about dogs. If we placed all dogs together, we would have large, short-haired, black dogs with four legs, short tails, pointed ears, and a deep rumbling bark. We would have large, long-haired, brown dogs with four legs, long bushy tails, big floppy ears, and a strong bark. We would have tiny, short-haired, gray dogs with four legs, long skinny tails, pointed ears, and a high-pitched yelping bark. We would have large, white dogs with medium-length hair, four legs, long thin tails, pointed ears, and a bark that sounds like a wailing child. We would have a continuing long list of dogs with widely varied characteristics. These animals are all *examples* of dogs. What characteristics are allowed? What characteristics do all dogs have in common?

But now let's think about some animals that are not included. Here is a small, brown, short-haired monkey with a long thin tail. Why is it not included with the dogs? Here is a large, short-haired, brown calf with four legs, large ears, and a long tail. Why is the calf not included with the dogs? Here is a small, black cat with short hair, four legs, a long thin tail, and a howl that sounds like a wailing child. Why is it not included with the dogs? These animals are *nonexamples* of dogs. What characteristics of dogs do these animals not have? What characteristics do these animals have that dogs do not have? Why are these animals not dogs?

What are the essential characteristics that make an animal a dog? What essential "dog characteristic" is not present in a monkey? *Dogs have four legs. Dogs cannot grasp things with their tails.* These are essential characteristics of dogs. What essential "dog characteristic" is not present in a calf? *Dogs have soft padded feet. Dogs can bark.* These are essential characteristics of dogs. What essential "dog characteristic" is not present in a cat? *Dogs can bark.* This is an essential characteristic of dogs.

In classification, the variety of included *examples lets us see what is allowed* in the class, but the variety of *nonexamples lets us see the essential characteristics* of the members of the class. It is important that we deal with both examples (why they were included) and nonexamples (why they were not included).

The attributes that distinguish learning classifications for young children are typically less complex than the characteristics of dogs. But, young children learn to tell the difference between cats and dogs even though these animals have so many common attributes. They are able to classify, and the reason they are able to classify is that they have been engaged in informal classification all their lives. We will now consider some classification activities that are fairly typical in the early childhood classroom.

A Simple Classification Activity

Activity 3.01   Buttons and Boys

Ask all the boys who are wearing shirts with buttons to come to the front of the class. Discuss the characteristics of the children in this group. Point out ways that members of this group are different and ask why they are in the same group. [They are boys wearing shirts with buttons.]

Point out a boy who is not in the group. Say, "He is a boy. Why isn't he in this group?" [He is not wearing a shirt with buttons.] Point out a girl who is wearing a shirt with buttons and ask why she is not in the group. [She is not a boy.]

A Classification Activity Related to a Story

Activity 3.02   Three Bears

Prepare flannel board cutouts of three bears—one large, one medium, and one small. Also prepare large, medium, and small cutouts of bowls, spoons, chairs, and beds.

Read the story *Goldilocks and the Three Bears* to the class.

Ask the children to tell what bears were in the story. As the father bear, the mother bear, and the baby bear are mentioned, place the large, medium, and small bear cutouts on the flannel board. Point out that these are the bears in the story. Ask if a large hare is part of this group. [No.] Why not? [It is not a bear.] Ask if Winnie-the-Pooh should be in this group. [No. Winnie-the-Pooh was not in the story.]

Show all the other cutouts (the bowls, spoons, chairs, and beds). Ask which of these things belong to Baby Bear. After all the small-sized objects are placed on the flannel board, ask why these things were chosen. [They are baby-bear sized. They are small.] Point out the large bed. Ask if it belongs in this group. Why not? [It is big. It is Father Bear's bed.]

Continue by classifying different groups of objects. Ask why they are included. Ask why other objects are not included.

Classification activities for young student might be teacher directed, as were the two preceding examples, or they might be self-directed. They could be activities for individual children, partners, groups, or the whole class. The classification activities included in this text include examples of all these types.

Pattern Recognition

The ability to recognize patterns is an important skill that is used to generalize concepts beginning in early childhood and continuing at every level in the study of mathematics. In the photo on page 26, students are following a pattern. At each place setting, there is a plate, a spoon, a fork, a napkin, and a cup. This is repeated for each place setting. This placement is an example of the kind of patterns all around us. In early childhood, children learn to identify simple color patterns like the following.

Show this arrangement of colored chips: white red white red

What color comes next?

Show this arrangement of colored chips: blue blue red blue blue red

What color comes next?

The students may learn to identify number patterns like the following.

Show this arrangement of numbers: 10 20 30 40

What number comes next?

Show this arrangement of numbers: 1 3 5 7

What number comes next? (Note that there are multiple correct answers.)

In the primary grades, students will make important generalizations like the following one based on patterns that they see in basic facts.

| Discover answers to | $3 + 0 = 3$ | $0 + 8 = 8$ | $4 + 0 = 4$ |
| these basic facts: | $7 + 0 = 7$ | $2 + 0 = 2$ | |

Notice that whenever 0 is added to any number, the answer is that number.

In every elementary grade, students use patterns to help them remember important concepts. Some patterns are repeating sequences; some are more complex, based on two or more criteria. Throughout this textbook, patterns will be used to develop children's abilities to generalize important concepts. For example, see the symmetry of the decimal number system on page 175. And, when the lesson uses the laboratory approach (see page 158), students are led to look for patterns and generalize concepts and skills from those patterns.

Teaching Comparison and Seriation

Comparison

Objects are compared by relating them with respect to some attribute. For example, if you are comparing two runners to see which one is faster, the attribute you are interested in is *speed*. One runner has more speed than the other runner. If you are comparing two pencils to see which is longer, the attribute you are interested in is *length*. One pencil has more length.

When some things are compared, the comparison could be made with respect to a variety of attributes. For example, if a male college student is comparing two female college students, a number of attributes might be the focus of the comparison, and the result of the comparison will vary depending on the attribute. One of the female students might be taller (more height). The other one might be prettier (more beauty). One might be smarter (intelligence). The other might be older (more age). One might be more popular. The other might be more wealthy. One might be heavier. The other might be more talented. Notice that some comparison attributes are objective (comparing height, age, or weight does not require a value judgment), whereas others are subjective (comparing beauty, popularity, or talent does require a value judgment). A comparison of intelligence or wealth may be either objective or subjective, depending on how it is done.

Before a child can make any comparison, he or she must have developed a sense of the attribute being compared. For example, a child cannot decide which of two objects is longer until a sense of *length* has been developed. Virtually all instruction to develop the ability to make comparisons centers around developing a sense of the comparison attribute. This instruction must use both examples and nonexamples to focus on what the attribute is and what the attribute is not. Size comparisons can be confusing to the child because there are so many different kinds of size—length, area, volume, mass (weight).

When the teacher says "longer," the student often thinks "bigger." So, for clarification, comparison *examples* must include both of these types:

Which is longer? **Which is longer?**

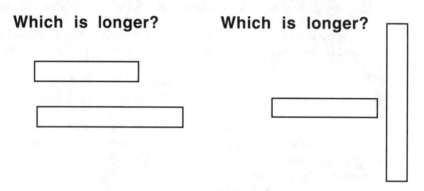

The above examples helps the child understand that we are not talking about thickness. We should also include each of the following types of examples:

Which is longer? **Which is longer?**

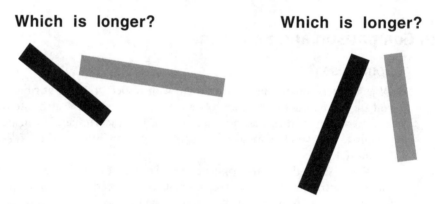

In this case, the above examples helps the child see that length does not depend on direction. We should also include each of the following types of examples:

Which is longer? **Which is longer?**

These examples help the child understand that the concept of length is different from the concept of color. The following example would help the child separate the kind of bigness that we call *area* from the notion of *length*:

Which is longer?

The child should also compare lengths of long objects that are very light and short objects that are very heavy to separate the concept of length from that of heaviness.

We see that in the development of understanding the attribute *length*, our examples must be varied enough to help the child rule out all the other attributes such as thickness, direction, color, area, and heaviness that might be confused with the one being learned. Also, our examples should begin with *gross comparisons*, in which a child who already understands the comparison attribute is easily able to tell which object has more of the comparison attribute. For example, if a teacher wants children to decide which child is taller, then he or she might begin by having them compare the shortest child and the tallest child. Or, if a teacher places objects of varying weights in bags and wants a child to decide which of two bags is heavier, the teacher would begin by comparing a very heavy bag with a very light bag.

After the child is able to make gross comparisons of obviously different objects, the examples should include more difficult comparisons (finer discriminations)—where the objects being compared are more nearly the same with respect to the comparison attribute. For example, if the lengths of objects are being compared, the objects might need to be placed side by side to see the difference. Or, if the weights of objects are being compared, a balance device might be needed to see the difference.

Two Simple Comparison Activities

Activity 3.03   Long and Short Shoes

Choose the tallest child, the shortest child, and three other children of varying sizes. Ask all five children to remove a shoe and then have them bring the shoes to the front of the room. Hold up the longest shoe and the shortest shoe so that they are about 3 feet apart. Ask which shoe is longer. Next, hold up two shoes that are about the same length. Ask which shoe is shorter.

Ask what could be done to make it easier to tell which is shorter. [Hold them next to each other.]

Activity 3.04   Stretch

Spread your hands as far apart as you can. Say, "See how far I can reach." Have all the students stand up and spread their hands out to see how far they can reach.

Have one child guess which child in the class can reach the farthest. Have that student come to the front and show everyone how far he or she can reach. Choose a second child to come forward and stand in front of the first child so the class can see who can reach farther.

If other children think they can reach farther than the first child, have them come forward so the class can make the comparison and decide.

Seriation

Seriation is the ordering of objects according to some consistent criterion. For example, in the photo above, the student is arranging the nested dolls in order of size. Comparison orders two objects, while seriation orders more than two objects.

The process of seriation can be thought of as a *series of comparisons*. This is both the most obvious and the most productive way to teach seriation. The following activity illustrates this process.

Activity 3.05   Tallest and Tallest and Tallest

Choose five children who have different heights, and have them come to the front of the room.

Have the class identify the tallest child in this group. Direct this child to stand next to every other child to verify that he or she is tallest. In other words, compare the height of this child to each of the other children. When the class is sure that the tallest child has been identified, have her or him stand to one side. Tell the class that this child is first in line. Follow the same process to identify the tallest child in the group that remains. Have this child stand second in line with the first tallest child.

Continue this process until all the children in the group have been lined up according to height.

This same process is illustrated in each of the following activities.

A Group Seriation Activity

Activity 3.06   Shorter Than a Yardstick

Hold up a yardstick. Tell the class that you want everyone to find a stick that is shorter than the yardstick and bring it to class tomorrow. You should bring several sticks the next day for children who forgot their sticks.

Form groups of four or five children. Direct them to compare sticks and identify the longest one. Then have them compare the remaining sticks to find the second-longest one. Have them continue this process until they have arranged their sticks in order.

Have each group show its result to the rest of the class.

Ask questions. Use, in context, appropriate length-comparison terminology: *long, short, longer, shorter, longest,* and *shortest.*

A Partner Seriation Activity

Activity 3.07   Up and Down

Have two children experiment with a balance by placing different weights in the pans.

After sufficient time has been allowed for experimentation, ask them why one side goes down and the other side goes up. Have them take turns holding two objects, one that is heavy and the other light. Show them that you are going to place one object on each side of the balance. Have them predict which object will go down and which will go up.

Give them three objects to arrange in order from heaviest to lightest. Monitor their work to be sure that they understand.

Have them show and tell the class what they did.

An Individual Seriation Activity

Activity 3.08   Ordering the Rods

Give an individual student a set of colored number rods:

Have the student make comparisons to arrange the rods in order:

Matching and Prenumber Comparisons

Another type of comparison involves early notions related to *number*. With these comparisons, the focus is not on the size of the objects, but on whether one group has more objects. The comparison is made by matching objects of one set with objects of the other set, one by one. When you run out of objects in one of the sets, then the other set has more. Two examples of this type of comparison follow.

Activity 3.09   More or Fewer

Form two groups of children, one with six children and the other with seven children. Ask the rest of the children how they could decide which group has more. If someone suggests a way to decide, try it to see if it works. If no one suggests the following method, demonstrate it.

Have each child from one group go hold hands with one person from the other group. One child will be leftover. Point out that this child makes the difference between the two groups. The group with the extra child has *more* children. This group has *one more* than the other group. The other group has *fewer* children.

Repeat the activity with groups of other sizes.

Activity 3.10   Birds and Nests

Make cutouts of 12 birds and 12 nests.

Place seven nests on the bulletin board where they can be reached by the children. Place eight birds on a table where the children can see them. Ask the children whether there are more birds or more nests.

Have children, one at a time, place the birds on nests. When there are no more nests, ask again whether there are more birds or more nests.

Repeat with different numbers of birds and nests.

Matching and Prenumber Seriation

A natural extension of using one-to-one matching to compare the numbers of objects in sets is using one-to-one matching to order three sets of objects according to the numbers of objects in the sets. The procedure for doing this is discussed in the activity.

Activity 3.11 The Most Pennies

Choose three children. Give each child a different number of pennies. Ask these children who has the most pennies. The child who thinks he or she has the most must use matching to show that he or she does have more pennies than each of the other children.

Then ask the remaining two children who has the most pennies. Have that child use matching to show that he or she has more.

Have the children line up in order according to the number of pennies they have.

The Beginning of Geometric Concepts: Relative Position

Relative position concepts (*above, below, between, near, far, inside, outside*) build spatial awareness and lay the groundwork for many mathematical concepts, particularly in the area of geometry. An effective way to develop relative position concepts and vocabulary is illustrated in the activities that follow. First, set up a situation where the concept is inherently present. Next, introduce the concept and the vocabulary. Then, use, and have the children use, the vocabulary in a natural context (Tucker, Weaver, & Singleton, 2000).

Above

Activity 3.12 Hold Up?

Give sheets of colored construction paper to four students. One child should have yellow. Another should have green. The others should have orange and purple. Have them hold the papers as pictured. Tell the children that the purple paper is above the orange one. Point to the green paper. Tell the children that the purple paper and the orange paper are both above the green one. Ask the children what colors are above the yellow. Have the children rearrange the papers. Point to a paper. Ask what colors are above the one that you point to. Repeat with other arrangements.

Below

Activity 3.13 What Colors Are Below?

Give sheets of colored construction paper to four students. One child should have yellow. Another should have green. The others should have orange and purple. Have them hold the papers as pictured. Tell the children that the yellow paper is below the green one. Point to the green paper. Tell them that the green paper is below the orange paper and also below the purple one. Ask the children what colors are below the purple. Have them rearrange the papers. Point to a paper. Ask what colors are below the one that you point to. Repeat with other arrangements.

Above and Below

Activity 3.14 Things Above, Things Below

Have four children bring objects such as a baseball cap, a shoe, a picture, a mug, or a book to the front of the room. Have them hold the objects in a vertical arrangement. Name any of the objects and have the children tell which ones are above and below the one you named.

Between

Activity 3.15 Stuff Between

Have the students cut out pictures of objects such as a baseball cap, a shoe, a dog, a tree, or a book and place them on the bulletin board in a vertical arrangement.

Point out two pictures that have another picture between them. Then point to the picture between them. Name the object in the picture and tell the children that it is between the others. Choose two other pictures that have another between them. Have the children tell what is between the ones you identified. Ask the children to move the objects into a horizontal arrangement and repeat the activity.

Activity 3.16 People Between

When the students are lined up to go to recess, art, or music, name two children and ask who is between the ones that you named.

Near and Far.   *Near* and *far* are relative terms. Objects are considered near to us or far from us only relative to other objects. For example, if you are considering people in a room, a person who is 30 feet away might be considered far away, but at a football game, another spectator who is 30 feet away would probably be considered near to you. Because of their relative nature, the *near* and *far* concepts are almost always dealt with together. Often the teacher will ask a child to decide which of two (or more) objects is near (compared to the other objects) and which is far (compared to the other objects). The next activities demonstrate how a teacher can help children to develop these concepts.

Activity 3.17 People Near and Far

When the students are lined up to go to recess, art, or music, identify two children and have each of them hold up a hand. Ask another child which of them is near and which is far away. Repeat with other students.

Activity 3.18 Table Shapes

Cut out three shapes: a square, a circle, and a triangle. Line them up on a table so that they are about 24 inches apart. Identify the first shape on the children's left. Ask which of the other shapes is near to the one you identified. Ask which shape is far from it. Rearrange the shapes and repeat the activity.

Move the middle shape so that it is near the one on the children's right. Call the attention of the class to the middle shape and ask the children which of the other shapes is near to it and which is far from it.

Inside and Outside

> ### Activity 3.19   It's in the Box!
>
> Stick a strip of masking tape on the floor. Place an open-topped box (about 12 inches wide by 18 inches long) about 7 feet from the line. Stand behind the line and toss a block into the box. Tell the children that the block is inside the box. Toss the block again and miss the box. Tell the children that now the block is outside the box.
>
> Toss the block several more times. After each toss, ask the children if the block is inside or outside the box.
>
> Have the students take turns tossing the block. After each toss, ask the class if the block is inside or outside the box.

> ### Activity 3.20   In the Circle
>
> Have about nine children hold hands in a circle. Have two children stand inside the circle and have two stand outside the circle. Ask the class who is inside and who is outside.
>
> Choose another group to form a circle. Call on other children to go stand either inside or outside the circle.

Open and Closed.   In young children, development of the geometric notion of *open or closed* nearly always makes use of the concept of *inside or outside*. We might talk about a dog's being able to get outside of the yard if the gate is left open. A person can tell if the fence is open or closed by whether or not the dog can get out.

> ### Activity 3.21   Can the Dog Get Out?
>
> ## Open or Closed?
>
>

Straight or Crooked.   There are three simple and easy-to-use tools for checking whether things are in a straight line: a stretched string, a sight line, and a folded sheet of paper. The following activities develop these tools and use them to check for straightness.

Activity 3.22　Straight as a String

Lay a 36-inch string on a table so that the string is crooked. Ask the children if the string is crooked or straight.

Pick up the string by its ends and stretch it out until it is straight. Explain to the children that a stretched string is straight.

Draw a freehand line that is about 24 inches long on the board. Ask if it is crooked or straight. Hold the stretched string next to the line to check whether it is straight.

Check some other things for straightness.

Activity 3.23　Make a Straight Edge

Form an odd-shaped sheet of paper by cutting away the corners and straight edges from a large sheet of paper.

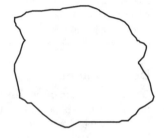

Show the resulting shape to the children. Point out that there are no straight sides. Tell them that you can make a straight side by folding the paper. Fold the paper and show the folded edge to the children. Stretch a length of string next to the folded edge to check its straightness.

Use the folded edge of the paper to check several things for straightness.

Activity 3.24　Looks Straight

Place three blocks on the table so that they are not in a straight line.

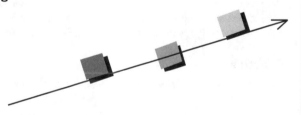

Have a child look along the line of blocks. Ask if the middle block is in line with the others or if it sticks out.

Have several other children also look.

Next, have a child look along the line of blocks while you slowly push the middle block into line. Tell the child to stop you when all three blocks are lined up. Have another child look also to check.

Stretch a length of string next to the blocks to check whether they are in a straight line.

Then use a folded edge of paper to check the line of blocks for straightness.

Have five children stand in a line. Have another child look down the line and move children until the line is straight.

A Revised Lesson

The following example of a lesson plan is similar to one that is based entirely on the suggestions provided in the teacher's guide of a kindergarten-level textbook. It is a good plan; however, its focus is on using the textbook pages, and the developmental part of the lesson is minimal. The example lesson plan is followed by a revised plan that expands the amount of developmental activity, increases the amount of visual input and kinesthetic activity, provides for increased communication among and from children, and makes monitoring the learning a more continuous process. Remember that these adaptations will make the lesson appropriate for virtually all students. But, remember also that some students with severe needs may require further instructional adaptations.

LESSON OBJECTIVE

The student will identify objects in specified positions: above, below, and between.

Lesson Opener

Ask the children to raise their hands on the basis of some criterion, such as color of clothing or eye color (for example, brown eyes). Ask each child meeting this criterion to raise one hand above his or her head and hold the other hand below his or her chin. Ask each child in this group to wiggle the fingers of the hand below his or her chin. Then have each child in the group wiggle the fingers of the hand above his or her head. Repeat with another variation on the criterion (for example, blue eyes) until all children have had a turn.

Development

Direct the attention of the class to the first example on the first page of the lesson. Point out that one cat is above the table and the other cat is below the table. Have the children trace the ring around the cat that is above the table. Have them trace the X that marks the cat below the table. Direct the attention of the children to the first example on the second page. Point out that the yellow toy is between the other two toys.

Monitoring Learning

Have the children look at the second example on the first page. Have them name the things that they see. [A dog in a doghouse and a cat on top of the doghouse.] Have them draw a ring around the animal that is above the other one. Have them mark an X on the animal that is below the other one. Have them complete the third example on the page. Provide individual help for children who do not understand. On the second page, have the children color the middle object yellow on the remaining two examples. Provide individual help for children who do not understand.

Practice

Assign the *Shape Reteaching Worksheet* to those who would benefit from reteaching. Assign the practice worksheet to the rest of the students.

We will now revise the lesson to make it more appropriate for diverse learners.

LESSON OBJECTIVE

The student will identify objects in specified positions: above, below, and between.

Lesson Opener

You will need a stepladder and three dolls. Choose three children to come to the front. Give each of them a doll to place on different steps of the ladder. Ask other children to tell which doll is highest, which doll is lowest, and which doll is in the middle on the ladder.

Repeat the activity with different children.

Tell the children that today they are going to learn to use the words *above*, *below*, and *between* to describe how things are arranged.

Development

Call on three new children to place the dolls on the ladder. Ask how many children have heard the word *above*. Explain that the doll that is highest on the ladder is above the others. Have someone identify the doll that is above the others. Rearrange the dolls. Ask which doll is above the others.

Monitoring Learning

Take note of any children who seem to have trouble understanding. Involve them as the activity is repeated.

Ask how many children have heard the word *below*. Ask who knows which doll is below the others. Rearrange the dolls several times and have someone tell which doll is below the others.

Monitoring Learning

Take note of any children who seem to have trouble understanding. Involve them as the activity is repeated.

Point to the doll in the middle. Ask if anyone knows a word that tells this doll's position. After children have had a chance to respond, tell them that this doll is *between* the others. Rearrange the dolls and ask which doll is between the others.

Place the dolls side by side on top of a table. Ask if any of the dolls is above the others. [No.] Ask if any of the dolls is below the others. [No.] Point out that the doll in the middle is still between the others.

Place three different-colored blocks in a line on the table. Ask which block is below the others. [None of them is below the others.] Ask which block is between the others.

Monitoring Learning

Some children may be confused by the change from a vertical arrangement of objects to a horizontal arrangement. Take note of any children who seem to have trouble understanding. Involve them as the activity is repeated.

Place three objects on the bulletin board in a diagonal arrangement. Ask which of these objects is between the others.

Choose two children to come forward. Have one of them lie on top of the table and have the other lie under the table. Ask, "Who is above? Who is below? Is anyone between them?"

Place four objects in a vertical arrangement on the bulletin board. Ask which object is above the others. Which is below the others? Point out that now there are *two things between* the top one and the bottom one.

Draw three objects on the board in a vertical arrangement. Have a child draw a ring around the one that is above the others. Have another child mark an X on the one that is below the others. Have a third child point to the one that is between the others. Repeat this with four objects. [Now there will be two things between.] Draw two objects and have a child draw an object between them.

Have the children work with partners. Give partners four different-colored blocks. Have them take turns stacking the blocks. The other child says which blocks are above, below, and between the others.

Monitoring Learning

Take note of any children having trouble. Provide individual assistance as it is needed.

Closure and Follow-Up

Ask if someone can tell what three words the class learned to use today. Have different children tell in their own words what each of these three words means. Have the children look at the pages from the textbook. Explain how to complete the pages. Have the children take the pages home and use them to explain to their parents about *above*, *below*, and *between*.

Exercises and Activities

1. Describe a classification activity for young children. Have the children form two groups of objects, one consisting of familiar objects with some specified attribute, the other consisting of familiar objects without that specified attribute.

2. Develop a classification activity based on a children's story like the one described in activity 3.02.

3. Develop a developmental length-comparison activity that uses objects familiar to young children.

4. Develop a practice activity on seriation that uses objects familiar to young children.

5. Develop a partner activity in which children use one-to-one matching to compare the size of two groups of objects familiar to young children.

6. Develop an outdoor activity that helps develop the concepts of *near* and *far* (developmental, not practice).

7. Study the traditional and adapted lesson plans in this chapter. Identify the changes in the adapted plan that would increase the:
   a. development of the concepts taught in the lesson;
   b. communication between and among the students about the concepts taught in the lesson;
   c. visual information about the concepts taught in the lesson;
   d. ways to provide for more kinesthetic activity; and
   e. continual assessment (monitoring of learning) in the lesson.

8. Write a complete lesson plan to teach the concepts of *open* and *closed*. Place heavy emphasis on development activity and kinesthetic activity.

9. Consider the following situation: the teacher showed some young children a doll, a book, a baseball, a toy car, a football, and some doll clothes, and then asked them to choose some things that go together. The teacher expected the children to choose the doll and the doll clothes or perhaps the two balls. However, the teacher was surprised when one child selected the baseball, the book, and the toy car.
   a. What do you think the child was thinking? Why do you think the child answered the way he or she did?
   b. What follow-up question might allow the teacher to understand what the child is thinking?

10. Suppose you have taught classification to your class of kindergartners. After the classification criterion has been given (for example, "Everything in this group of objects has corners") and a group of objects that meet that criterion has been formed, the children should be able to decide whether other objects belong, or do not belong, in that group. Design an activity for the children that you can observe to determine which children understand and which children do not understand.

References and Related Readings

Baroody, A. J. (1987). *Children's mathematical thinking: A developmental framework for preschool, primary and special education teachers.* New York: Teachers College Press.

Baroody, A. J. (1996). An investigative approach to the mathematics instruction of children classified as learning disabled. In D. K. Reid, W. P. Hresko, & H. L. Swanson (Eds.), *Cognitive approaches to learning disabilities* (pp. 545–615). Austin, TX: PRO-ED.

Court, S. R. A. (1920). Numbers, time, and space in the first five years of a child's life. *Pedagogical Seminary, 27,* 71–89.

National Council of Teachers of Mathematics. (1989). *Curriculum and evaluation standards for school mathematics.* Reston, VA: Author.

National Council of Teachers of Mathematics. (2000). *Principles and standards for school mathematics.* Reston, VA: Author.

Tucker, B. F., Weaver, T. L., & Singleton, A. (2000). Relative position concepts are whole-body concepts. *The Journal of Early Education and Family Review, 8*(1), 23–28.

Websites

www.ldonline.org/indepth/adhd
Links to resources on ADHD.

www.ldonline.org/ld_indepth/parenting/johnson_helping.html
Help for parents of children with learning disabilities. Links, links, links.

www.math.about.com
Resources for mathematics prek–4.

www.pbs.org/kcts/preciouschildren/diversity/read_linguistic.html
Language and cultural diversity in early childhood.

four

WHOLE NUMBERS AND NUMERATION

Naming and Writing Quantity

CHAPTER OUTLINE

Number Sense

The standards of the National Council of Teachers of Mathematics (NCTM, 1989, 2000) emphasized the importance of the development of *number sense*. "Number sense is an intuition about numbers that is drawn from all the varied meanings of number" (NCTM, 1989, p. 39). The NCTM (1989) indicated that number sense has five components: developing number meanings, exploring relationships with manipulatives, understanding the relative magnitudes of numbers, developing intuitions about the relative effect of operating on numbers, and developing referents for measures of common objects and situations. *Principles and Standards for School Mathematics* (NCTM, 2000) also emphasized the importance of understanding numbers. The NCTM (2000) indicated that students should use numbers in flexible ways, including relating, composing, and decomposing them.

In this text, suggestions for the development of number sense are found in several different chapters. To help the reader understand that number sense is developed within a variety of topics and at a variety of different ages, we will use the symbol shown in the margin at the left to indicate instruction that will help develop number sense. *Remember:* When you see that symbol, the discussion in the text is about developing number sense.

Foundations of Algebra

Although *algebra* is generally considered to be a secondary school subject, the NCTM (2000) included an algebra standard for elementary school students. The algebra standard (NCTM, 2000) states that all students should understand patterns, relations, and functions; be able to represent and analyze mathematical situations and structures by using algebraic symbols; be able to use mathematical models to represent and understand quantitative relationships; and be able to analyze change in various contexts.

In this chapter and in several of the chapters that follow, the foundations of algebra are introduced. To help the reader understand how the foundations of algebra are developed within a variety of topics and at a variety of different ages, we will use the symbol shown in the margin at the left to indicate instruction that will help develop understanding of the foundations of algebra.

Building on What Children Already Know

Before learning to name and write numbers, children will already have developed considerable number sense (Greenes, Schulman, & Spungin, 1993; NCTM, 1989) that can be used as a foundation for new learning about numbers. Good teaching invariably builds on existing knowledge so smoothly that nothing seems new to the child. Rather, each concept or skill that is taught seems merely to be an extension of what is already known. Not only is this good teaching but it is also efficient teaching, because more is learned and it is learned more quickly. In addition to being good and efficient teaching, it is also effective teaching, because what is learned is better understood, more likely to be remembered, and easier to apply in varied settings.

Before working on number concepts, children will have been encouraged to use *prenumber quantitative vocabulary* to describe their environment. For example, they have had a lifetime of experiences with the number *one*:

"I have some cookies. You have only *one*."
"Here is *one* of your shoes. Where is the other *one*?"
"There are some pencils on the desk. Will you bring me *one*?"
"No, you can't have a piece of candy. You've already had *one*."

Children also have a strong sense of the meaning of *more*. They have had years of experience with this concept. Often, the word *more* is in the form *one more*:

"I have *more* than you have."
"Share with your sister. You have *more* than she has."
"I want you to eat *one more* bite of carrots."
"I'll read you *one more* book. Then you have to go to sleep."
"If you do that *one more* time, you'll be in big trouble!"
"All right, you may hit the ball *one more* time. Then your turn will be over."

Other examples of prenumber quantitative vocabulary can be developed by using one-to-one correspondence, a skill already emphasized. Using one-to-one correspondence, children are able to continue their development of prenumber quantitative vocabulary. *As many as, more than,* and *less than* can describe many situations, as the following illustrate:

"There are just *as many* desks in the room *as* there are children."
"There are *as many* cartons of milk *as* there are children."
"I have a lot *more* crayons *than* he does."
"There are *more* girls *than* boys here today at school."
"There are *more* chairs in the room *than* there are children."

Therefore, as we examine each topic, we consider what the child already knows that can serve as the basis for building the new idea. We then explore how that already-available knowledge can be extended to include the new idea.

Students need to make the connection that the language they use to describe natural activities in their lives and the language used to describe mathematical activities in the classroom are the same. The following activity describes how this natural connection can be made.

Activity 4.01 M&Ms

Give the following directions to your students: "When I give you a bag of M&Ms, carefully put them into groups and be ready to describe your bag of M&Ms without using numbers."

Discuss the students' bags of M&Ms by encouraging them to use prenumber quantitative vocabulary such as:

"I have *more* brown M&Ms *than* any other color."

"I have the *same amount* of red M&Ms *as* I do yellow M&Ms."

"*Some* of my M&Ms have chipped edges."

"*All* of my M&Ms are chocolate."

Use food very cautiously when planning activities to develop mathematical concepts. A compelling reason for this caution is the high prevalence of children with food allergies, and, at best, candy is not conducive to good dental hygiene and encourages poor food choices so prevalent in today's world. The M&M activity is described here because it is a natural connection between the language students use when they are describing the real world in which they interact and the language teachers use in describing the mathematical world in which they participate in the classroom. This activity can easily be adapted by using bags of small toys or cutouts from a die-cut machine.

As students become proficient in describing relationships between quantities, they are ready to describe their surroundings in more detail. They should be led to discover the importance of using quantitative concepts in their descriptions. To do this, they must understand whole numbers.

The Big Picture

Students should understand the concept of the quantitative value before the written expression is introduced. Unfortunately, if the number *two* is the topic of the day, often teachers will begin their lesson by showing the children the numeral 2 on the board first, and then they will begin the developmental activities. A teacher should provide many examples of *two* before introducing the written numeral. For example:

"I have two eyes."
"I have two hands."
"I have two ears."
"Here are two books."
"Here are two crayons."

These examples demonstrate the quantitative concept to the child.

After the teacher has identified the quantity *two* for the children, that knowledge should be reinforced by having them show the quantity *two*. For example:

"Show me two crayons."
"Show me two fingers."
"Clap two times."

After the child has learned the concept of "*twoness*" and then demonstrated the quantity of *twoness*, nonexamples should be included with examples to ensure complete understanding. For example:

"Do I have two noses?"
"Do I have two feet?"
"Do I have two necks?"
"Do I have two desks in this room?"

After the children have fully developed this concept of *twoness*, they are ready to learn the symbolic notation for this number. It is important to remember that the language used in writing 2 must match the model it describes.

Development of Numbers and Numeration

The activities described in this chapter promote the children's ability to attain the following three goals: First, they will be able to identify the quantity that is named by the number. Second, they will be able to name the number or say it. Third, they will be able to write the number clearly using standard notation. The following six objectives convey these important abilities:

1. When the students are shown a quantity (that is, some number of objects), they will be able to say the number that names the quantity.
2. When the students are shown a quantity, they will be able to write the numeral that names the quantity.
3. Shown a numeral (a written number), the children will be able to show that quantity (that many objects).
4. Shown a numeral, the children will be able to say the number.
5. Given a number orally, the students will be able to show that quantity.
6. Given a number orally, the children will be able to write that quantity.

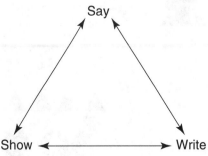

Counting is an important skill in the development of children's knowledge of numbers. However, it is important to remember that the ability to say the numbers in their correct order does not ensure an understanding of the process of counting. For example, a very young child can say the numbers 1 to 5 in a rote fashion. Yet, when a key ring with three keys on it is presented, the child might "count to five" while touching the three keys.

The ability to assign a number for each unit added during counting is related to *one-to-one correspondence*. Because using one-to-one correspondence is important in counting, teachers should physically count as well as verbally count in order to demonstrate this concept. For example, the teacher should touch each pencil as it is counted or touch each child as the child is counted. After the children fully understand the concept of one-to-one correspondence, the teacher could stand close to each student as he or she is counted. Eventually, the teacher will simply be able to point to each student as he or she is counted. The important thing is for the children to understand that something is being counted instead of just hearing numbers recited orally.

One-Digit Numbers

The meaning that a child attaches to a number depends on the mental image that he or she associates with that number. Young children think *concretely*—that is, in terms of mental images of things existing in their world. Therefore, the mental image for the number *three*, or any number, should not be an abstract symbol:

Rather, the image should be of three objects. And, often, the child will place those three objects in some particular arrangement:

 Remembering that one goal is to establish mental imagery for numbers, teachers must be aware of a problem related to establishing that mental imagery. To illustrate this problem with a rather extreme example, we next show three numbers represented by linear arrangements of objects. At a glance, it is nearly impossible to recognize the numbers being represented:

After the objects are rearranged to "organize" the mental imagery, notice how much easier it is to recognize the numbers:

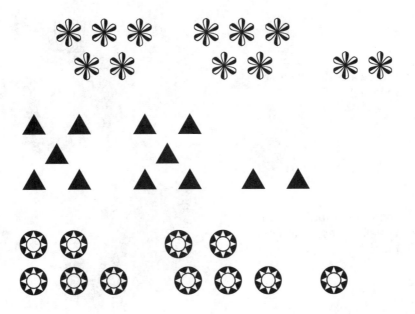

Linear arrangements of objects for numbers greater than 3 should be avoided. Rather, use arrangements that help the child recognize quantity without counting.

When teaching the numbers 1 to 9, take the time to develop each number thoroughly before another number is introduced. In other words, if a teacher uses the following scope and sequence for teaching one-digit numbers—1, 2, 3, 4, 0, 5, 6, 7, 8, and 9—the number 2 needs to be fully developed before progression to the number 3.

What is meant by "full development"? As already mentioned, the students should have many opportunities to see the concept. For example, students can be taught to see the number *seven* by using concrete or pictorial examples. Students also need to express orally that what they are being shown is *seven*. Then they should be given opportunities to show *seven*. When children have had sufficient opportunities in experiencing *seven*, then, and only then, should they be shown how to write the numeral 7. For a smooth transition, the teacher should use the same language when describing concrete situations, pictorial situations, and symbolic situations of the number.

For example, the teacher may demonstrate *seven* by counting seven books and saying, "Here are seven books." The teacher could also draw seven books on the board and say, "Here are seven books." Then, the teacher could write on the board "7 books" and say, "This says 'seven books.'" The teacher's use of consistent language will enable the children to understand that all three representations describe the same situation: seven books.

Only after the students fully understand the concept of *seven* and have been taught to write the number 7 should the teacher introduce the next concept. The teacher should give full attention to the development of the new concept and use the same types of activities as described in the development of the concept of *seven*. Again, the teacher should make sure that the children know what this new concept looks like, know how to say the number when they see it described, know how to model it, and then know how to write its corresponding numeral.

Numbers will be meaningful for children when the numbers are connected to what the children already know and when they are developed out of experiences that provide mental images for numbers. For example, building on the concept of *one more*, children should understand 7 and be able to visualize 7 as "6 and one more":

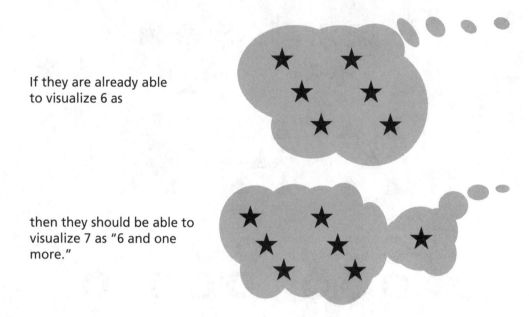

If they are already able to visualize 6 as

then they should be able to visualize 7 as "6 and one more."

The students should see and understand 7 as a composition of many combinations of numbers that they already know:

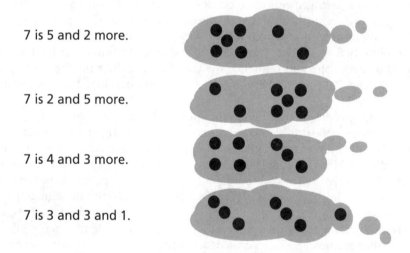

7 is 5 and 2 more.

7 is 2 and 5 more.

7 is 4 and 3 more.

7 is 3 and 3 and 1.

Domino patterns provide efficient and easily recalled mental images for small numbers. There are, in fact, a number of effective instructional activities using dominoes.

Two activities that help children learn to combine numbers to form a larger number are described next.

Activity 4.02   Domino Match

Form a group of two or three children. Place a set of dominoes faceup on the table. One child starts by choosing a domino and places it to the side. The children count to see how many dots are on that domino.

Then they take turns finding another domino with the same number of dots. When they cannot find any more dominoes with that many dots, another child selects a domino and they start over.

Form a group of two or three children. Place a set of dominoes faceup on the table. One child starts by choosing a domino and places it to the side. The children count to see how many dots are on that domino.

Then they take turns finding another domino with one more dot than that one. When they cannot find any more dominoes with one more dot, another child selects a domino and they start over.

It is not important to follow the preceding instructional sequence exactly. What is important is that each number is given full attention and the students completely understand each number's meaning before they are introduced to and taught how to write its symbol. The concept of *zero* should be taught only after several numbers, because it is easier to understand *nothing* after the concept of *something* has been taught.

The use of nonexamples is as important in developing number sense as it is in the development of any concept (Ehrenburg, 1981). After the students have been given ample experience with a particular concept, the teacher should show them examples that do not contain the concept being studied, emphasizing that this is *not* an example of the concept. As more and more numbers are learned, these nonexamples could be previously learned numbers; therefore, meaningful review of past numbers becomes a natural part of the day's math lesson.

One structured format for ensuring long-term retention is to plan a review lesson following each newly learned concept. For example, after the students have learned about the number 2 and are currently learning the number 3, a review lesson emphasizing both numbers 2 and 3 should follow. The number 4 is taught next. A review lesson emphasizing the numbers 3 and 4 follows, and then a review lesson emphasizing the numbers 2, 3, and 4. Numbers 1 through 9 are taught in this format. Even though it may seem as if a large proportion of the math lesson consists of review, the more time spent developing these important basic concepts, the less time needed to remediate later. Activities 4.04 to 4.07 illustrate how a teacher might develop the concept of *four*. Activity 4.08 illustrates how a teacher may introduce the concept *zero*.

Activity 4.04   I Have Four

Fill a box with various school supplies, including four of each of the items—for example, four pencils, four erasers, four boxes of crayons, four bottles of glue, and so on.

Tell the students that you have a box of school supplies. You need to know what's in it. Ask them to help you figure out exactly what is in the box.

First, let the students help you group each kind of item together. Then, count each group and announce each time that you have four of these. After counting each group, ask the students to count with you. As a closing activity, ask the students how these groups are alike. [Each group has four in it.]

Activity 4.05   Move and Count

Fill a small plastic bag for each child with various counters, including four of each of the counters. Before you give each student his or her bag, explain that when they get their bags, they should put the counters into groups. After distributing the bags, use an overhead projector to demonstrate the grouping. As you arrange each group on one side, ask your students to put their groups on one side. Now you are ready to move and count. Ask your students to slide each counter over to the other side as they count. Count each group of counters in this fashion, emphasizing that each group has four in it.

Activity 4.06   Four-Leaf Clovers

Draw several stems for four-leaf clovers on a piece of drawing paper, or make the stems using brown yarn. Cut out the leaves for the students to use, or let them cut the leaves out if time permits.

Tell the students that today they will make four-leaf clovers. Ask if anyone has ever seen a four-leaf clover. Have a short discussion about what a four-leaf clover looks like. Emphasize that each four-leaf clover has four leaves. Using a projector, demonstrate how the students can make their own four-leaf clovers. Have the children count with you each time you make one. Ask how many leaves their four-leaf clovers will have.

Activity 4.07   Four or Not Four

Make a worksheet by drawing several flowers, some having four petals, some having fewer than four petals, and some having more than four petals. Tell the students they are going to color only the flowers with four petals.

Use a projector to show and discuss each flower and have the students count with you to decide if it should be colored. *Remember:* The emphasis is on whether the flowers have exactly four petals or not. It is all right to name the numbers already learned, but the emphasis is on the development of the concept of *four*.

Activity 4.08   Nothing's There

Using a paper bag, put in one chip. Ask the children, "How many chips are in the bag?" Have a child check. Then empty the bag. Next, put four chips (one at a time) in the bag. Ask the students, "How many chips are in the bag?" Have a child check. Empty the bag so that the children can see that it is empty. Ask, "How many chips are in the bag?" After the students' responses, explain, "When there are no chips, we say that the number of chips is zero." Repeat the sequence with objects set on a table.

Two-Digit Numbers

The previously discussed instructional sequence for teaching one-digit numbers is also followed in teaching two-digit numbers. The numbers are introduced as quantities and are related to already-learned numbers (quantities) before the written notation is taught. You want the child to know what the number (the quantity) "looks like" before learning to write the number. The mental image for the number *twelve*, for example, should not be an abstract symbol. Rather, the mental image should be of 12 objects. Unfortunately, when the number is greater than 10, that many objects often appears to the child as a "bunch." Groups of 11, 12, or 13 objects are virtually indistinguishable:

The mental image may be "organized" by helping the child to see *twelve* as an easily recognizable arrangement of that many objects (Schram, Feiman-Nemser, & Ball, 1990). When this is done, the new number is represented as some combination of already-recognizable quantities. For example, *twelve* could be shown in many ways:

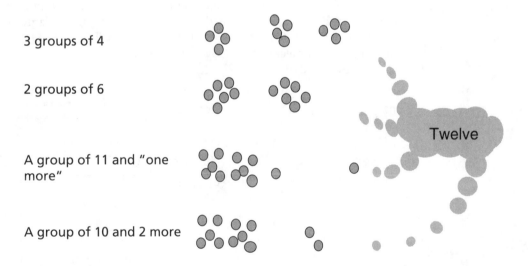

3 groups of 4

2 groups of 6

A group of 11 and "one more"

A group of 10 and 2 more

Twelve

Since numbers greater than 10 are named as a combination of tens and ones, the last of the images shown for *twelve* (10 and 2 more) is an important one. A device called the *10-frame* is an effective way to structure the mental image for numbers in the teens. The 10-frame helps the child see the number as tens and ones:

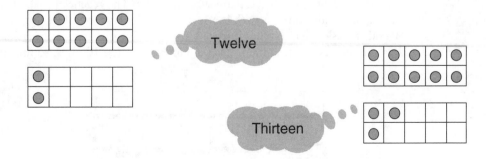

Twelve

Thirteen

Bundled sticks are another excellent model for helping children develop mental imagery for two-digit numbers. Twelve sticks in a pile just look like a bunch of sticks, but when 10 of them are bundled together, it is easy to see *twelve* as 10 and 2 more.

Similarly, 14 can be seen as 10 and 4 more.

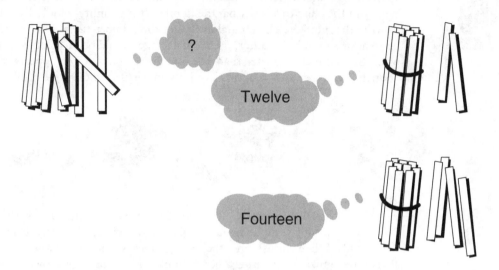

Base-10 blocks are another effective model for two-digit numbers. *Base-10 blocks* consist of small cubes, rods (sometimes called *longs*), flats, and large cubes. The *small cubes* represent ones. *Rods* are equal in length to 10 small cubes and represent tens. *Flats,* which are the equivalent of 10 longs, represent hundreds. *Large cubes,* 10 flats in size, represent thousands.

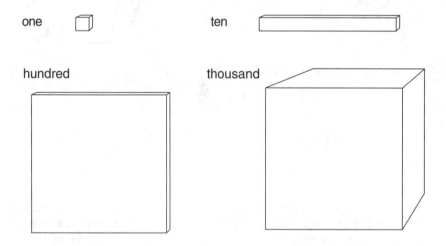

When introducing the base-10 blocks, the teacher should build on the one-digit-number concepts that the students already know. The teacher usually begins by representing one-digit numbers with the small cubes. Then she or he shows the children the 10-rod and asks what number it represents. By lining up 1-cubes alongside the rod, children can understand that the rod is the same amount as 10 ones, so they must be equal:

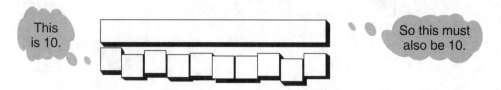

The student can see that there are two ways to represent 10: with ten 1-cubes or with one 10-rod. Similarly, other numbers can be represented in two ways—as ones or as ten and ones:

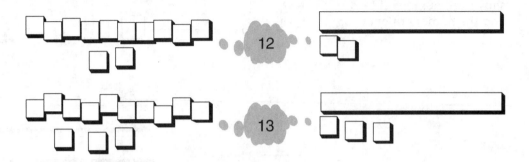

The children should have many experiences representing teen numbers by using tens and ones. In each example, the teacher emphasizes, so the children understand, that using tens and ones is just another way to show the same amount. But, the children should also understand that it is easier to recognize the number at sight when tens and ones are used, because the mental imagery is better.

As the students visualize the teens as ten and ones, written notation should be introduced. Although many children are already able to write 10, 11, and 12, and possibly other two-digit numbers, it is important that the teacher emphasize that the written symbol actually indicates the 1 ten and the number of ones:

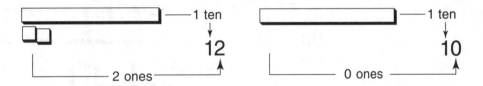

When the child is thinking of the teen numbers as tens and ones, it is easy to move on to understanding other two-digit numbers. *Nineteen* is 10 and 9 ones. One more than 19 is 20, so 20 is 10 and 10 ones, or 2 tens and no ones:

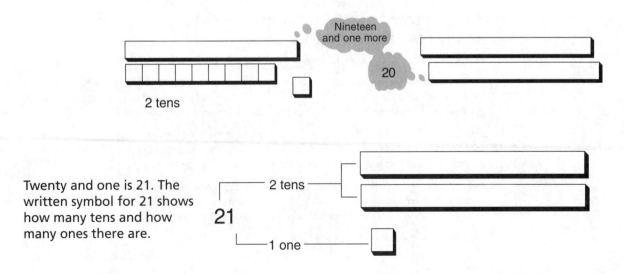

Twenty and one is 21. The written symbol for 21 shows how many tens and how many ones there are.

Twenty and five ones is 25, and the written symbol shows the number of tens and the number of ones.

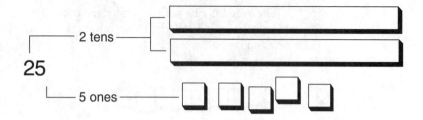

25

2 tens

5 ones

Thirty is 3 tens. Thirty and 4 ones is 34.

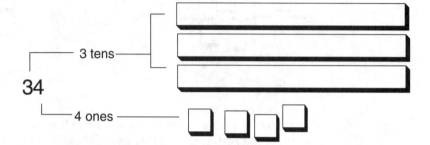

34

3 tens

4 ones

Sixty is 6 tens. Sixty and 3 ones is 63.

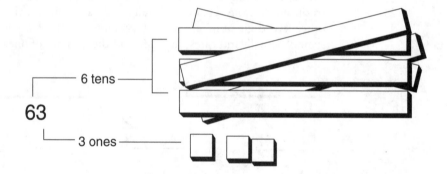

63

6 tens

3 ones

The following activities illustrate how a teacher might develop the concepts of two-digit numbers.

Activity 4.09   Bundle Them Up

Place 20 Popsicle sticks in a bag for each student. Keep 20 sticks for your own use.

Tell the students that you have some sticks and that you need to know how many you have. Have them count with you as you count 20 sticks. Count 10 sticks and place a rubber band around them. Ask how many are in the bundle. Do the same thing to form another bundle of 10.

Ask how many bundles of 10 you have. [two] Remind them that there were 20 sticks altogether, so 2 tens must be the same as 20. Remove the rubber bands and count out 12 sticks. Then bundle 10 of them so that you have one group of 10 and 2 single sticks.

Pass out the bags of sticks. Have everyone count out 15 sticks and lay the extra sticks aside. Then have the children bundle 10 of the 15 sticks. Ask how many sticks they have altogether. [15] Ask how many bundles of 10 there are and how many other sticks there are. [1 ten and 5 single sticks]

Lead the class to show all of the teen numbers.

Activity 4.10   Let's Trade

From a set of base-10 blocks, place 1 10-rod and 19 1-cubes in a bag for each student. Keep a set for your own use.

Show 6 cubes and ask how many there are. Do the same for 3 cubes and 9 cubes. Allow someone to count them if necessary. Show 10 cubes and have someone count them. Line up the 10 cubes beside a 10-rod so that the children can see that they equal the same amount. Ask what number name should be given to the rod. [ten] Ask how many cubes you should trade for 1 rod if it is an even trade. [10] Show 12 cubes. Ask if there are enough to trade for a 10. Do that and point out that 12 is the same as 10 and 2.

Pass out the bags of base-10 blocks. Have everyone count out 15 cubes. Then have the children trade 10 cubes for a 10-rod. Ask the students to tell another name for 15.

Repeat with all of the teen numbers.

Activity 4.11   Match

Using base-10 blocks, place representations of two-digit numbers in paper bags. Represent each number two or three different ways. For example, 27 might be represented as 27 ones, as 1 ten and 17 ones, and as 2 tens and 7 ones.

Hand out the bags to the children. Have them look at the numbers in their bags and write the numbers that they have on the outside of the bags.

Then have them move around the room and get together with everyone else with the same number. Finally, have each group look at the numbers in the bags to make sure the same number is in all the bags in the group.

Have each group report to the class the different names that it has for the different representations of the same number.

Activity 4.12   See and Say

Have sets of nine 10-rods and 30 1-cubes ready for groups of students. Keep a set for your own use.

Form groups of two or three children. Give each group a set of base-10 blocks.

Write 23 on the chalkboard. Have the groups figure out how to show the numbers by using the fewest pieces from the base-10 blocks. After checking to see that everyone understands and that the students represented 23 as 2 tens and 3 ones, write several other two-digit numbers on the board and have the groups represent them as tens and ones.

Activity 4.13   Too Many

Have each child draw and cut out a picture of a boy.

Read the poem "Too Many Daves," by Dr. Seuss. Using 23 of the boys that were drawn by the children, group the boys into groups of 10 as the story of Mrs. McCave's dilemma of having 23 sons, all with the name of Dave, unfolds with alternative names.

Activity 4.14   Moira's Birthday

Moira's Birthday, by Robert Munsch, is a delightful children's book that uses numbers in a variety of ways—for example, the number of children to be invited to a party, the number of pizzas ordered for the party, and the number of presents brought to the party. Resolution of the chaos also presents and uses numbers. Read the book and discuss the ways that numbers are used. Emphasize how numbers are used to help us understand *how much*.

Three or More Digits

The introduction and development of three-digit numbers, as well as numbers with more than three digits, can easily be connected to the children's knowledge of two-digit numbers. The mental imagery previously developed for two-digit numbers can be extended by using any of the models that allow the children to see the basic units: base-10 blocks (add the hundreds-block and, later, the thousands-block); bundled sticks (add bundles consisting of 10 tens); play money (add hundred dollar bills and thousand dollar bills).

It is still important that the children see numbers visually represented before they learn the number names or write the numerals. If base-10 blocks are being used, the teacher might have the children combine 10 tens and show that they are the same amount as the larger block. If the children can count rationally to 100, they might also combine 100 ones to see that they are also the same amount as the larger block. Then, the number name for the larger block (one hundred) can be introduced with meaning:

If bundled sticks are used, 10 bundles of 10 can be combined into a larger bundle. The number name for this larger quantity is one hundred. The individual sticks can then be counted to verify that the large bundle does contain 100 sticks.

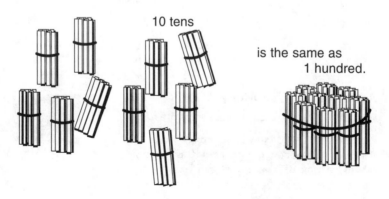

Children need to visualize and think of these new numbers in terms of their basic units. For example, we do not want a child to think of the number 247 as 247 of something. Rather, the child should think of this number as 2 of something (hundreds), and 4 of another thing (tens), and 7 of still another thing (ones). The children should be able to recognize these numbers, write these numbers, and read or say these numbers. When the children are presented with a three- or four-digit number in any of these forms, they should be able to respond by giving that same number back in each of the other two forms.

As the children use these larger numbers, they should be taught not only to write them using standard notation but also to read them in the standard way. It is correct to think of the number 384 as "three hundred and eighty-four." It is equally correct to think of 384 as "three hundred and eighty and four." However, the standard way to read and write this number is "three hundred eighty-four."

Students should be encouraged and led by the teacher to use the standard language. The teacher should consistently use standard mathematical language. However, the teacher should not overreact when an occasional "and" creeps into the reading and writing of multidigit whole numbers. A gentle correction followed by moving on to more important things is generally the most productive way to bring the children to consistent standard language. The following sequence of activities illustrates how a teacher might develop three-digit numbers.

Activity 4.15   Too Many to Write? Make a Bundle

Have a child come forward and use bundled sticks to represent 35. Have the child place the number in a box. Ask how many bundles of 10 are in the box. [3] How many extra sticks? [5]

Have the children watch as you drop three more sticks into the box. Ask how many tens are in the box. [3] How many ones are in the box? [8] What number is in the box? [38]

Drop five more sticks into the box. Ask how many tens are in the box. [3] How many ones are in the box? [13] Ask what we need to do before we can write the new number. [Make a trade, or make a new bundle.] Take 10 sticks out of the box and use a rubber band to bundle them together. Drop the new bundle into the box. Ask what is in the box now. [4 tens and 3 ones]

Do another similar example. Place 58 sticks in the box, then add 6 more sticks. Make a new bundle and name the new number. Emphasize that when you have too many ones to write the number, make a bundle.

Activity 4.16   Too Many to Write? Make a Big Bundle

Have a child come forward and use bundled sticks to represent 85. Have the child place the number in a box. Ask how many bundles of 10 are in the box. [8] How many extra sticks? [5] Have the children watch as you remove a 10 from the box. Ask how many tens are in the box. [7] How many ones are in the box? [5] What number is in the box? [75]

Drop five more bundles of 10 into the box. Ask how many tens are in the box. [12] How many ones are in the box? [5] Point out that 12 tens is too many to write. Have the children watch while you take 10 tens out of the box and place a rubber band around them to make a big bundle. Tell the children that the big bundle contains 100 sticks. One hundred equals 10 tens. Place the big bundle into the box and ask what is in the box. [1 hundred, 2 tens, and 5 ones] Show the class how to write this number.

Do another similar example. Place 98 in the box, then add six more bundles of 10. Make a big bundle and name the new number. Emphasize that when you have too many tens to write the number, make a big bundle.

Activity 4.17 Trading Ten

Follow the procedures of Activities 4.15 and 4.16, except use base-10 blocks to represent the numbers. When you have too many to write, trade 10 ones for a ten or trade 10 tens for a hundred.

Activity 4.18 See, Say, and Show

Form the class into groups of four students. Give each group a set of base-10 blocks.

Use the blocks to show the number 381. Ask how many hundreds, tens, and ones there are. Demonstrate how to say the number. ["Three hundred eighty-one"] Use the blocks to show the number 526. Demonstrate how to say the number. ["Five hundred twenty-six"] Use the blocks to show the number 642. Ask a child to say the number.

Place the number 354 in a box. Have a child come forward, look in the box, and say the number. Then each group should use its blocks to show that number. When everyone is finished, take the 3 hundreds out of the box and show them to the class. Did all the groups have the right number of hundreds? Do the same with the tens and then with the ones. Have everyone say the number together. Repeat this procedure with 269, 524, and 915.

Activity 4.19 Hear, Show, and Write

Form the class into groups of four students. Give each group a set of base-10 blocks. Write 538 on a sheet of paper. Have a child come forward and read the number to the class.

Each group should then use its base-10 blocks to show the number. After showing the number with the blocks, the group should agree on how to write the number correctly and someone in the group should write the number.

When all the groups are finished, hold up your number so each group can see it and check its own number. Repeat this procedure with 219, 526, and 645.

Activity 4.20 One Amount, Many Names

On the chalkboard, write a base-10 chart like the one pictured.

Use base-10 blocks to represent the number 645. Record the number on the base-10 chart.

Trade a ten for 10 ones and record the result. Point out that we still have the same amount, but this is another way to name that amount.

Trade a hundred for 10 tens and record the result. This is just another name for the same amount. Make other trades to get other names for the same amount.

Start with another number and make trades to get other names for the same amount.

Hundreds	Tens	Ones
6	4	5
6	3	15
5	13	15

Rounding Numbers

The most effective way to develop the concept of rounding numbers is to help the children to visualize the numbers on the number line. If the tens are highlighted on the number line, it is not difficult for the children to decide which ten the number is closest to. For example, if you want to round 87 to the nearest ten, first draw a number line that has the tens written in a *different color*:

Then, locate the number 87 on the number line:

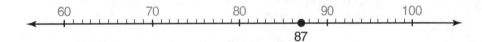

The children will see that 87 is between 80 and 90, but it is closer to 90. So, since 90 is the nearest ten, we say that 87, rounded to the nearest ten, is 90.

Similarly, we would say that 32, rounded to the nearest ten, is 30:

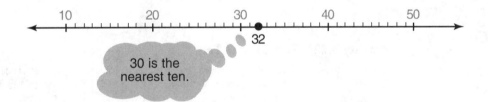

Sixty-five is exactly halfway between 60 and 70. Neither of these tens is nearer to 65 than the other:

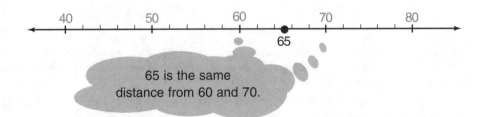

In cases like this, there are a number of conventions that can be adopted, but the most common at the elementary school level is to round numbers like this up to the next higher ten:

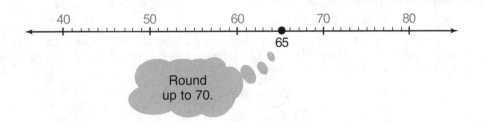

As the students are exposed to a variety of examples, they may be able to generalize the rule: If the ones digit is 5 or more, round up. If the ones digit is less than 5, round down. It is important that the rule not be presented rotely. Rather, arrive at the rule as a generalization of many examples. Ideally, the children should be led to state the rule themselves as a summary of what they have discovered. Then the children will understand the rule. Retention of the rule will be much better because it is always easier to remember things that we can visualize and connect to other things that we know.

The following activity sequence suggests how a teacher could develop the concept of rounding numbers to the nearest ten.

Activity 4.21   The Closest Girl

Line up 15 chairs at the front of the room. Have three girls come forward and seat one girl in the third chair, one in the eighth chair, and one in the thirteenth chair.

Then have a boy come and sit in any of the empty chairs. Ask which girl the boy is closest to. Repeat the activity with several other boys.

Next seat three boys in the chairs, have a girl sit in an empty chair, and decide which boy is closest. Repeat the activity with several other girls.

Activity 4.22   The Closest Ten

Line up 15 chairs at the front of the room, with their backs toward the children. Tape the number 20 to the back of the third chair, and tape the number 30 to the back of the thirteenth chair.

Point to the chair with 20 on its back and ask, "If this is chair number 20, then what number chair would the next one be?" [21] Have the children figure out the numbers for several other chairs.

Next, have a child sit in any chair. Ask, "What is the number of that chair?" Then ask if 20 or 30 is closest. If the child sits in chair number 25, be sure that everyone agrees that chair is the same distance from 20 and from 30.

Repeat the activity with several other children.

Have the children line up 25 chairs in the hallway and label the second chair with a 40, the twelfth chair with a 50, and the twenty-second chair with a 60. Follow the same procedures just described.

Activity 4.23   Find the Nearest Ten

Draw a number line on the chalkboard. Label the tens with colored chalk, but do not label the rest of the numbers. Prepare cards with all the missing numbers. Shuffle the number cards and pass them out to the class.

Have the children come forward, one at a time, and tape their numbers in the proper place on the number line. After taping the numbers to the number line, have them tell which is the nearest ten.

Repeat the activity with several other children.

Adapting a Lesson

Now we examine a lesson from grade 1. The lesson plan parallels the teaching activities that would typically be suggested in a teacher's guide. We have organized the plan around the components: objective, lesson opener, development, monitoring learning, practice, and closure.

LESSON OBJECTIVE

The student will recognize and write numbers from 13 through 19.

Lesson Opener

Write the numbers 7 through 12 on the board and place about 20 counters on the table. Point to the 8 and call on a child to tell what that number is. Have another child come forward and give you that many counters. Then have a third child check to see if it is the correct number of counters. Repeat the process with the number 12. Tell the children that today they will learn to recognize and write the numbers 13 through 19.

Development

Show the students 14 Popsicle sticks. Tell them that there are 14 sticks. While they watch, count out 10 of the sticks and put a rubber band around those 10 sticks. Show them that there are 4 leftover sticks, and tell them that 14 is 10 and 4. Record the number on a place-value chart. Explain that this is how we write 14, and then write 14 next to the chart.

Repeat this process with the numbers 16 and 19.

Direct the attention of the children to the first page of the lesson in the student book. Lead them through the first example. Point out that one group has 10 dots and the other group has 5 dots. Point out how the number 15 is written.

Monitoring Learning

Have the children complete the rest of the teaching examples on the page. Move around the room, observing the children's work. Identify those who are having difficulty.

Practice

Have the class complete the practice exercises on the second page of the student lesson. Have students who are having difficulty complete the *Reteaching Worksheet* instead.

Closure

When you are getting near the end of the math period, get the attention of the children, and remind them that today they learned how to recognize and write the numbers 13 through 19.

Adapting the Lesson for a Diverse Group of Students

To adapt this traditional lesson plan into one that is appropriate for all learners, you need to accomplish the following five goals:

1. **Increase the amount of development.** You want to develop the concepts more thoroughly and relate the "new" numbers more completely to other numbers with which the children are already familiar.
2. **Provide more visual information.** The original lesson did a good job of providing visual information, but you need to expand the use of visuals to be sure that the

children acquire strong mental imagery for their number concepts. Every time a new mathematical concept is introduced, the children should "see what it looks like."

3. **Add more kinesthetic activity.** You want the children to be up, out of their seats, doing math. Children need to be active participants in demonstrating concepts, in addition to the teacher's showing them. Active physical involvement encourages active intellectual involvement.

4. **Plan for more oral communication about mathematics from and among the children.** Encourage the children to question and conjecture. You want them to discuss and explain. Ask questions instead of lecturing.

5. **Plan for continual monitoring of learning.** You need to be aware of how well the children are learning during every part of the lesson. Continual assessment of learning allows you to know who understands and who does not, who can use the skills being taught and who cannot, which students might be grouped together for remedial instruction, what content needs to be retaught, and when content needs to be taught with a different approach.

Remember that these adaptations make the lesson appropriate for almost all students. But remember also that some students with severe needs may require further instructional adaptations.

LESSON OBJECTIVE

The student will recognize and write numbers from 13 through 19.

Lesson Opener

Prepare sets of three cards for each of the numbers 5 through 12. One card should have the numeral, one card should have a picture of that many dots without any apparent grouping, and the third card should have a picture of that many dots grouped by fives and tens. See the following examples:

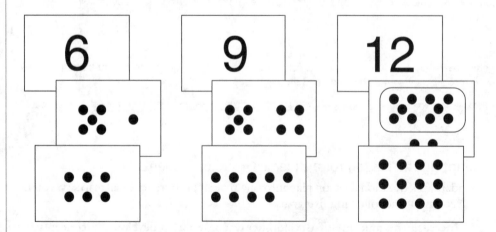

Shuffle the cards and pass them out to the children. Have the students get together with others who have the same number. When all the children are with their partners, have them explain what is on their cards. [For example, "I have the number 9." "I have nine dots." "I have five dots and four dots. That's the same as nine dots."]

Monitoring Understanding

Observe to be sure that all the children understand how to find their partners. Provide further explanation to children who are having difficulty.

For the numbers 10, 11, and 12, use a place-value chart to show how we write numbers that are 10 or more.

Explain to the children that today they will learn about the numbers 13 through 19.

TEN	ONES
1	2

12

Development

Have the children work with one or two partners. Give each set of partners 13 Popsicle sticks. Tell them to separate their sticks into two groups. Ask how many sticks they placed in each of the two groups. Have children come forward and record combinations that they have discovered. Discuss all the different combinations that the children discovered. [For example, "Thirteen is the same as 9 and 4 more." "Six and 7 more is also 13." "Eleven and 2 is 13."] Be sure the discussion includes 12 and "1 more" and 10 and "3 more." Use the place-value chart to show how to write 13.

Monitoring Understanding

Listen to the children explain the different combinations that they found. Ask leading questions when they need help to understand. Observe to be sure the children are able to record their results.

Give the partners one additional stick (now they have 14). Tell them to discover and record as many combinations as they can. Discuss what they find. Ask which combinations tell them the most about the number 14. During the discussion, emphasize the importance of 10 + 4 and 13 + 1. Use the place-value chart to show how to write 14.

Monitoring Understanding

Move around the room, observing and listening to the children's discussion. Ask leading questions when they need help to understand. Be sure the children understand how to record their results.

Repeat the process with the numbers 16 and 18.

Direct the attention of the students to the first page of the lesson in the student book. Lead them through the first example. Point out that one group has 10 dots and the other group has 5 dots. Have a child come to the board and record that number on a place-value chart. Have another child come forward and show how the number 15 is written without using the place-value chart.

Monitoring Learning

Have the children complete the rest of the teaching examples on the first page of the lesson. Move around the room, observing the children's work. Identify those who are having difficulty.

Practice

Pair the children with partners. Have them complete the practice exercises on the second page of the student lesson, one at a time. After both partners have completed an example, they should compare results to see if they agree. If they have different results, they should discuss the example and agree on an answer.

Monitoring Learning

Move around the room, observing the children's work. Identify those who are having difficulty and provide assistance. Emphasize forming a group of 10 and then counting to see how many are left.

Closure

Near the end of the math period, ask the children what they have learned today. Ask how to write the numbers 13 through 19.

Follow-Up

Pass out copies of a sheet of paper with 17 dots on it. Have the children take the paper home and use it to show a parent how to write the number.

Exercises and Activities

1. Read "Standard 6: Number Sense and Numeration" on pages 38–40 of *Curriculum and Evaluation Standards for School Mathematics*, published in 1989 by the NCTM. Also read the discussion of the Number and Operations Standard on pages 32–36 of *Principles and Standards for School Mathematics*, also published by the NCTM (2000). Compare and contrast the recommendations in the standards with the recommendations in this chapter.

2. Study the sample adapted lesson plan in this chapter. Identify activities in the plan that implement the recommendations in Standard 6 of *Curriculum and Evaluation Standards for School Mathematics* and *Principles and Standards for School Mathematics*.

3. Study the traditional and adapted lesson plans in this chapter. Identify the changes in the adapted lesson plan that increase:
   a. the development of number concepts;
   b. opportunities for communication from and among students;
   c. the visual information about the number concepts;
   d. kinesthetic activities in the lesson; and
   e. continual assessment (monitoring of learning) of the lesson plan.

4. Suppose you have taught your class to round numbers to the nearest hundred.
   a. Write an objective test item to test whether your students understand rounding of numbers to the nearest hundred.
   b. Design an activity that you can observe to determine which children understand and which children do not understand rounding of numbers to the nearest hundred.

References and Related Readings

Ehrenburg, S. D. (1981). Concept learning: How to make it happen in the classroom. *Educational Leadership, 39*(1), 36–43.

Greenes, C., Schulman, L., & Spungin, R. (1993). Developing sense about numbers. *Arithmetic Teacher: Mathematics Education through the Middle Grades, 40,* 279–284.

National Council of Teachers of Mathematics. (1989). *Curriculum and evaluation standards for school mathematics.* Reston, VA: Author.

National Council of Teachers of Mathematics. (2000). *Principles and standards for school mathematics.* Reston, VA: Author.

Schram, P., Feiman-Nemser, S., & Ball, D. L. (1990). *Thinking about teaching subtraction with regrouping: A comparison of beginning and experienced teachers' responses to textbooks.* (NCRTE Research Rep. 89–5). East Lansing: Michigan State University.

Sztajn, P. (2002). Celebrating 100 with number sense. *Teaching Children Mathematics, 9,* 212–217.

Websites

http://math.about.com/
Resources for mathematics.

www.sasked.gov.sk.ca/docs/elemath/numop.html
A scope and sequence chart for numbers and operations.

www.teacherlink.org/content/math/interactive/probability/numbersense/numbersense/home.html
Introduction to number sense.

www.learnnc.org/
Use the search engine to find articles and lessons on mathematics.

five

ADDING AND SUBTRACTING WHOLE NUMBERS

Combining and Separating Quantities

An Overview of the Development of Computation

When teaching any operation on whole numbers, the teacher must complete three distinct instructional tasks: developing the meaning of the operation, developing the basic facts, and developing the algorithm(s). A closer examination of these instructional tasks yields a clear pattern of development.

The Meaning of the Operation

When teaching the meaning of the operation, teachers need to lead the child to accomplish two things. First, the child must associate the arithmetic operation with some physical operation. This association provides a basis for modeling the operation and establishes mental imagery for the operation. Second, the child must learn to use some already-available skill to figure out the answer. When established in this way, the meaning of the operation provides the child with a way to discover answers to specific examples.

The Basic Facts

Some facts are committed to memory, whereas others are "figured out" by using a step-by-step procedure. Basic facts are those needed to figure out the others. In other words, basic facts serve as the basis for the rest of the facts. Normally, children are initially taught a body of easy basic facts for an operation, and then later they are taught the harder basic facts for that operation. However, for both the easy basic facts and the hard basic facts, there are three things that the children should be led to do.

First, the children should discover the answers for themselves. The meaning of the operation is applied to find answers to the easy facts. However, as the numbers get larger, the skills used in the application of the meaning become too inefficient. So, more-efficient thinking strategies need to be developed for finding answers to the hard basic facts.

Second, the children should recognize relationships that exist among the facts. There are two major benefits of this emphasis on relationships. The emphasis on relationships improves retention, because it is easier to remember things that are related to other things that students already know. Also, recognition of those relationships drastically reduces the amount of memorization needed.

Third, the children should commit the facts to memory. Of course, if the meaning of the operation has been effectively taught, the child can figure out the answers to basic facts. So, why is it important that they be memorized? Remember that the basic facts are used to find computation answers. If the basic facts are not memorized, the computation process becomes so slow and tedious that mathematics learning grinds nearly to a stop. If the basic facts are not memorized, children develop a sense of "can't do."

The Algorithm(s)

The algorithms are the step-by-step computation procedures that are followed to complete multidigit examples. Since the algorithms are procedures, it is tempting to resort to teaching a series of rote rules that describe the procedures. Memorization of rote rules has traditionally been the predominant method for learning algorithms for arithmetic operations. Rules are generalizations, usually important ones. However, effective teachers deemphasize rote rules. The problem with learning rules rotely is that rote rules are meaningless rules. The word *rote* literally means "mechanically and without intelligent attention."

Rote rules are also confusing. Students often learn them slightly wrong. Rote rules are often only slightly different from other rote rules, and children mix them up. They tend to use them in the wrong context. Retention is also poor. Although the teacher may get what appears to be quick mastery after intense practice of a rote rule, that so-called mastery often goes away as soon as the practice stops. A weekend away from practice will have a devastating effect on retention. And, if we carefully consider the content of rote rules as they are taught, most of them are not even true. Every rote rule that is commonly taught is true only within some very narrow context. Eventually, as the setting changes, the rule has to be corrected with a new rule. This adds to the confusion. The child's dilemma becomes: When do I use that rule? When do I use this rule? Is either rule the right one?

Instead of teaching rote rules, the teacher should emphasize big ideas that explain the process (Thornton, Tucker, Dossey, & Bazik, 1983). *Big ideas* are ideas that are constantly recurring. Each recurrence of a big idea becomes an extension of something already learned. The algorithms should be taught with effective physical or pictorial models. Modeling a concept or skill lets the children see what the concept or skill looks like and helps the children to develop clear mental imagery. Modeling gives meaning to the algorithms. Note that we are not contending that children should not learn rules in mathematics. Indeed, with meaningful teaching, *the children still learn rules*. However, the *rules arise out of patterns observed by the children* as they use appropriate models that allow them to visualize the mathematical procedures. Rules are simply *statements of helpful ways to do the work*. Meaningful rules *make sense to the children* and are not "what we do because the teacher told us to."

Now we examine this developmental sequence as it is applied to establishing the meaning of addition.

Teaching Addition of Whole Numbers

Developing the Meaning of Addition

Children need to *associate addition with the combining of quantities*. This association should become so strong that when the children see the symbols 3 + 4, they visualize three things being combined with four things. When seeing a situation where quantities are being combined, the child thinks, "That's addition!" After addition has been mastered, the child will see problem settings where things are being combined and will think, "I can use addition to solve this problem." But association of addition with the combining of quantities is not enough. After those quantities have been combined, children must understand that they can *count to find the answer*. The following activity illustrates how a teacher might begin development of the meaning of addition.

Activity 5.01   Altogether

Write the number 4 on the board. Have a child place that many blocks in your hands. Ask the other children how many blocks you have. Place the four blocks into a box, out of sight. Ask the children how many blocks are in the box. On the board, write the number 2 about 10 inches to the right of the number 4. Have a child give you two blocks. Ask the other children how many blocks are in your hands.

Place these two blocks into the box with the first four blocks. Point out that you put four blocks into the box and then put two more blocks into the box. Ask if anyone can tell you how many blocks are in the box now. Have someone count them to see how many.

Repeat the activity with other pairs of numbers.

Tell the children that when you put two amounts together, you are adding.

This first activity starts out as if it is just another activity relating number and numeral. But then the physical operation, combining, is introduced and the mathematical name for it (adding) is introduced. Notice that no effort is made at this time to introduce the plus sign. That comes very soon, but for now, we are modeling addition (combining quantities) and introducing the new term, *add*. When the children see addition modeled, they should be able to tell what they see using appropriate mathematical language:

Modeled addition ⟶ Verbal description

In the next activities, the plus sign and then the equal sign are introduced, and we begin using the written notation for addition:

Modeled addition ⟶ Written notation

An Activity to Introduce the Plus Sign

Activity 5.02 Give Me a Sign

Write the numbers 3 and 6 side by side and about 8 inches apart on the board. Have a child place three blocks on the table. Have another child place six blocks on the table. Tell the children to watch what you do. Place the three blocks and then the six blocks into a box, out of sight. Ask the children, "What do we call it when we put two amounts together?" [Adding.]

Tell the children that we use a plus sign to show that the two numbers have been added. Write a plus sign between the numbers. Point to it and say, "This is a plus sign." Tell the children that what is written on the board is "three plus six." Ask what it means. [3 and 6 are added.]

Repeat the activity with other pairs of numbers.

An Activity to Introduce the Equal Sign

Activity 5.03 This Equals That

Place a group of two blocks and a group of five blocks on the table. Have a child come forward, count the blocks in each group, and announce the numbers to the class. Tell the children to watch what you do. Place the two blocks and then the five blocks into a box, out of sight. Ask the children, "What do we call it when we put two amounts together?" [Adding.] Ask a child to come forward and write the addition on the board, using a plus sign to show the addition.

Next, ask a child to come forward and check to see how many blocks there are altogether. Tell the children that we use an equal sign to tell how many blocks there are altogether. Write $2 + 5 = 7$ on the board. Point to each symbol as you read it.

Repeat the activity with other pairs of numbers. Have different children write the symbols and other children read what is written.

Finally, the children should learn to model addition examples that they are given either in writing or verbally:

Written example $\longrightarrow$ Modeled form

Spoken example $\longrightarrow$ Modeled form

An Activity to Introduce the Process of Finding Answers

Activity 5.04 Show Me Sum

Place some blocks and a box on the table. Choose a child to come to the table. Tell this child to listen carefully and then use the blocks and the box to show the addition that you are going to say. Slowly say, "Two plus three." If the child has difficulty, allow other children to make suggestions.

After the child has combined the blocks together in the box, ask how to find how many there are altogether. [Count them.]

Have someone count the blocks to see how many there are. Then say the result, "So, two plus three equals five." Have someone come forward and write the facts on the board.

Repeat the activity with several other examples. Point out again that the children know how to figure out answers by themselves.

To reinforce the meaning of addition, the teacher should expose the children to a wide variety of addition examples using objects that are familiar to them, such as lunch boxes, pencils, ball caps, cookies, or even other children. The children should use appropriate terminology to describe verbally the addition and use the plus sign and equal sign to write it. In every example, the children should figure out the answer for themselves, and the teacher should continually emphasize how easy this is. They can find the answers by themselves.

Making the Process of Finding Answers More Efficient. Of course, the meaning of the operation is dependent on counting to find the answer. For example, to find the answer to 6 + 3, the process would look something like this:

First, count out six objects.

Next, count out three objects.

Then combine these two groups.

And finally count all the objects to see how many.

You will note that the process requires a lot of counting. Anything that can speed up the process should be done. In the preceding example, when we counted the nine objects that we have altogether, we recounted objects that had already been counted. We do not need to recount the group of six; we already know that there are six objects in that group. So, instead, start with that group and add the objects from the other group to it, one at a time:

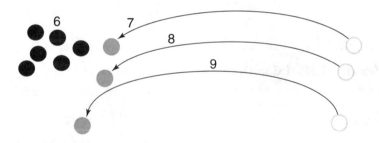

Start with six in the larger group. Add one of the objects from the other group; now there are seven. Add the next object from the other group; now there are eight. Add the last object from the other group; now there are nine. There are nine altogether. *Counting on* is the process in which we count on from the largest number to find the sum. Since we do not have to recount the larger group, it is a quicker and more efficient way to find the answer.

Developing the Easy Basic Addition Facts

As the children begin developing the basic addition facts, the first focus is on mastery of the easier ones (Thornton et al., 1983). This generally includes basic facts with sums of 10 or less. The children should not be given the facts with answers included. Rather, it is important that the children find the answers for themselves. The benefits that result from the children's finding basic fact answers for themselves are the following:

- Since they use the meaning of the operation to find the answers, the process of finding those answers reinforces the meaning.
- They realize that they do not need to rely on someone else for an answer. They can do it themselves, and they become more confident.
- They know that the answers are correct because they figured them out.

- If there is ever a question about the accuracy of an answer, they do not have to rely on someone else to tell them. They can check their own answers.
- As their self-esteem improves, they develop an "I can do it" approach to basic facts. This positive approach spills over into the development of other mathematics concepts and skills.

Activities to Help Children Discover the Facts. The process of finding answers should be as interesting as you can make it. The following series of activities illustrates the variety of methods that could be employed.

Activity 5.05 Fact Finder

Assign the children to work in pairs. Give each pair 10 objects, such as 10 pencils, 10 blocks, 10 frog cutouts, or 10 crayons.

The children take turns going first. One child takes some of the objects. The other child takes some of the remaining objects.

Both children write both numbers with a plus sign between them. Then they combine the objects that were chosen, and each child figures out how many there are altogether. Each child writes an equal sign and the answer. Then they compare results to see if both did the addition correctly.

Repeat the activity to do other additions.

Activity 5.06 I Can Do Sum

Form groups of three or four children. Each child should have 10 counters. Each group should have two cubes with numbers printed on the faces. The first cube should have the numbers 4, 5, 6, 4, 5, and 6. The second cube should have the numbers 0, 1, 2, 3, 3, and 4.

Children take turns tossing the two cubes. After each toss, each child uses his or her counters to find the sum of the two numbers showing on the cubes. After finding the answer, the child should record the fact on a sheet of paper.

When everyone is finished, the children compare results and correct errors.

Activity 5.07 Finger Split

Have the children work with partners. Each pair of partners will need a 10-inch piece of colored yarn.

One child holds his or her hands up, with both hands open and palms outward. The partner hangs the yarn between any two of the first child's fingers. This separates the 10 fingers into two groups. The children identify the addition fact and record it on a sheet of paper.

This fact is 4 + 6 = 10.

Repeat the activity to find other sums of 10.

Discovering Relationships among the Facts.   After the children have found answers for a body of easy basic addition facts, the teacher should lead the class through the process of accumulating these facts into an organized list. The facts should be organized in many different ways to help the children see patterns. The patterns that the children see will help them discover relationships that exist among the facts.

For example, you might have the children make a list of all the facts where 1 is being added. The children could then see that when they add 1 to a number, they get the next number (next in the counting sequence). When listing all the facts where 0 is being added, the children can easily see that whenever 0 is added, they get the same number. If you point out 2 + 3 = 5 and 3 + 2 = 5, 5 + 1 = 6 and 1 + 5 = 6, 5 + 3 = 8 and 3 + 5 = 8, and other similar pairs, the children can see that rearranging the numbers does not change the answer. If the children are led to organize the facts so that facts with the same answer are together, they will discover that there are many different ways to name a number. For example, 6 + 1, 4 + 3, 1 + 6, 2 + 5, 0 + 7, 5 + 2, 3 + 4, and 7 + 0 are all names for the same number, 7.

The emphasis on relationships provides two benefits. First, the interrelationships among the facts make them easier to remember. And, once the facts have been memorized, the interrelationships will improve retention. *It is always easier to remember things that are related to other things that we know.*

Second, the emphasis on relationships substantially reduces the quantity of information to be learned. Suppose we consider the addition facts with sums of 10 or less to be easy basic addition facts. These facts are displayed in the following illustration. Note that there is a total of 64 easy facts. That's a lot to have to learn.

+	0	1	2	3	4	5	6	7	8	9
0	0	1	2	3	4	5	6	7	8	9
1	1	2	3	4	5	6	7	8	9	10
2	2	3	4	5	6	7	8	9	10	
3	3	4	5	6	7	8	9	10		
4	4	5	6	7	8	9	10			
5	5	6	7	8	9	10				
6	6	7	8	9	10					
7	7	8	9	10						
8	8	9	10							
9	9	10								

Notice that there are 19 facts that involve addition of 0. But when we study relationships among the facts, we find that when adding 0, we always get the other number. That is only 1 thing to learn instead of 19 things:

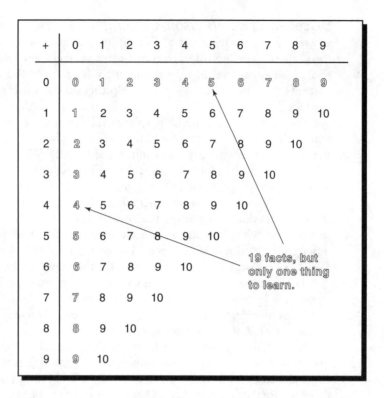

+	0	1	2	3	4	5	6	7	8	9
0	0	1	2	3	4	5	6	7	8	9
1	1	2	3	4	5	6	7	8	9	10
2	2	3	4	5	6	7	8	9	10	
3	3	4	5	6	7	8	9	10		
4	4	5	6	7	8	9	10			
5	5	6	7	8	9	10				
6	6	7	8	9	10					
7	7	8	9	10						
8	8	9	10							
9	9	10								

19 facts, but only one thing to learn.

The facts $1 + 0$ and $0 + 1$ were included in the preceding illustration. There are 17 other facts where 1 is being added. In the exploration of patterns and relationships, the children have already seen that when they add 1, they get the next number in the counting sequence. So, instead of needing to learn these 17 facts as separate things, the children have only 1 thing to learn:

+	0	1	2	3	4	5	6	7	8	9
0	0	1	2	3	4	5	6	7	8	9
1	1	2	3	4	5	6	7	8	9	10
2	2	3	4	5	6	7	8	9	10	
3	3	4	5	6	7	8	9	10		
4	4	5	6	7	8	9	10			
5	5	6	7	8	9	10				
6	6	7	8	9	10					
7	7	8	9	10						
8	8	9	10							
9	9	10								

17 facts, but only one thing to learn.

Now, if the children have seen that rearranging the numbers does not change the answer, 6 + 3 and 3 + 6 can be learned together, not as 2 things to learn, but as 1 thing. This is, of course, what mathematicians call the *commutative property of addition*. Similarly, 2 + 8 and 8 + 2 become 1 thing to learn. In the 64 easy basic facts that we are considering, there are 12 of these commutative pairs. That is, 24 facts, but only 12 things to learn:

+	0	1	2	3	4	5	6	7	8	9
0	0	1	2	3	4	5	6	7	8	9
1	1	2	3	4	5	6	7	8	9	10
2	2	3	4	5	6	7	8	9	10	
3	3	4	5	6	7	8	9	10		
4	4	5	6	7	8	9	10			
5	5	6	7	8	9	10				
6	6	7	8	9	10					
7	7	8	9	10						
8	8	9	10							
9	9	10								

12 of these pairs. That's 24 facts, but only 12 things to learn.

We have now considered all but four of the easy basic addition facts. These are the doubles: 2 + 2, 3 + 3, 4 + 4, and 5 + 5. They must be learned as separate facts, but children generally find them relatively easy to learn. Let's review how these few relationships reduce the amount of memorization that is necessary:

Group of Facts	Number of Facts	Things to Learn
Adding 0	19	1
Adding 1	17	1
Commutative pairs	24	12
Doubles	4	4
All easy facts	64	18

Activities for Exploring Relationships

The following activities illustrate ways to help students explore patterns and discover relationships among the addition facts.

Adding One

Activity 5.08   Just Another One

You will need a box and 10 blocks.

Show the children that the box is empty. Place the box on a table or desk where all the children can see. Tell them to watch and listen carefully. Drop 3 blocks into the box, one at a time. Ask how many blocks are in the box. Tell the children that you are going to add 1 more block. Drop another block into the box. Ask how many blocks are in the box. [4] Write 3 + 1 = 4 on the board.

Repeat the activity, starting with different numbers (for example, 6, 4, or 9). In each case, record the result. [6 + 1 = 7, 4 + 1 = 5, and so on.]

Place 15 blocks into the box. Tell the children that there are 15 blocks. Have them watch and listen as you add 1 more block. Ask how many there are now. Write 15 + 1 = 16.

Write 11 + 1 = on the board. Ask what the answer is. If no one knows, use the blocks and box to find the answer. Continue with other examples until the children have generalized the notion that *when we add 1, we get the next number* in the counting sequence.

Adding Zero

Activity 5.09   The Empty Box

Form groups of three or four children. Each group will need three boxes and 10 blocks.

Write 6 on the board. Have someone in each group place that many blocks into one of the boxes. Write 0 on the board, about 6 inches to the right of the 6. Point to the 0 and have someone in each group put that many blocks in another box.

Write a plus sign between the two numbers and tell the children that we are going to add the two numbers. Have them empty the blocks from the first box and the blocks from the second box into the third box. Ask how many there are altogether. Does everyone agree?

Repeat the activity with 0 + 8, 4 + 0, and 0 + 9. Then write 7 + 0 = on the board and ask if anyone knows the answer. Repeat with 0 + 13. Ask, "What is always true?"

Rearranging Pairs

Activity 5.10   Number Split

Have the children work with partners. Each pair needs 10 counters and a 12-inch length of yarn. Have them place some of the counters on the table between them. (For example, they might place 8 of the counters on the table.)

Then have them use the yarn to separate the counters into two groups.

Help them see that when the two parts are added, the answer is all of the counters. Have them write the two facts that are shown by the counters and yarn. [3 + 5 = 8 and 5 + 3 = 8.]

Have them repeat the process to produce other pairs of facts. Have the children report the pairs of facts that they found.

Record the facts on the board. Have the children look at the pairs of facts and explain the pattern. What happens to the answer if you rearrange the numbers? [It does not change.]

Activity 5.11 Another One Like the Other One

On large cards (about 8.5 inches by 5.5 inches), print two facts. Each pair should demonstrate one of the relationships discussed earlier. One fact should have the answer; the other should not:

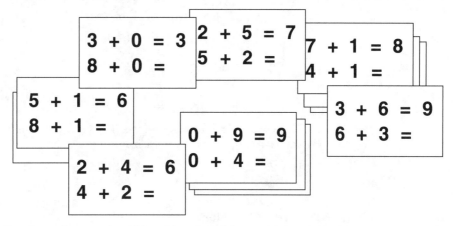

Pass the cards out to the children. Have the children explain how what they know about the first fact can help them figure out the second fact.

Memorization of the Easy Basic Addition Facts. After the easy basic facts have been investigated for helpful relationships, there needs to be a concentrated and sustained effort to help the children commit those facts to memory. As practice activities with the objective of memorization are planned, eight principles should be kept in mind:

1. Children should be aware that the objective is to memorize the facts. They should be told to remember. (Surprisingly, children are often not told to remember the facts.)

2. The activities should use an interesting and fun format.

3. The activities should have a high level of involvement. Minimize time spent waiting. Maximize time spent thinking about the facts.

4. The activities should focus on a small number of unmemorized facts at any given time.

5. Some already-memorized facts should be mixed in with the target unmemorized facts. This will improve retention.

6. If a child does not know an answer, he or she should be required to figure it out. This implies that the child will have time to figure it out.

7. To figure out an answer, the child should think about what he or she already knows that will help find the answer. What other already-known facts will help? What already-known relationship will help? Counting should be used only as a last resort.

8. Emphasize accuracy, not speed. Accuracy is of great importance. Speed is of little importance. Speed will come after accuracy and confidence.

The following are examples of activities that might be used when children are working on memorization of the easy basic addition facts.

Activity 5.12 Facts of the Day

Identify two "Facts of the Day." Have the children find the answers. Write the facts on the board and then tape a sheet of paper over the answer to each fact. Tell the children to remember these facts. Call on a child and ask for the answer to one of the facts. If the child does not know, ask her or him to figure it out. Then tell the child to remember it.

Throughout the day, ask different children for the answers to these facts. Have the children write the facts and put the written facts in their pockets.

Activity 5.13 Easy Ones

Prepare flash cards with the numbers 0 to 9 printed on them. Also prepare flash cards with these facts printed on them:

0 + 1 =	1 + 0 =	1 + 1 =	2 + 1 =
1 + 2 =	3 + 1 =	1 + 3 =	4 + 1 =
1 + 4 =	5 + 1 =	1 + 5 =	6 + 1 =
1 + 6 =	7 + 1 =	1 + 7 =	8 + 1 =
1 + 8 =	9 + 1 =	1 + 9 =	

Call on a child. Show one of the numbers. Have the child tell you the number that is one more. When the children can correctly give the number that is one more, switch to the addition-fact flash cards.

Activity 5.14 One More

Prepare flash cards for addition facts through sums of eight.

Show a card. Have the child give the answer. If he or she cannot, have the child figure it out.

Then ask for the answer to a fact that is one more. For example, after the child gives the answer to 4 + 2 =, ask, "What is 4 + 3?" After the child has answered 4 + 3 =, ask, "What is 4 + 4?" After the child has answered 4 + 4 =, ask, "What is 4 + 5?"

Developing the Hard Basic Addition Facts

Thinking Strategies for Hard Basic Addition Facts.   When developing the hard basic addition facts (sums of 11 through 18), children can still find answers by counting. However, with the larger numbers, counting is inefficient and consequently very slow. So, at this point in the development, more-efficient strategies are needed to allow the child to find answers quickly and accurately (Thornton et al., 1983). A wide variety of fact strategies are taught to students. The objective is to commit these facts to memory. Some fact strategies seem to lead to memorization, whereas others do not. The strategies that successfully lead to memorization have two common characteristics.

First, *successful strategies are mental strategies.* They consist of a series of quick, easy, mental procedures. They are not pencil-and-paper strategies, although they can be recorded by using mathematical notation. They are not mechanical strategies. They are not performed by manipulating fingers or other objects, although the fingers or other physical materials could be used to establish mental imagery for the strategies.

Second, *successful strategies require the child to use facts that are already memorized to figure out the facts that are not yet memorized.* The children should be constantly thinking about what they already know that can help them figure out what they do not know. The students should have a sense of building on what is already known. New knowledge is closely related to existing knowledge, and it is always easier to remember things that are related to other things that are known.

One More   The simplest thinking strategy for hard basic addition facts is the *one-more strategy.* The thinking is simple, so it is an easy strategy for children to use. Every hard fact can be thought of as being one more than another fact. Think of that other fact and then add one more:

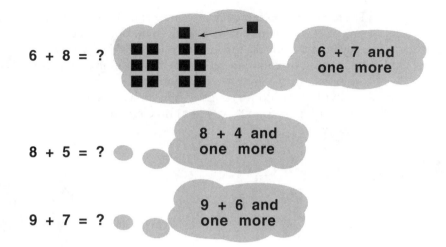

6 + 8 = ?   6 + 7 and one more

8 + 5 = ?   8 + 4 and one more

9 + 7 = ?   9 + 6 and one more

Of course, a child cannot use this strategy to find 6 + 8 unless he or she already knows 6 + 7. He or she cannot find 8 + 5 unless 8 + 4 is already known. The answer to 9 + 7 cannot be found unless 9 + 6 is known.

This strategy works particularly well in a clinical setting where the instructor is working with one child. However, in the classroom, children learn the facts at different rates. They do not learn them in the same sequence. One child may know 6 + 8 = 14, but the next child may not know that fact. One child is able to use the one-more strategy to find the answer to 6 + 9, but another cannot. To use this strategy successfully, the teacher must know exactly which facts the child already knows in order to know which one the child will be able to figure out. With one child, this is possible, but with a classroom full of children, it is not. So, even though the one-more strategy is easiest for the child to use, and even though the strategy works well with an individual child, it is not manageable with a class.

Doubles Researchers (Thornton et al., 1983) have found that the doubles (6 + 6, 8 + 8, and so on) tend to be easier for children to commit to memory than are other hard basic addition facts. A reasonable approach might be to get the doubles memorized and then build on them to find answers to other facts. In fact, the doubles strategy is one of the more successful ones:

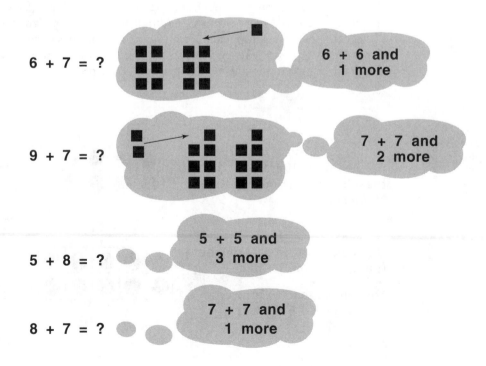

6 + 7 = ?   6 + 6 and 1 more

9 + 7 = ?   7 + 7 and 2 more

5 + 8 = ?   5 + 5 and 3 more

8 + 7 = ?   7 + 7 and 1 more

The thinking process requires "counting on" from the double. Counting on is easy if the target fact is only one or two away from the double. However, if the fact is three or more away from the double, the strategy is less effective.

Adding by counting on requires two simultaneous counts. For example, to find the answer to 8 + 6 we would begin with 8 and count on from there: 9, 10, 11, 12, . . . But how far do we count? When do we stop counting? At the same time that we are counting on from 8, we must also count from 1. Otherwise, we don't know when to stop:

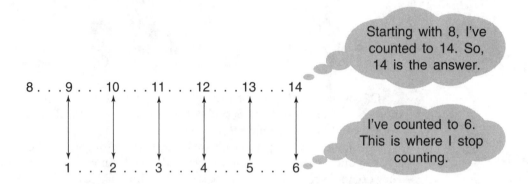

Because the doubles method requires two simultaneous counts starting with different numbers, when the target fact is more than two away from a double, children are usually unable to complete the process mentally. They typically do one count mentally and keep the other count on their fingers. Finger counting slows the process down and becomes more mechanical. The mental link between the problem and its answer is cluttered. Practice using this strategy does not effectively lead to memorization of facts that are more than two away from the double.

Make Ten   Another strategy that has been shown to be effective is the *make-10 strategy*. It is based on the understanding that basic addition facts with sums of 10 are typically learned before the basic addition facts with sums greater than 10. In this strategy, the purpose is to mentally rearrange the quantities being combined to form a group of 10 and some leftovers. The strategy is taught easily when some device such as a 10-frame is used to provide mental imagery for the process:

To find 8 + 6, place the larger number in the 10-frame and place the other number outside the 10-frame.

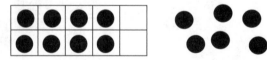

Use some of the smaller number (the 6) to fill the 10-frame.

You can see that the answer is 10 + 4. So, 8 + 6 = 14.

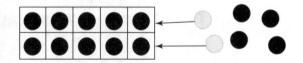

To find 3 + 9, place 9 in the 10-frame and place 3 outside the 10-frame.

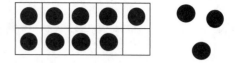

You need to move 1 to fill the 10-frame. That leaves 2 outside the 10-frame. The answer is 12. So, 3 + 9 = 12.

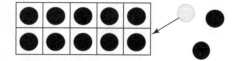

The children should practice using the 10-frame to find answers until mental imagery for the process is established. Then children are able to get answers by just thinking about how they would use the 10-frame. For example, finding the answer to 8 + 7 requires the following series of mental steps:

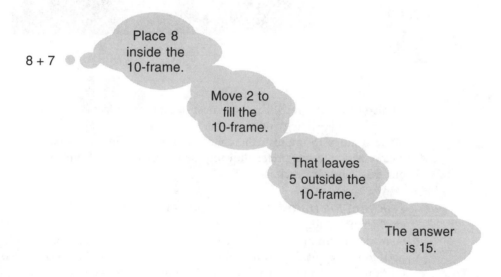

The child can easily learn the process through a series of self-directed questions. To find 7 + 9, he or she must answer these questions:

What number goes inside? [9]
How many do I move? [1]
What's left outside? [6]
What's the answer? [16]

The make-10 strategy is a general strategy in that it works for all of the hard basic addition facts. As a result, the children can always use it without having to decide what to do with each fact. It uses a process very much like the regrouping process used in the addition algorithm, so learning the make-10 strategy makes it easier to learn the addition algorithm.

Choice of Strategies Teachers must decide which fact strategy to teach and whether to use a single strategy or a combination of strategies. Some teachers prefer to use a single strategy to improve the child's speed in finding answers, which also speeds up memorization. Some prefer allowing the child to choose from a variety of strategies the one that is best for each fact.

Teaching the Hard Basic Addition Facts.

After the children have learned to use an efficient strategy to find answers to the hard basic addition facts, rapid progress can be made toward mastery of those facts. As when working on the easy facts, the children need to figure out the answers to the hard facts. The children should recognize and use relationships among the hard facts and commit them to memory.

If children do not know a hard fact, saying "I don't know" is not acceptable. They need to figure out the answer. Because you want them to do that efficiently and quickly, you should encourage (almost require) them to use the thinking strategy that they learned. The children have, at this point, been using counting for over a year to find addition-fact answers. They are comfortable with counting—even when it takes a long time. Consequently, they will automatically fall back on counting because they are so comfortable with it. So, you must continually lead the children to use the thinking strategy instead of counting.

If children do not know the answer to a fact, they need to think about what they already know that will help them find that answer. If they continually think about the relationships among the facts, they end up with fewer things to learn, and their retention of what they have learned is better.

Memorization of the Hard Basic Addition Facts.

The following sequence of activities illustrates how a teacher might help the students memorize the hard basic addition facts.

Activity 5.15 *What Do You Know That Helps?*

This activity requires a set of addition-fact flash cards. Select some cards that show facts that have already been mastered. Mix in some cards for facts that are not yet mastered. Shuffle the cards.

Show a flash card to a child. If he or she gives an answer, ask the rest of the class if it is correct. If the child does not know the answer, show related facts and ask if they help.

For example, if the fact on the flash card is 6 + 8, ask if the child knows 8 + 6. Does the child know 6 + 6? Does the child know 8 + 5? If none of the related facts helps, then lead the child through a thinking strategy to find the answer.

Activity 5.16 *Match Me*

Prepare large cards showing facts without answers. Include pairs of facts with the same answer. Mix in some facts that have already been mastered with facts that are not yet mastered. Shuffle the cards. Give a card to each child. Have everyone find a partner whose fact has the same answer. If there is an odd number of children, the teacher should participate so everyone has a partner.

Have the children stand in a circle with partners standing together. They should hold their cards so everyone else can see. Then ask the children to check to see if all the partners match.

Collect the cards, reshuffle them, and repeat the activity.

Activity 5.17 *Fact War*

Prepare a set of cards with one-digit numbers on them. Make five cards for each number.

Form a group of three or four children. Shuffle the deck and place it facedown on the table.

On each play, all players take two cards from the top of the deck. Each child lays his or her cards faceup and

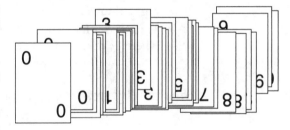

says the sum. Whoever has the greatest sum takes the cards used in that play. When all the cards have been played, the child who has taken the most cards is the winner.

If there is a disagreement about a sum or about which is greater, the children should use counters to discover who is right.

Activity 5.18 *Make Eleven*

Use cards like those described in activity 5.17. Form a group of three or four children. Shuffle the cards and place the deck facedown on the table. Turn three starter cards faceup on the table.

Players take turns. On each play, the player takes the top card from the deck and places it faceup on the table with the starter cards. The player then looks at all the cards that are faceup. If two of them have a sum of 11, the player takes those two cards, and her or his turn is over. If the player is unable to find two cards with a sum of 11, the turn is over. The number of starter cards for each player will increase or decrease depending on whether the previous player found two cards with a sum of 11.

When all the cards have been played, the child who has taken the most cards is the winner.

Activity 5.19 Make Twelve

Use cards like those described in activity 5.17. Form a group of three or four children. Shuffle the cards and place the deck facedown on the table. Turn three starter cards faceup on the table.

Follow the procedures of activity 5.18, except the players find two cards with a sum of 12.

Teaching the Addition Algorithm

After mastery of the basic addition facts, the students are ready to begin work on the addition algorithm. Remember that the addition algorithm is the step-by-step process by which the basic facts are used to find answers to any other whole-number addition example. To say it another way, the addition algorithm is what we use to do multidigit addition, addition of numbers with more than one digit. Remember that when teaching the algorithm, you want to do several things:

- **Let the children see what it looks like.** Carefully model the operation with an appropriate physical or pictorial model. Use a model that lets the children see what happens to the basic units—ones, tens, hundreds, and so on—when they add.
- **Deemphasize rote rules.** You might end up with rules, but they should be meaningful. They should arise out of the modeling process.
- **Emphasize big ideas.** These are the important generalizations that describe the process. They arise out of the modeling process.
- **Let the written algorithm simply be a recording of what happens when the algorithm is modeled.** Everything you write should match something you do.
- **Watch your language.** The language you use should describe what the children see when the operation is modeled, not language that describes what you write down.

The First Big Idea. The next two activities introduce the first of the big ideas.

Activity 5.20 Gloves and Socks

Bring nine gloves and nine socks to class.

Have a child come forward and place six gloves and one sock into a box. Record on the board what was placed in the box.   6 gloves   1 sock

Have another child come forward and place three more gloves and two more socks into the box. Record on the board what was placed in the box.

Ask how many gloves and how many socks in the box.   6 gloves   1 sock
Ask how the children know. Repeat the activity with   3 gloves   2 socks
different numbers of gloves and socks.

Activity 5.21 What's in the Box?

Use single Popsicle sticks and bundles of 10 Popsicle sticks.

Write the number 26 on the board.   26

Have a child come forward and show the number by using the bundled sticks and the single sticks. Place the sticks that the child selected into a box. Then write the number 53 about 6 inches to the right of the 26. Have a child come forward and show   26   53 the number by using the bundled sticks and the single sticks. Place those sticks into the box also. Point out that you have put those two numbers together. Ask what we call it when you do that. [Adding.]

Write a plus sign between the numbers. 26 + 53

Now ask what is in the box altogether. Ask how the children know.

Repeat the activity with different numbers and then with three-digit numbers.

The First Big Idea in Addition Is Always Add Like Units Out of experiences like those illustrated previously, it becomes apparent to the children that to decide what is in the box, they need to think about only what was put into the box. If sticks and stones are in the box, then they need to think about how many sticks and how many stones are in the box. If gloves and socks are put into the box and later some more gloves and socks are put into the box, then to tell what is in the box they need to think about only how many gloves are in the box and how many socks are in the box. And how can they figure this out? Add the number of gloves that were put into the box at first to the number of gloves put into the box later. To decide how many socks are in the box, add the number of socks that were put into the box at first to the number of socks that were put into the box later. This is so obvious to the children that it rarely needs to be pointed out. Why do they not add the number of gloves to the number of socks? Because in this setting that would make no sense.

When adding 26 and 53 by representing these numbers with bundled sticks and single sticks allows the children to see the basic units and then combining the numbers together, the children know the answer because they can see what it looks like. They can see that they need to tell only how many tens there are and how many ones there are. There is no tendency to add the number of tens to the number of ones. That makes no sense.

If they use the model to add 142 + 35, they will not be inclined to add the 1 and the 3. That does not make sense. However, if the typical rote rules are taught, children frequently combine "always go left to right" and "you must line up the columns" to get:

$$
\begin{array}{r}
142 \\
+\ 35 \\
\hline
\end{array}
$$

This is obviously not correct. It makes no sense. When an appropriate model is used to help the children see what multidigit addition looks like, they will not make this common error. They can see what needs to be added to what (Tucker, 1989):

142 + 35   Add the ones.
We need to know
how many ones
there are.

142 + 35   Add the tens.
We need to know
how many tens
there are.

142 + 35   We have only
1 hundred.

We add ones to ones. We add tens to tens. *We always add like units.* This is the first of two big ideas that are used in the addition algorithm. Let's consider this big idea.

First, addition of like units is a constantly recurring idea. How do we add decimals? We add like units.

2.481 + 47.2 = 49.681   To find out how many tenths there are, tenths are added to tenths. *We must add like units.*

Why is it easier to add $\frac{2}{5} + \frac{1}{5}$ than to add $\frac{2}{5} + \frac{1}{3}$? Because in $\frac{2}{5} + \frac{1}{5}$, the fractional units are the same in both fractions. In $\frac{2}{5} + \frac{1}{3}$, the fractional units are not the same. *We add like units.* In this case, we call them *like denominators*, but it is the same big idea.

When adding polynomials in algebra, we would add as follows:

$$(2x + 5y + 4xy) + (7x + 3xy) = 9x + 5y + 7xy$$

Why do we add the xs together? Why do we add the xys together? Why did we not add the $5y$ to anything? Because *we add like units*. In this case, we call them *like terms*, but it is the same big idea.

Although we don't need to point it out to first-grade children, this big idea (*always add like units*) is really an application of the *distributive property*:

$$
\begin{aligned}
23 + 42 &= (20 + 3) + (40 + 2) \\
&= 2 \times 10 + 3 \times 1 + 4 \times 10 + 2 \times 1 \\
&= 2 \times 10 + 4 \times 10 + 3 \times 1 + 2 \times 1 \\
&= |2 + 4| \times 10 + |3 + 2| \times 1 \\
&= 6 \times 10 + 5 \times 1 \\
&= 65
\end{aligned}
$$

The Second Big Idea. The second of the two big ideas that are the basis of the addition algorithm also arises out of the modeling process. We first provide experiences to establish that a number can be named in many ways. We then create an addition dilemma and use the children's understanding of renaming numbers to resolve it. The following activities illustrate how this can be done.

Activity 5.22   AKA

Ask the children if they know what *AKA* means. [It stands for Also Known As. It is another name for something or someone.] Write 45 on the board. Tell the children that 45 has a lot of names. Below the 45, write AKA 40 + 5. Tell the children to get out pencil and paper and write another name for 45. Have them share with the class their AKAs. Record the different names for 45. The AKAs might include 44 + 1, 43 + 2, 42 + 3, 10 + 35, 30 + 15, and so on. If necessary, remind the children of the new names they get if they unbundle a ten.

Activity 5.23   Too Many to Write

Write the addition problem 54 + 28 on the board in vertical form.

$$
\begin{array}{r}
54 \\
+\ 28 \\
\hline
\end{array}
$$

Have a child come forward and represent the two numbers by using bundled Popsicle sticks or base-10 blocks. Have the child place the numbers into a box. Ask the class to tell you what is in the box. How many tens are there? [7] Record this under the tens.

$$
\begin{array}{r}
54 \\
+\ 28 \\
\hline
7
\end{array}
$$

Ask how many ones are in the box. [12] Record this under the ones. Restate that we have 7 tens and 12 ones. Point to the answer on the board. Ask if this looks like 7 tens and 12 ones. [No, it looks like 7 hundreds, 1 ten, and 2 ones.]

$$
\begin{array}{r}
54 \\
+\ 28 \\
\hline
712
\end{array}
$$

Ask if anyone knows what is wrong. [When you write 12 ones, it does not look like 12 ones.] Point out that we have room, in each position, for only a one-digit number. In this case, *we have too many to write.* Ask what we can do to get rid of this problem. [Trade 10 ones for a ten.]

Have the children help you make a trade. Ask, "What do we have after the trade?" Point out that this is another name for the same number.

Repeat the activity with other numbers.

The Second Big Idea in Addition Is When There Are Too Many to Write, Make a Trade The second of the two big ideas that are the basis for the addition algorithm is: *when there are too many to write, make a trade*, meaning too many to write in standard notation. If the example given in activity 5.23 had been done by using a base-10 chart, there would have been no confusion caused by the way the answer was written. But, neither would there have been a need to make the trade.

tens	ones
5	4
+2	8
7	12

Use of the Addition Algorithm. So, building on the children's experiences with the model, you can show that there are only two things in the addition algorithm to do: add like units and when there are too many to write, make a trade. That is all there is to the addition algorithm. When the children learn these two things, they can add any two whole numbers. It does not make any difference whether they are adding three-digit numbers without regrouping, adding two-digit numbers with regrouping from ones to tens, adding five-digit numbers with regrouping from tens to hundreds and also regrouping from hundreds to thousands, or adding any combination of whole numbers. And, looking ahead to addition of decimals, there will not be anything new, because we just add like units and make a trade when there are too many to write.

Summary of the Developmental Sequence for Addition

Establish the meaning of the operation
1. Associate addition with combining quantities.
2. Learn to use counting to find answers.

Develop the easy basic facts
1. Find the answers by using the meaning of addition.
2. Discover relationships among the facts.
3. Memorize the facts.

Develop thinking strategies for hard addition facts
1. Use mental strategies.
2. Use memorized easy facts to find answers for the hard facts.

Develop the hard basic facts
1. Find the answers by using the thinking strategies.
2. Review helpful relationships among the facts.
3. Memorize the facts.

Develop the algorithm
1. Always add like units.
2. If there are too many to write, make a trade.

Teaching Subtraction of Whole Numbers

The developmental sequence for teaching whole-number subtraction is similar to that for addition. The first step is to establish the meaning of the operation by associating subtraction with a physical operation. Two physical settings are related to subtraction. One setting calls for comparison subtraction, and the other calls for take-away subtraction.

Developing the Meaning of Subtraction

Comparison Subtraction. We first consider *comparison subtraction*. Beginning with two quantities, we compare them to find the difference.

Activity 5.24   So, What's the Difference?

Show the children a group of 4 shoes and a group of 10 socks.

Ask if there are the same number of shoes and socks. Ask if there are more socks or more shoes. Have children come forward and match a shoe with a sock until you run out of shoes.

Point out that the extras are the difference. The difference is 6 socks. Tell the children that this is a kind of subtraction. Write the subtraction sentence on the board. Explain each of the symbols used.

The process used to find the difference is one-to-one matching. Children can easily learn to use this matching process to find answers to specific subtraction examples. The next activity illustrates how to lead the children to find answers in comparison subtraction.

Activity 5.25   Compare for Differences

Write 8 − 3 on the board. Tell the children, "Today we are going to find the difference between 8 and 3."

Use counters to show the two numbers.

Then match counters from the first number with counters from the second number so the children can see that the difference is 5. Record the answer on the board.

Repeat the activity with several other examples. Sometimes have a child write the problem or have a child get the counters to show the two numbers. Other times have a child do the matching or have a child write the answer. Sometimes have a child do the whole thing.

Take-Away Subtraction. Now we consider the second of the physical settings that children should associate with subtraction. In this setting, you start with one number, take some of it away, and find the remainder (Page, 1994). The following activity can be used with children to illustrate *take-away subtraction.*

> **Activity 5.26   It's in the Bag**
>
> Have the children work with partners. Give each pair of partners a paper bag, 10 crayons, and pencil and paper. They take turns going first.
>
> The first child places some of the crayons in the bag. He or she writes the number (for example, 8) on the paper to show how many crayons are in the bag.   8
>
> The second child takes some of the crayons out of the bag and records how many crayons were taken out of the bag (for example, 3).   8 − 3
>
> The first child counts to see how many crayons are left in the bag and records the rest of the subtraction sentence.   8 − 3 = 5
>
> The children should continue the activity until they have generated at least 10 subtraction examples.

Notice that there are two distinct types of subtraction. Children need to become familiar with both comparison and take-away situations and to relate both to subtraction. They will encounter both kinds of situations in solving problems. They need to recognize that *we can use subtraction here*. However, once the meaning of subtraction has been established, take-away subtraction is used almost exclusively in the development of whole-number subtraction.

Developing the Easy Basic Subtraction Facts

The students should find the answers to the easy basic subtraction facts. Their understanding of the meaning of subtraction allows them to do this. Activities such as activity 5.26, It's in the Bag, are effective for this purpose. As they discover the facts, their results should be compiled in some organized form. As the facts are organized, lead the children to discover several relationships.

They should notice that any time a number is subtracted from itself, the answer is 0. There are 10 of these facts, but once they see the relationship, there is only one thing to remember. The children should notice that whenever they subtract 0 from a number, the answer will be that same number. There are also 10 of these facts, but only one thing to remember. They should notice that when they subtract 1 from any number, they get the number that comes before it in the counting sequence. There are 10 of these facts, but again only one thing to remember. Recognition of these relationships reduces the amount of memorization that is necessary.

There are other relationships that should also be discovered because they provide connections to other things that the child knows. And, *it is always easier to remember things that are related to other things that we know.* Every subtraction fact is related to an addition fact. For example:

$$8 - 2 = 6 \qquad 5 - 1 = 4 \qquad 10 - 7 = 3 \qquad 9 - 3 = 6$$
$$6 + 2 = 8 \qquad 4 + 1 = 5 \qquad 3 + 7 = 10 \qquad 6 + 3 = 9$$

Every subtraction fact is related to another subtraction fact. For example:

$$5 - 2 = 3 \qquad 8 - 1 = 7 \qquad 10 - 6 = 4 \qquad 7 - 2 = 5$$
$$5 - 3 = 2 \qquad 8 - 7 = 1 \qquad 10 - 4 = 6 \qquad 7 - 5 = 2$$

The children need to see what these relationships look like. So, as the relationships are being discovered, the children should be exposed to physical representations of those relationships. The following activities illustrate how this can be accomplished.

Activity 5.27   Let Me See: Subtracting a Number from Itself

As children are noticing that all subtraction facts such as 3 − 3, 7 − 7, 2 − 2, or 9 − 9 have 0 as the answer, illustrate the facts with counters. Show several examples:

 Take away 5.

Start with 5.

Then, to generalize the notion, place a handful of counters on the table. Ask how many will be left if the children take them all away. [0] What if there were 52? What would be the answer to 52 − 52?

What if there were 24? What if there were 124?

Activity 5.28   Let Me See: Subtracting Zero

As children are noticing that all subtraction facts such as 3 − 0, 7 − 0, 2 − 0, or 9 − 0 have the beginning number as the answer, illustrate the facts with counters. Show several examples:

 Start with 5.   Cover them with a sheet of paper.

Wave your hand over the paper and ask, "How many did I take away?" [0] Ask how many are left under the paper. [5] So, 5 − 0 = 5.

Then, to generalize this idea, place a handful of counters on the table. Cover them. Wave your hand over the paper and ask how many were taken away. Ask how many are left if there were 57 counters under the paper. [57] What would be the answer to 57 − 0? What if there were 29? What is the answer to 29 − 0? What if there were 247?

Activity 5.29   Let Me See: Related Subtraction and Addition Facts

As the children are noticing that subtraction facts are related to addition facts—for example, 3 − 1 = 2 and 2 + 1 = 3, 7 − 4 = 3 and 3 + 4 = 7, or 9 − 5 = 4 and 4 + 5 = 9—illustrate the facts with counters. Show several examples:

If I start with 8 and take away 3, I have 5 left. That's 8 − 3 = 5.

Then, if I put those 3 back with the 5 that were left, I have 8 again. That's 5 + 3 = 8.

Then, to generalize, place a handful of counters on the table. Tell the children that you think there are 51 counters. Take away all but 3 of them. Ask how many are left. [3] Replace the counters that were taken away. Ask how many there are now. [51—as many as we started with.] Write 128 − 54 = 74 on the board. Tell the children that this means we started with 128, took 54 away and had 74 left. Ask how many there would be if we put the 54 back with the 74 that were left. [128]

Activity 5.30 Let Me See: Related Subtraction Facts

As the children are noticing that there are pairs of related subtraction facts such as 3 − 1 = 2 and 3 − 2 = 1, 7 − 4 = 3 and 7 − 3 = 4, or 9 − 5 = 4 and 9 − 4 = 5, illustrate the relationship with counters. Show several examples:

Show eight counters. Lay a length of yarn through the counters to separate them into a group of three and a group of five.

Show the children that if you take away the group of three counters, you are left with the group of five. That's 8 − 3 = 5.

On the other hand, if you take away the group of five counters, you are left with the group of three. That's 8 − 5 = 3.

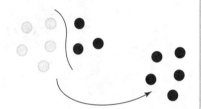

After discovering these helpful relationships, the children are ready to begin memorization of the easy basic subtraction facts. Some of the memorization activities that follow emphasize thinking about the relationships.

Activity 5.31 Related Pairs

Prepare large cards with pairs of related subtraction facts on them. The answer should be included for one of the facts, but not for the other:

| 8 − 2 = 6 | 4 − 1 = 3 | 8 − 5 = 3 | 6 − 2 = 4 | 9 − 3 = 6 |
| 8 − 6 = | 4 − 3 = | 8 − 3 = | 6 − 4 = | 9 − 6 = |

Show the cards one at a time. Have children give the missing answer. Ask how the first answer can help them get the missing answer. If they cannot give the missing answer, ask how the first answer can help them figure it out.

Use counters to show the related facts if needed (see activity 5.30).

Activity 5.32 Put Them Together and Take Them Apart

Prepare flash cards for the following subtraction facts:

8 − 3 =	5 − 2 =	9 − 6 =	6 − 3 =
4 − 2 =	7 − 5 =	8 − 4 =	6 − 4 =
7 − 4 =	8 − 6 =	9 − 4 =	9 − 2 =

Write these addition facts on the board:

2 + 2 = 4	3 + 2 = 5	3 + 3 = 6	1 + 4 = 6
2 + 5 = 7	3 + 4 = 7	5 + 3 = 8	4 + 4 = 8
2 + 6 = 8	3 + 6 = 9	5 + 4 = 9	7 + 2 = 9

Show a flash card. Whether or not the child can give the answer, ask which of the addition facts on the board helps in figuring out the answer. Use counters to show the related facts if needed (see activity 5.29).

Activity 5.33 Peek If You Need To

When an individual child is having difficulty remembering a particular fact—for example, $9 - 4$—fold a small piece of paper, write the problem on the outside, write the answer on the inside, and tape it to the child's desk.

Each time the child is asked this fact, she or he tries to remember the answer. If the child cannot remember, she or he is allowed to look inside at the answer. The child is told each time to remember the answer and is then asked, "What is $9 - 4$?"

Developing the Hard Basic Subtraction Facts

Thinking Strategies for the Hard Basic Subtraction Facts. Answers to the hard basic subtraction facts (minuends of 11 through 18) can still be found by counting. However, with the larger numbers, counting is inefficient and slow. At this point, more-efficient strategies need to be developed that allow the child to find answers to the hard basic subtraction facts quickly and accurately.

Our objective is for these facts to be committed to memory, and the strategies that successfully lead to memorization have two common characteristics. They are mental strategies, and they require the child to use facts that are already memorized to figure out the facts that are not yet memorized. The children should be constantly thinking about what they already know that can help them figure out what they do not know. The children should build on what they already know. New knowledge is closely related to old knowledge, and it is always easier to remember things that are related to other things that are already known.

Think of a Related Addition Fact Among the thinking strategies for hard basic subtraction facts that have been used, two have been particularly successful. The first of these is the one most loved by mathematicians—think of a related addition fact. This strategy is based on the inverse-operation relationship between subtraction and addition, which allows subtraction to be defined in terms of addition: $a - b = c$, where c is the unique number such that $c + b = a$. So, if we want to find the answer to $a - b = ?$ we can think about what number can be added to b to produce a sum of a ($? + b = a$).

What do I add to 7 to get 12?

$12 - 7 = ?$

This is a good strategy. It is mathematically strong and it is a universal strategy; that is, it will work for all hard basic subtraction facts. However, as a strategy for finding answers to hard subtraction facts, it has one flaw. Using this strategy to find $12 - 7 = 5$ requires that the child already know $5 + 7 = 12$. To find $17 - 9 = 8$, the child must already know $8 + 9 = 17$. This strategy requires that the child already know the hard addition facts. Unfortunately, children who are having difficulty mastering the hard subtraction facts are most frequently the same children who have not yet mastered the hard addition facts. This strategy will not work for these children.

Subtract from Ten A second strategy that has proven successful for finding answers to the hard basic subtraction facts requires the children to already know the facts having a minuend of 10 ($10 - 5$, $10 - 7$, $10 - 4$, and so on). It uses the idea that the teen numbers can be thought of as "10 and some more."

This strategy is the reverse of the make-10 strategy that was suggested for finding answers to the hard addition facts. Because subtraction from 10 is easy, have the children subtract from 10 to find answers to all the hard basic subtraction facts. The 10-frame is an effective tool for developing understanding of and mental imagery for the subtract-from-10 thinking strategy. For example, suppose a student wants to find the answer to $13 - 7$. She or he will begin by using the 10-frame to represent 13, the number that the child will start with:

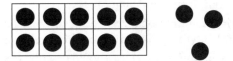

When she or he takes away 7, the child will take seven counters from the 10-frame:

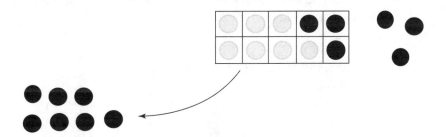

Three counters are left in the 10-frame. Altogether, $3 + 3$, or six, counters are left. So, $13 - 7 = 6$. Or, suppose a child wants to find $14 - 8$:

Start with 14.

Take 8 from the 10.

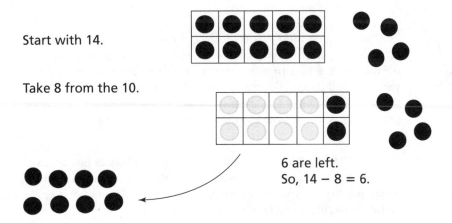

6 are left.
So, $14 - 8 = 6$.

This is a nice way to record the steps:

$$\begin{array}{c}13\\ \underline{-7}\end{array} \longrightarrow \begin{array}{c}10+3\\ \underline{-7}\end{array} \longrightarrow \begin{array}{c}10+3\\ \underline{-7}\\ 3\end{array} \longrightarrow \begin{array}{c}10+3\\ \underline{-7}\\ 3+3=6\end{array}$$

The subtract-from-10 strategy is easy to teach. It is a universal strategy that can be used for all the hard basic subtraction facts. And, it requires the children to know only easy facts.

Teaching the Subtraction Algorithm

After mastery of the basic subtraction facts, the students are ready to begin work on the subtraction algorithm. Remember that the subtraction algorithm is the step-by-step process by which we can use the basic facts to find answers to any other whole-number subtraction example. Remember, also, that when teaching the algorithm, you want to do several things:

- **Let them see what it looks like.** Carefully model the operation with an appropriate physical or pictorial model. Use a model that lets the children see what happens to the basic units—ones, tens, hundreds, and so on—when they subtract.
- **Deemphasize rote rules.** You might end up with rules, but they should be meaningful. They should arise out of the modeling process.
- **Emphasize big ideas.** These are the important generalizations that describe the process. They also arise out of the modeling process.
- **Let the written algorithm simply be a recording of what happens when the algorithm is modeled.** Everything you write should match something you do.
- **Watch your language.** The language you use should describe what the children see when the operation is modeled, not language that describes what you write down.

The First Big Idea.   In the next activity, we introduce the first of the two big ideas that are the basis for the subtraction algorithm.

> ### Activity 5.34   What's Left in the Box?
>
> Write 74 on the board. Have a child come forward and get the base-10 blocks that represent 74. Put them in a box. Write −31 to the right of the 74. Ask what this means. [Take away 31 from 74.]
>
> Have a child come forward and take 31 out of the box. Ask how many tens are left in the box. [4] Ask how the child knows that. How many ones are left in the box? [3] Ask how the child knows that. Record the answer on the board.
>
> Repeat the process with other examples, but do not use examples that require regrouping. Use some examples with three-digit numbers. Record some examples horizontally and record some vertically.

The children will never try to take the ones from the tens or take the tens from the hundreds. That makes no sense when they see what it looks like. It is not necessary to tell the children how to subtract two- and three-digit numbers. The children's common sense will tell them. We take the hundreds from the hundreds. We take the ones from the ones. We take the tens from the tens. *We always subtract like units.* This is the first of two big ideas that are used in the subtraction algorithm.

The Second Big Idea.   The second big idea comes just as naturally as did the first one. Set up an example in which the children encounter a dilemma and then let the children tell you how to deal with it. Activity 5.35, which is really a continuation of activity 5.34, illustrates how this might be done.

Activity 5.35　What's the Problem? What'll We Do?

Write 75 on the board. Have a child come forward and get the base-10 blocks that represent 75. Put them into a box. Write −27 below the 75. Ask what this means. [Take away 27 from 75.]

Have a child come forward to take 27 out of the box. Suggest that the child take the 7 ones out of the box first. When the child cannot do it, ask what the problem is. [There are not enough ones.] Ask the other children what to do. Ask, "How can we get more ones?" [Trade a ten for 10 ones.] Have the child make that trade.

Have the children tell what you have after the trade. Now, how many tens are there? How many ones are there? Record the trade.

Ask if there are enough ones now to take away 7 ones.

Complete the subtraction, recording each step as it is completed.

$$\begin{array}{r} \overset{6\,15}{\cancel{7}\cancel{5}} \\ -27 \\ \hline \end{array}$$

Repeat the process with other examples. Use some examples with three-digit numbers. Record them vertically. Do some examples where there are not enough ones and some where there are not enough tens. Do some examples where there are not enough ones and also not enough tens. Emphasize that it does not make any difference what you are short of, whenever you do not have enough, you make a trade.

Have children do the modeling and the writing.

Activities like the preceding one illustrate the second of the two big ideas that are the basis for the subtraction algorithm: *When there are not enough, make a trade.*

Use of the Subtraction Algorithm.

Out of the children's experiences with the model, we can show that there are only two things that we do in the subtraction algorithm: *Subtract like units and when there are not enough, make a trade.* That is all there is to the subtraction algorithm. When the children learn to do these two things, they can complete any whole-number subtraction example. It does not make any difference whether they are subtracting three-digit numbers without regrouping, subtracting two-digit numbers with regrouping from tens to ones, subtracting five-digit numbers with regrouping from hundreds to tens and also regrouping from thousands to hundreds, or any combination of whole numbers. *Always subtract like units. When there are not enough, make a trade.* And, looking ahead to subtraction of decimals, there will not be anything new, because we just subtract like units and make a trade when there are not enough.

Summary of the Developmental Sequence for Subtraction

Establish the meaning of the operation
1. Associate subtraction with comparison and with take away.
2. Learn to use counting to find answers.

Develop the easy basic facts
1. Find the answers by using the meaning of subtraction.
2. Discover relationships among the facts.
3. Memorize the facts.

Develop thinking strategies for hard subtraction facts that
1. Use mental strategies.
2. Use memorized easy facts to find answers for the hard facts.

Develop the hard basic facts	1. Find the answers by using the thinking strategies.
	2. Review relationships among the facts.
	3. Memorize the facts.
Develop the algorithm	1. Always subtract like units.
	2. If there are not enough, make a trade.

Adapting a Lesson

Now, we adapt another lesson—this time, an early lesson on subtraction. Again, we begin with a traditional plan, taken directly from suggestions that might be found in a teacher's guide of a published program. You should note that this plan is a good one. However, its focus is to teach the textbook page. This lesson will be adapted to make it more effective in meeting the learning needs in a diverse classroom.

LESSON OBJECTIVE

The student will create subtraction sentences with minuends of 1 to 6.

Lesson Opener

Show four counters and two boxes. Tell the children that you are going to put some of the counters into one box and the rest into the other box. Ask, "If you place three counters into one box, how many will be in the other box?" "If you place two into one box, how many will be in the other box?" Tell the children that today they will be creating subtraction sentences.

Development

Make a transparency like the visual on the right. Place the blue lake transparency on the overhead projector. Place four fish cutouts in the lake. Take one of the fish out of the lake. Ask how many fish are left in the lake. Write the subtraction sentence, 4 − 1 = 3, on the board.

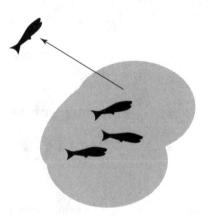

Tell the children to watch while you do another example. Place three fish in the lake and then remove two of them. Ask what subtraction sentence tells what you did. Write the subtraction sentence on the board.

Monitoring Learning

Have everyone do the *Check Understanding* example. Observe to identify children who do not understand.

Practice

Have children who had difficulties with the *Check Understanding* example complete the *Reteaching Worksheet*. Have the rest of the children use their lake work mats and fish counters to complete the examples on the practice page.

Closure

At the end of math time, point out to the children that they have been using their fish counters to create subtraction sentences.

The adapted lesson plan that follows includes an increased amount of developmental instruction. Notice the shift in instructional emphasis from teaching the pages of the student book toward an emphasis on teaching the concept. We have also increased visual input, kinesthetic activity, student communication, and monitoring of learning. Remember that these adaptations will make the lesson appropriate for almost all students. But remember also that some students with severe needs may require further instructional adaptations.

LESSON OBJECTIVE

The student will create subtraction sentences with minuends of 1 to 6.

Lesson Opener

Show four counters and a box. Tell the children that you want to put some of the counters into the box. Have a child come forward to help. Ask the class how many to place into the box. Have the child who is helping place that many into the box. Without showing the remaining counters, ask how many are left. Have your helper check to see if the children were right. Have two children come forward to help. Show the class five counters. Have one helper put them into the box. Ask how many are in the box. Have the second helper write that number on the board. Tell the children that you want to take some out of the box. Ask how many they want to take out of the box. Ask what we call it when you start with a number and then take some away. [Subtraction.] Ask how many were subtracted. Have your helper who is writing on the board record this subtraction. Ask how many are left in the box. Have the first helper look in the box to check the answer. Have the second helper record the answer. **Monitor understanding**. Observe the children carefully throughout this activity. Ask leading questions of children who may not understand. Provide further explanation or additional examples as needed.

Monitoring Understanding

Explain that when we write a subtraction fact in horizontal form, we call it a *subtraction sentence*. Tell the class that today they will be creating subtraction sentences.

Development

Direct the attention of the class to the bulletin board. (Before school, you should place three bird cutouts on the bulletin board.) Call on a child to come forward and remove two of the birds. Ask how many birds we started with. Ask how many were taken away. Ask how many are left. Have another child come forward and write the subtraction sentence. **Monitor understanding**. Observe the children carefully throughout this activity. Ask leading questions of children who may not understand. Provide further explanation or additional examples as needed.

Place six chairs in a line at the front of the room. Have six children come sit in the chairs. Tell four children get up and go to the back of the room. Ask how many children we started with. Ask how many moved to the back of the room. Ask how many are left. Have a child come forward and write the subtraction sentence. **Monitor understanding**. Observe the children carefully throughout this activity. Ask leading questions of children who may not understand. Provide further explanation or additional examples as needed.

Place the blue lake transparency on the overhead projector. Tell the class that you have six fish. Ask how many of your fish you should place in the lake. Have a child come to the front to help. Tell the class that your helper is fishing in the lake. Ask the class how many of the fish they think your helper will catch. Have your helper remove that many fish from the lake. Ask how many fish are left in the lake. Ask how many fish were in the lake to start with. Ask how many were taken out of the lake, then ask how many are left. Have another child come forward and write the subtraction sentence on the board.

Use the fish to complete another example, except have all the children use pencil and paper to write the subtraction sentence at their seats. **Monitor understanding**. Move around and check the children's work. Ask leading questions of children who may not understand. Provide extra explanations as needed.

Direct the children's attention to the *Check Understanding* example. Have the children use their lake work mats and fish counters to complete the example. **Monitor understanding**. Move around the room to check the children's work. Ask questions of students who may not understand. Provide extra explanations as needed.

Practice

Have children work with partners and use their lake work mats and fish counters to complete the first four examples on the practice page.

Closure

At the end of the math time, ask the students what they have been doing today. Ask what they have learned how to do. Do one more example using sunflower seeds. Have the children tell you what the subtraction sentence is.

Follow-Up

Give each child a small plastic bag with six sunflower seeds. Tell the children that you want them to take the sunflower seeds home and use them to explain to their parents what they learned today.

Teaching Problem Solving Using Addition and Subtraction

Problem solving is a high-priority topic in the elementary school mathematics curriculum. An early part of the development of the ability to use addition and subtraction to solve problems is found in the way that the meanings of the operations are developed. When the arithmetic operations are related to physical operations, the child is better able to look at problem situations and determine if addition or subtraction can be used to find the solution.

If the essence of the problem is that some of a quantity is being taken away, the child can look at the situation and tell that subtraction should be used to find the answer. If the essence of the problem situation is that quantities are being combined and we want to find how many altogether, the child can look at the situation and tell that addition should be used to find the answer. If the essence of the problem situation is that two quantities are being compared and you want to find which is more and how much more, the child can look at the situation and tell that subtraction should be used.

Translate Word Problems into Situations. When problems are posed as word problems, the children should not be taught to look for key words like *and* or *of*, but rather they should think about the situation being described and think about what is happening to the quantities. They should think about what operation they see happening in the problem. The reason many children are unable to solve word problems is that they have not learned to convert the word problem (a bunch of words) into a situation. It is not that they lack the needed mathematical understanding and ability. Most often, once they are able to "see" the situation, the solution is simple for them.

Sometimes special help must be provided so that the children can make the conversion from a bunch of words to a situation. Among techniques that have proven to be successful are *dramatization of the problem, modeling the problem, partnering*, and *group explanations*. These techniques are illustrated in the following activities.

Activity 5.36   Act It Out

Form groups of children. Give each group a word problem. Have each group plan how to act out its problem for the rest of the class. When the groups are ready, have each group act out its problem and then ask the question that needs to be answered. The other class members must figure out the answer. The teacher should use some children to show an example.

Activity 5.37   Show It with Stuff

Form groups of children. Give each group a word problem. Have each group plan how to use materials like counters and boxes to show its problem to the rest of the class. When the groups are ready, have each group show its problem and then ask the question that needs to be answered. The other class members must figure out the answer. The teacher should show an example.

Activity 5.38   Partners Can

Have the children work with partners. Give the partners a word problem. Have them discuss the problem and agree on how to explain what is happening in the problem. When the partners are ready, the teacher should go to them and have them explain the problem. What is happening? What do we want to find out?

Activity 5.39   Teacher's a Dummy

Have the children look at a word problem. Tell them that you don't understand the problem. You don't know what to do. Ask them to explain the problem to you. Try to get even the weakest students involved. Play dumb. Ask really stupid questions. Loosen up and have fun with it.

Use Things That Children Care About.   Suppose a friend poses a problem that you do not care about. When this happens, the friend has the problem but you really do not have the problem because you just don't care. A "problem" is not a problem to you unless you want to get a solution. You might play along with your friend to help solve the problem, but you will be easily bored by it. And if something comes along that is important to you, you will quickly drop the "problem" and do what is important to you.

Remember that children are like that, too. If they don't really care about getting a solution, finding a solution will have a low priority. Anything else that they do care about will draw their attention away. But, there is something that will help keep the children involved. Read on.

Use Things That Are Real to Children.   It is important that children experience problems that come from everyday situations. The problems they experience should include numerical situations involving things that they are familiar with, and things encountered in natural settings. If they are farm children, problems about chickens or cows might make sense. If they are city children, similar mathematical situations that involve taxicabs would probably be more meaningful and more interesting.

It is recommended that the teacher find out what objects are common to each child in the class and pose problems involving objects from the world of each child. Whenever others do not know about those objects, that child can then be the "expert" and explain about them. In this way, a thoughtful teacher can arrange circumstances so that every child, at some time, can be looked on by the other children as an expert.

Use Mixed Problem Examples.
It is also important that problem solving be mixed. It is not enough for the child to be able to use addition to solve problems included in the unit on addition. He or she must be able to decide when to add *and when not to add*. Within the unit on addition, the child should encounter examples of addition problems *and nonexamples of addition problems*. He or she should be required to think about the problem setting and decide when to add, when to subtract, and when not to do either. This will happen only when there is a conscious effort to provide an effective mix of problem settings.

Activity 5.40 What's Happening? What Do I Do?

Prepare several word problems on overhead transparencies. Also prepare a card for each child with a large plus sign on one side and a large minus sign on the other side. And, finally, prepare three what's-happening cards for each child, one with the words *put together*, one with the words *take away*, and one with the word *compare*. Give each child a set of four cards.

Use the projector to show a word problem. Ask what's happening. The children then hold up the what's-happening card that tells what is happening in the problem. Talk about it. What is being put together? What is being taken away? Taken away from what? What is being compared to what?

Then the children hold up the plus sign or the minus sign to show what to do.

Watch for children who are having difficulty. Provide extra discussion for clarification or provide individual help.

Translate Situations into Arithmetic.
An emphasis should be placed on writing the number sentences that relate to problem situations (Parmar & Cawley, 1991). This, of course, is simply an extension of work that was already done when the meaning of the operations was taught. An excellent activity for this follows.

Activity 5.41 Headlines

Show the children two or three articles in a newspaper. Point out the headline for each article. Explain that the *headline* tells, in a very small amount of space, what is in the story.

Show this story on the overhead projector. Talk about the story. Since some of Billy's cars are being taken away, we can write it as subtraction. The subtraction sentence that goes with the story is 10 − 4 = 6.

> Billy brought 10 toy cars to school. He gave 4 of the cars to his friend Ben to play with. He had 6 cars left.

Since this subtraction sentence tells what is in the story, it would make a good headline for the story. Write 10 − 4 = 6 above the story.

Repeat the process with an addition story. Write the addition sentence above the story as a headline.

Give the children several number stories. Have them work with partners to write a headline above each story.

Give them some headlines. Have them work with their partners to make up a story that goes with each headline.

Exercises and Activities

1. Compare the two earlier subtraction lesson plans.
   a. Identify where the adapted plan provides more kinesthetic activity.
   b. Identify where the adapted plan provides more opportunity for communication from the children.
   c. Identify where the adapted plan provides more opportunity for communication among the children.

2. Adapt activity 5.30 so that it could be used with a child with a severe visual impairment.

3. Choose a lesson plan on either addition or subtraction of whole numbers from a published elementary school mathematics textbook series.
   a. Indentify the parts of the lesson plan that develop the concept(s) or skill(s).
   b. Expand the lesson plan by adding activities that provide more visual information about the concepts or skills being taught.
   c. Add more kinesthetic activity to the lesson plan.
   d. Add more opportunities for communication from and among students to the lesson plan.
   e. Add more continual assessment (monitoring of learning) to the lesson plan.

4. An interesting process can be used to change a hard subtraction fact into an easier one. If we think of the answer as the difference between the two numbers, that difference can be illustrated on the number line:

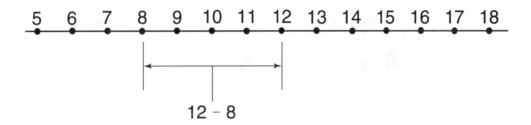

Notice that if 2 is added to both numbers, they shift two spaces to the right on the number line, but they are the same distance apart:

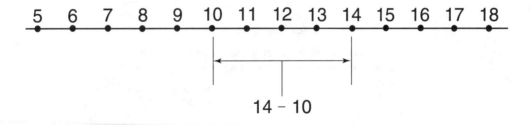

Adding the same number to both numbers does not change the difference. Notice that although the difference (the answer) is the same, this new fact is a lot easier.
   a. Use this equal-additions process to change 15 – 8 into an easier fact.
   b. Develop an activity to teach the children to use this strategy to find answers to the hard basic subtraction facts.

5. The following addition results illustrate an error pattern like those that were related by Robert Ashlock in his book, *Error Patterns in Computation: Using Error Patterns to Improve Instruction:*

$$
\begin{array}{r} 8\ 4 \\ +5\ 6 \\ \hline 1310 \end{array}
\qquad
\begin{array}{r} 35 \\ +72 \\ \hline 107 \end{array}
\qquad
\begin{array}{r} 6\ 9 \\ +2\ 8 \\ \hline 817 \end{array}
\qquad
\begin{array}{r} 1\ 8 \\ +9\ 7 \\ \hline 1015 \end{array}
$$

a. What is this student's error pattern? What is she or he doing to produce the incorrect answers?

b. Plan a mini-lesson to correct this student's error pattern.

References and Related Readings

Ashlock, R. B. (2002). *Error patterns in computation: Using error patterns to improve instruction* (8th ed.). Upper Saddle River, NJ: Prentice Hall.

National Council of Teachers of Mathematics. (1989). *Curriculum and evaluation standards for school mathematics.* Reston, VA: Author.

National Council of Teachers of Mathematics. (2000). *Principles and standards for school mathematics.* Reston, VA: Author.

Page, A. (1994). Helping children understand subtraction. *Teaching Children Mathematics, 1,* 140–143.

Parmar, R. S., & Cawley, J. F. (1991). Challenging the routines and passivity that characterize arithmetic instruction for children with mild handicaps. *Remedial and Special Education, 12*(5), 23–32, 43.

Thornton, C. A., Tucker, B. F., Dossey, J. A., & Bazik, E. F. (1983). *Teaching mathematics to children with special needs.* Menlo Park, CA: Addison-Wesley.

Tucker, B. F. (1981). Give and take: Getting ready to regroup. *The Arithmetic Teacher, 28*(8), 24–26.

Tucker, B. F. (1989). Seeing addition: A diagnosis/remediation case study. *The Arithmetic Teacher, 36*(5), 10–11.

Websites

http://www.corestandards.org/the-standards/mathematics
The Common Core State Standards for Mathematics can be found at this site.

www.proteacher.com/100009.shtml
Lesson plans on addition and subtraction, by teachers.

http://mathforum.org/
Math forum links to math discussions and ideas.

www.sasked.gov.sk.ca/docs/elemath/numop.html
A scope and sequence chart for numbers and operations.

six

MULTIPLYING AND DIVIDING WHOLE NUMBERS

Combining Equal-Sized Groups and Separating Quantities into Equal-Sized Groups

CHAPTER OUTLINE

Teaching Multiplication of Whole Numbers

Now we examine the developmental sequence as it is applied to teaching whole-number multiplication. As when teaching addition and subtraction, the teacher must first establish the meaning of multiplication.

Developing the Meaning of Multiplication

Children need to *associate multiplication with the combining of equal-sized quantities*. The association must be so strong that when children see the symbols 3 × 4, they visualize three groups of four things being combined. When the children see a situation where

101

equal quantities are being combined, they will think, "That's multiplication!" After multiplication has been mastered, the children will see problem settings where equal quantities are being combined and think, "I can use multiplication to solve this problem."

Counting.   The children must also realize that, after equal quantities have been combined, they can *count to find how many there are altogether*.

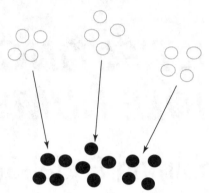

If I combine three groups of 4,

I can count them to see that there are 12 altogether. So, $3 \times 4 = 12$.

Addition.   Since counting so many objects becomes tedious and is time consuming, you want to lead the children to understand that they can also use addition to find the answer:

Start with three groups of 4.

Combine two of the groups.
That's 4 + 4

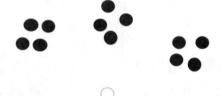

Then, I can add the other group of 4. That's 4 + 4 + 4.

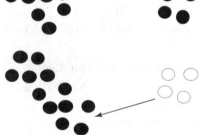

Teaching Both Counting and Addition.   There are two ways to figure out the answer to multiplication examples: children can count to get the answer, or they can add to get the answer. If the children have already developed a level of proficiency with simple addition, it is easier and quicker to get multiplication answers by adding. Both ways work, but the children should be encouraged to use the most efficient method.

The teacher should introduce the operation of multiplication by using physical materials. During this introduction, the teacher should use concepts and language that are already available to the students. In this natural setting, the teacher should then introduce the new mathematical terms and the notation that is used to write them.

In the next activities, multiplication is introduced as a physical operation on equal-sized groups. Then, the language of multiplication is introduced along with the times sign. Finally, they begin using the written notation for multiplication.

Activity 6.01   Putting Bunches Together

Bring about 25 small sticks that are about the same size to class.

Using rubber bands, have the children make three bunches of five sticks and put the three bunches into a box. Write on the board what is in the box. [three bunches of 5] Ask how we can figure out how many sticks are in the box. [We count them.]

Point out that the bunches are being combined. Ask, "What do we call it when we put numbers of things together?" [Addition] Show how addition can be used to find how many sticks. [First, put two bunches together into the box. That's 5 + 5. Then add the other bunch. That's 5 + 5 + 5.] Have the children find how many sticks are in the box by using both methods. Write the answer. [Three bunches of 5 is 15.]

Repeat the activity with other numbers.

Activity 6.02   Money in My Pocket

Bring to class about 30 pennies. Have four children come forward. Give each of them 6 pennies and tell them to put the pennies in their pockets. Have the class figure out how to find how many pennies there are in all four pockets. [By taking them out, combining them, and counting. By adding.] Have the children find the answer both ways.

Repeat the activity with different numbers.

Activity 6.03   The Way to Say It

Ask six children to come to the front of the room and give each of them four blocks. Then have the other children watch carefully as your six helpers, one at a time, place their blocks in a paper bag.

Ask the class to describe what was done. [Four was placed in the bag 6 times.] Have the children figure out how many blocks are in the bag. Write, "Four, 6 times = 24" on the board.

Do another example (for example, seven, 3 times) and write it on the board. Then explain to the children that instead of four, 6 times, we usually say "6 times 4." Point to the other example and ask how we usually say it. [3 times 7]

Finally, introduce the multiplication sign [×] and show how to use it to write the examples. [6 × 4 = 24, 3 × 7 = 21] Tell the children how to read each example. [6 times 4 equals 24, 3 times 7 equals 21]

Do other examples with the blocks and paper bag. Have the children use multiplication language and notation to say, write, and read the examples.

Developing the Easy Basic Multiplication Facts

To reinforce the meaning of multiplication, the teacher should expose the children to a wide variety of multiplication examples using objects that are familiar to them. The students should use appropriate terminology to describe the multiplication verbally and use the times sign and equal sign to write it. In every example, the children should figure out the answer for themselves, and the teacher should continually emphasize how easy it is. They can find the answers by themselves. The following instructional activity illustrates how this can be accomplished.

Activity 6.04   How Much Paper Do I Need?

Tell the children that you are thinking about doing an art activity where each person needs five sheets of paper. Ask the class to figure out how many sheets of paper are needed for a group of four children.

Get out some paper, and use it to check the answer.

Note that this process requires a lot of adding. You want to speed it up as much as possible. One way to accomplish this is to have the children think about what multiplication they have already done that might help with this one. Often, several related multiplications are done together or in succession. For example, if the children have just found the answer to 3×6 by adding $6 + 6 + 6$, then 4×6 is easy:

$$4 \times 6 = 6 + 6 + 6 + 6$$

I already know that this is 18, so the answer to 4×6 is

$$4 \times 6 = 18 + 6$$
$$= 24$$

The teacher should continually emphasize that with every problem that the children face, they should first think about what they already know that will help.

Discovering Relationships among the Easy Basic Multiplication Facts.

After the meaning of multiplication has been established and the children can confidently find answers on their own, focus on the easier basic multiplication facts, with your goal being for the children to commit those facts to memory. Which multiplication facts are included in the easy ones will vary from program to program, but whichever ones are included, there is a sense that these are easier than the others. For purposes of our discussion here, we will consider multiplication facts with multipliers of 0 to 3 to be the easy ones. There are 64 of these easy basic multiplication facts.

While focusing on the easy facts, in addition to figuring out the answers for themselves, the children need to discover helpful relationships that exist among the multiplication facts. In particular, you need to ensure that the children discover four relationships.

First, the children should recognize that the facts where one of the numbers being multiplied is 0 all have something in common. The answer for these facts is always 0:

X	0	1	2	3	4	5	6	7	8	9
0	0	0	0	0	0	0	0	0	0	0
1	0	1	2	3	4	5	6	7	8	9
2	0	2	4	6	8	10	12	14	16	18
3	0	3	6	9	12	15	18	21	24	27
4	0	4	8	12						
5	0	5	10	15						
6	0	6	12	18						
7	0	7	14	21						
8	0	8	16	24						
9	0	9	18	27						

$$0 \times 4 = 0 \quad\quad 0 \times 7 = 0 \quad\quad 6 \times 0 = 0$$
$$9 \times 0 = 0 \quad\quad 0 \times 3 = 0 \quad\quad 4 \times 0 = 0$$
$$0 \times 8 = 0 \quad\quad 1 \times 0 = 0$$

There are 19 facts with the multiplier or the multiplicand equal to 0. That's 19 of the 64 easy basic multiplication facts, but because of this relationship, it is only one thing for the children to learn.

A second important relationship is evident in the next group of facts:

$$1 \times 4 = 4 \quad\quad 1 \times 7 = 7 \quad\quad 6 \times 1 = 6$$
$$9 \times 1 = 9 \quad\quad 1 \times 3 = 3 \quad\quad 4 \times 1 = 4$$
$$1 \times 8 = 8 \quad\quad 1 \times 1 = 1$$

There are 19 basic multiplication facts in which one of the numbers being multiplied is 1. In each of these cases, the answer will be the other number. Two of those are $0 \times 1 = 0$ and $1 \times 0 = 0$, and they have been dealt with earlier. So, we have 17 new facts in this group. But, because of this relationship, it is only one thing to learn.

A third, important relationship between other pairs of facts should also be recognized by the children. This time, the relationship is between certain multiplication facts and certain addition facts:

$$2 \times 4 = 8 \quad \text{and} \quad 4 + 4 = 8$$
$$2 \times 9 = 18 \quad \text{and} \quad 9 + 9 = 18$$
$$2 \times 5 = 10 \quad \text{and} \quad 5 + 5 = 10$$
$$2 \times 8 = 16 \quad \text{and} \quad 8 + 8 = 16$$

Multiplying 2 times a number is exactly the same as adding that number to itself. This is a direct result of the meaning of multiplication. Children who recognize this relationship realize that these are just the doubles that were already memorized as addition facts, so there is nothing new to learn here. Also, since the numbers being multiplied may be rearranged without affecting the answer, $4 \times 2 = 2 \times 4$. Therefore, 4×2 is also a double. There are 15 of these doubles that have not been previously dealt with as multiplication by 0 or by 1. If the children are aware of how multiplication is related to addition, they will already know these 15 facts. That's 15 facts, but nothing new to learn.

The fourth relationship that we want the children to recognize is that certain pairs of facts are related:

$$3 \times 4 = 12 \quad \text{and} \quad 4 \times 3 = 12$$
$$5 \times 3 = 15 \quad \text{and} \quad 3 \times 5 = 15$$
$$6 \times 4 = 24 \quad \text{and} \quad 4 \times 6 = 24$$
$$9 \times 3 = 27 \quad \text{and} \quad 3 \times 9 = 27$$

Students should recognize from these pairs of facts that changing the order of the numbers being multiplied does not change the answer. This rearrangement principle shows that the answer to 5×6 is also the answer to 6×5. The answer to 3×9 is also the answer to 9×3. And, 8×74 has the same answer as 74×8. These pairs are known as *commutative pairs*.

There are just six remaining rearranged pairs that were not included in multiplication by 0, by 1, or by 2. That's 12 multiplication facts, but if the child has learned that rearranging the numbers does not change the product, it is only six new things to learn. So, of the 64 easy basic multiplication facts, the only one not yet discussed is $3 \times 3 = 9$. That's 1 fact to learn. Let's summarize the impact of such an emphasis on relationships:

Group of Facts	Number of Facts	Things to Learn
$\times 0$	19	1
$\times 1$	17	1
$\times 2$	15	0
Commutative pairs	12	6
3×3	1	1
All easy facts	**64**	**9**

The emphasis on relationships provides a tremendous advantage to the child. The 64 easy basic multiplication facts can be mastered by learning only nine new things. This certainly increases the number of children who actually have the facts committed to memory and increases the speed with which memorization takes place. But, even more important, it significantly increases retention of those facts once they have been memorized. *Remember: It is always easier to remember things that are related to other things that are already known.*

Memorization of the Easy Basic Multiplication Facts.
After the children understand the relationships among the facts, they should commit the easy basic multiplication facts to memory. The instructional activities that are selected to lead the children to memorizing the easy basic multiplication facts should have certain characteristics. These are the same eight characteristics presented in Chapter 5 for addition facts:

1. Children should be aware that the objective is to memorize the facts. Tell them to remember the facts.
2. The activities should use an interesting and fun format.
3. Activities should have a high level of involvement. Minimize waiting time. Maximize thinking time.
4. Activities should focus on a small number of unmemorized facts at any given time.
5. Some already-memorized facts should be mixed in with the target unmemorized facts. This will improve retention.
6. If a child does not know an answer, then he or she should figure it out. Allow enough time to figure it out. Discourage guessing by asking, "How did you figure that out?"
7. To figure out an answer, the child should think about what he or she already knows that will help find the answer, asking herself or himself, "What other facts do I know that will help? What relationship that I know will help?" Counting or adding should be used only as a last resort.
8. Accuracy, not speed, should be emphasized. Accuracy is of great importance. Speed is of little importance. Speed will come after accuracy and confidence.

The following examples of memorization activities demonstrate these characteristics.

Activity 6.05   They're Still Doubles

Have a student come to the front and demonstrate 2 × 6 by using counters. As the child shows six objects 2 times and then combines them, say, "But that looks like 6 + 6." Repeat the process with a child showing 2 × 4. As he or she shows four objects 2 times and then combines them, say, "But that looks like 4 + 4." Repeat with several other doubles to ensure that the children see that multiplication by 2 is the same as a double in addition.

Then have them think about the doubles in addition as they figure out answers when multiplying by 2. Emphasize that they already know these answers.

Activity 6.06   Doubles and One More

Have a student come to the front and demonstrate 3 × 6 by using counters. After the child has shown three groups of 6, suggest that he or she start by combining two of the groups. Call attention to the two groups of 6 that have been combined. Point out that is 6 + 6, and that it is also 2 × 6. Then point out that there is still one more 6. Three 6s are the same as two 6s and one more 6. Write it on the board:

$$3 \times 6 = 2 \times 6 + 6$$

Emphasize that the students already know the double, so they just need to add one more 6.

Repeat this process with other multiplications by 3 : 3 × 7, 3 × 5, 3 × 9, 3 × 4, 3 × 8, 3 × 3.

Activity 6.07   Facts of the Day

Identify two facts that a student needs to work on. Have the child figure out the answers and write each fact on a piece of paper. Tell him or her to remember both of the facts. Immediately ask the child for both answers. Tell the child again to remember the facts. Frequently during the day, ask the child to give you one or the other of these answers. Each time, remind the child to remember. At the end of the day, send the two pieces of paper with the facts written on them home with the child, along with a note explaining what you are doing. Have the parents ask their child to give them the answers to both facts.

Developing the Hard Basic Multiplication Facts

Thinking Strategies for the Hard Basic Multiplication Facts.   During development of the hard basic multiplication facts (for example, those with multipliers greater than 3), answers can still be found by counting or by adding. However, with the larger numbers, both counting and adding are inefficient and consequently very slow. At this point in the development, more-efficient strategies are needed that allow the child to find answers quickly and accurately.

The objective is for the children to commit these facts to memory. Remember from our discussion of strategies for the hard basic addition facts that some strategies seem to lead to memorization while others do not. Recall, also, that the strategies that are successful have two common characteristics.

 Successful strategies are mental strategies. They consist of a series of quick, easy, mental procedures. They are not pencil-and-paper strategies, nor are they performed by manipulating fingers or other objects. Also, *successful strategies require the child to use facts that are already memorized to figure out the facts that are not yet memorized.* The child is constantly thinking about what he or she already knows that can help figure out what he or she does not know. The child has a sense of building on what is already known. New knowledge is closely related to existing knowledge, and it is always easier to remember things that are related to other things that we know.

One More   The simplest thinking strategy for hard basic multiplication facts is the *one-more strategy*. The thinking is very simple, so it is easy for children to use. Every hard basic multiplication fact can be found by using this strategy. If we want to find 6 × 8, we think of six 8s as being five 8s and one more 8. We visualize 6 × 8 as six rows of 8 objects:

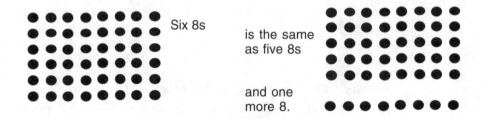

If we know what five 8s is equal to, then we simply need to add one more 8. That will give the answer to six 8s:

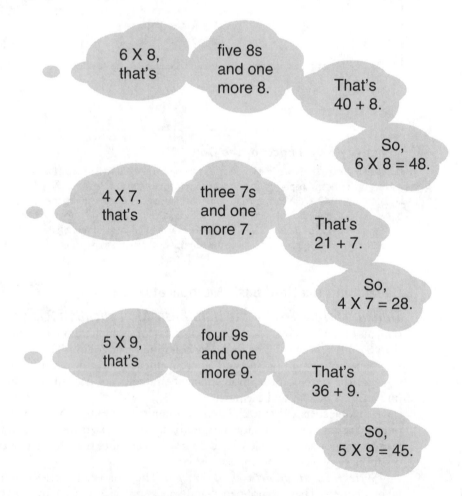

To use the one-more strategy to find answers to a hard basic multiplication fact, the student must, in each case, know another fact first. For example, to find 6 × 8, the child must already know 5 × 8. To find 7 × 9, she or he must already know 6 × 9. To find 5 × 7, the child must already know 4 × 7. To find 6 × 6, the child must already know 5 × 6.

Textbooks frequently use the one-more strategy to develop the hard facts in a carefully controlled sequence. The authors know which facts have previously been developed, and all new facts build on them. However, in practice, the *children do not memorize the facts* in the same sequence in which they are developed in the textbook. They typically remember some and not others. As a result, at any given time, the children in any class will have mastered varied combinations of facts, and, of course, they will not have mastered other combinations.

When it is time for the children to figure out the answer to 6×8, you cannot be sure that they already know 5×8. When you are ready for the children to figure out the answer to 7×9, you cannot depend on their already knowing 6×9. Some children already know the necessary facts. Some do not. Although the one-more strategy works well in the textbook, and though it may work well when you are working with a single child (when you can keep track of which facts are already memorized), it is difficult to use in a large group setting (when it is hard to keep track of which facts each child has already memorized). But there is another thinking strategy that seems to work more effectively in a whole-class setting.

Partial-Products Strategy   The other thinking strategy for hard basic multiplication facts that has proven to be more successful in a whole-class environment is the *partial-products strategy*. In fact, the one-more strategy is really a special case of the partial-products strategy. The simplest description of this strategy is that the students takes the "big" fact that they do not know and *break it into easier facts* that they do know. For example, suppose a student does not know the answer to 6×7. Tell the child to visualize this as 6 rows of 7 objects. Explain to her or him to break it into two easy parts and then combine those two parts:

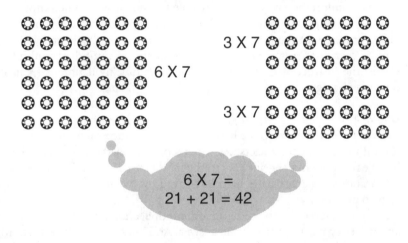

Other examples of this strategy are given next:

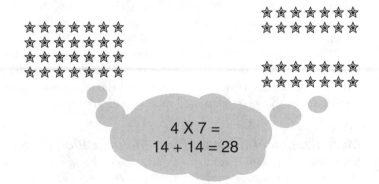

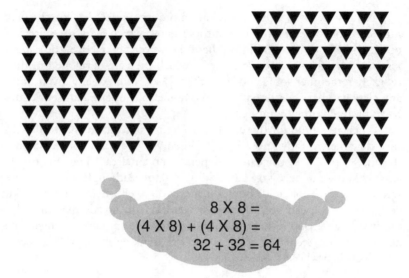

Success with this strategy depends on getting the children to think about *what easier facts they already know* that can help them find the answer. This kind of thinking is good problem-solving behavior, and we would want them to think like this even if it did not help them with their multiplication facts.

Teachers who use the partial-products strategy find that a fair amount of time and effort is required to get the children to use this thinking pattern. But, after the children become comfortable with it, they are able to find answers much more quickly, and they make rapid progress toward mastery of the multiplication facts. In addition to providing quicker mastery of the hard basic multiplication facts, this strategy introduces the concept of *partial products*, which will be used later in multidigit multiplication. In other words, the instructional goal is achieved more quickly if time is spent on learning the thinking strategies.

Use of the Thinking Strategies After the children have learned to use an efficient strategy to find answers to the hard basic multiplication facts, rapid progress can be made toward mastery of these facts. As when working on the easy facts, the children should be able to figure out the answers to the hard facts. They children need to recognize and use relationships among the hard facts. And, we want the children to commit the hard facts to memory.

If the children do not know a hard multiplication fact, they cannot just say, "I don't know." They must figure out the answer. And because you want them to figure out the answer efficiently and quickly, encourage (almost require) them to use the thinking strategy that has been learned. The children have, at this point, been using repeated addition for over a year to find multiplication-fact answers. They are comfortable using repeated addition—even when it takes a long time. Consequently, they will automatically fall back on repeated addition because they are comfortable with this process. So, you must continually lead the children to use the thinking strategy instead.

If the children do not know the answer to a hard basic multiplication fact, *they need to think about what they already know that will help them with the fact that they do not know.* If the children continually think about the relationships among the facts, they end up with fewer things to learn, and their retention of what they have learned is better.

Memorization of the Hard Basic Multiplication Facts.

The following activities demonstrate how a teacher can *help students to think about what they already know that will help them with what they are trying to figure out.*

Activity 6.08 Splitting Sixes

Begin by reviewing facts with multipliers of 3: $3 \times 4 = 12$, $3 \times 5 = 15$, $3 \times 6 = 18$, $3 \times 7 = 21$, $3 \times 8 = 24$, $3 \times 9 = 27$. Next, show how multiplication by 6 can be split into two multiplications by 3:

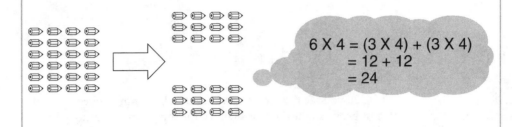

$$6 \times 4 = (3 \times 4) + (3 \times 4)$$
$$= 12 + 12$$
$$= 24$$

As the children practice the 6s, have them find answers by using this method:

$$6 \times 8 = 24 + 24 = 48, 6 \times 7 = 21 + 21 = 42, \text{etc.}$$

Activity 6.09 Scavenger Hunt

Prepare five lists of answers to multiplication facts. Each list should have seven answers. Also prepare cards showing the multiplication facts that have the answers on the lists, but do not include the answers on these cards. Be sure that there is a fact card for each answer on each list, but include some extra fact cards that do not go with any of the answers.

Tape the fact cards on the walls all around the classroom. Form five teams and give each team one of the lists of answers. Tell the teams that they must find facts to go with all the answers on their lists.

The first team to collect facts for all their answers wins.

Teaching the Multiplication Algorithm

When the basic multiplication facts have been mastered, the child is ready to begin work on the multiplication algorithm. The multiplication algorithm is the step-by-step process by which we use the basic facts to find answers to any other whole-number multiplication example. We use the multiplication algorithm to do multidigit multiplication. Several principles related to teaching algorithms have been mentioned earlier. Let's review those principles:

- **Let them see what it looks like.** Carefully model the operation with an appropriate physical or pictorial model. Use a model that lets the children see what happens to the basic units—ones, tens, hundreds, and so on—when they multiply.
- **Deemphasize rote rules.** You might end up with rules, but they should be meaningful. They should arise out of the modeling process.
- **Emphasize big ideas.** These are the important generalizations that describe the procedures. They also come from the modeling process.
- **Let the written algorithm simply be a recording of what happens when the algorithm is modeled.** Everything the child writes should match something the child does.
- **Watch our language.** The children should use language that describes what they see when the operation is modeled, not language that describes what they write down.

The First Big Idea

Multiplication by Ten   The first of the big ideas that form the basis of the multiplication algorithm is *multiplication by 10*. It is important that the child discover that multiplication by 10 is really easy. It is not unusual to see a child multiply by 10 something like this:

$$\begin{array}{r} 236 \\ \times\ 10 \\ \hline 000 \\ 236\ \ \\ \hline 2360 \end{array}$$

When you see this, you know that the algorithm has been taught rotely, and the child has not been taught the first big idea for the multiplication algorithm. Most adults know (and who knows how they learned it) that when multiplying by 10, we simply "add a zero." Multiplication by 10 is easy. But you do not want to just give the children this "rule" without teaching it meaningfully. To do this, you need a model for numbers that lets the child see ones, tens, and hundreds. For our discussion here, we begin by using bundled sticks:

We begin by using the bundled sticks
to represent 21.

Then, we use the bundled sticks to represent 21 ten times,
and we write 10 × 21 on the board.

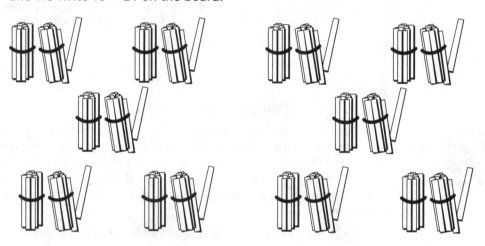

Next, we put all the tens together and put all the ones together.

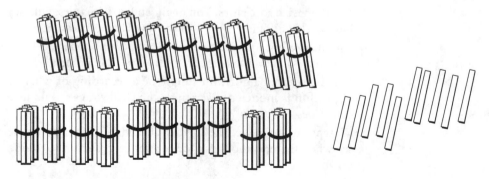

And, finally, we group the tens together
to make hundreds and group the ones
together to make a ten.

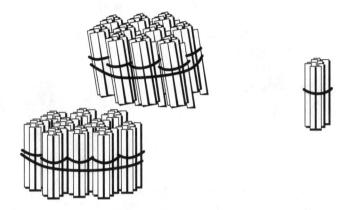

We record the result on the board: 10 × 21 = 210.

We repeat this process with a variety of examples and record all the results together on the board. For example, you might use:

$$10 \times 21 = 210$$

$$12 \times 10 = 120 \; (10, \text{twelve times})$$

$$10 \times 36 = 360$$

$$42 \times 10 = 420$$

$$10 \times \;\; 8 = 80$$

When these examples have been completed by using the model to get the answers, ask the students if they see a pattern. Do they see how they might get the answer without using the model? When it has been suggested that someone could just "add" a zero to get the answer, write another example (for example, 10 × 18) on the board, and ask what the answer is. Record the answer that the children give, but then do this example with the model to verify that the children's answers are correct.

Out of experiences like those just illustrated, it becomes apparent to the children that multiplication by 10 is easy, that you "just add a zero." The next step is to extend the notion of multiplication by 10 as follows:

This is 30.

$$30 \times 7 = 10 \times 3 \times 7$$

We have a basic fact (3 × 7) and a multiplication by 10.

The answer is 10 × 21 = 210.

Similarly, 50 × 9 = 10 × 5 × 9 = 10 × 45 = 450. Again, we have a basic fact and a multiplication by 10. Another example is 4 × 60 = 4 × 6 × 10 = 240, which is also a basic fact and a multiplication by 10. Answers to all of the examples—70 × 8, 30 × 6, 7 × 20, 40 × 3, 5 × 80, and so on—are easily found by multiplying the answer to a basic fact by 10.

The answer to an example like 30×70 can be found by extending the notion of multiplication by 10 still further:

$$30 \times 70 = \overset{30}{\overbrace{10 \times 3}} \times \overset{70}{\overbrace{10 \times 7}} = 10 \times 10 \times 3 \times 7 = 2100$$

In this case, we end up with a basic fact and two multiplications by 10. Each multiplication by 10 "adds a zero." Similar examples also result in a basic fact and two multiplications by 10:

$$40 \times 30 = 4 \times 3 \times 10 \times 10 = 1200$$
$$20 \times 90 = 2 \times 9 \times 10 \times 10 = 1800$$
$$50 \times 70 = 5 \times 7 \times 10 \times 10 = 3500$$
$$80 \times 50 = 8 \times 5 \times 10 \times 10 = 4000$$

> This one has 3 zeros. Why?

One final extension of multiplication by 10 is needed. Since $100 = 10 \times 10$ and $1000 = 10 \times 10 \times 10$, and $600 = 6 \times 10 \times 10$ and $4000 = 4 \times 10 \times 10 \times 10$, it follows then, that

$7 \times 600 = 7 \times 6 \times 10 \times 10 = 4200$
(A basic fact and two multiplications by 10)

$70 \times 600 = 7 \times 6 \times 10 \times 10 \times 10 = 42000$
(A basic fact and three multiplications by 10)

$4000 \times 30 = 4 \times 3 \times 10 \times 10 \times 10 \times 10 = 120,000$
(A basic fact and four multiplications by 10)

$60 \times 500 = 6 \times 5 \times 10 \times 10 \times 10 = 30,000$
(A basic fact and three multiplications by 10)

> This one has 4 zeros. Why?

After each step in the development of the concept of multiplication by 10 and the extensions of that concept, the children need to have a variety of experiences where they practice and apply their current level of understanding. The following activity illustrates how to practice this concept.

Activity 6.10   That One!!!

Prepare a set of about 30 cards with multiplication examples like 6 × 80, 200 × 4, 30 × 60, 800 × 70, 300 × 200, 90 × 80, and 600 × 6.

Have two children play the game. Shuffle the deck and place it face-down between the players. On each play, both players take 1 card. At the same time, they place the 2 cards faceup on the table. The players decide which card has the greatest product. The first player to touch that card and say "That one!" takes both cards. After all the cards have been played, the player who has taken the most cards is the winner of the game.

The children should settle any disputes by discussing the basic fact and how many multiplications by 10 there are.

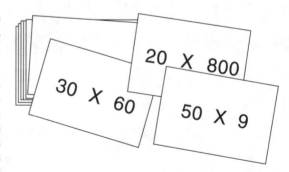

The Second Big Idea

Partial Products The second of the two big ideas that are the basis of the multiplication algorithm also develops from the modeling process. This big idea was used earlier when we worked on the hard basic multiplication facts. It is the notion of *partial products*. Recall that when the students were faced with a hard multiplication fact that they did not know the answer to, they could use partial products to break it into easier facts that they already knew. For example, 8×7 can be broken into $4 \times 7 + 4 \times 7$:

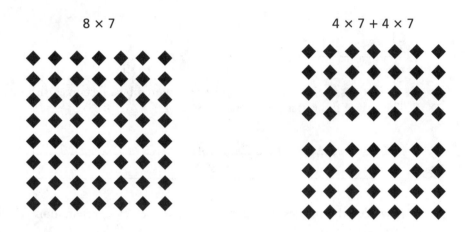

Similarly, if the students want to multiply a one-digit number by a two-digit number, they can break this hard-to-find product into two easy parts, called *partial products*. To multiply 12×7, they do this:

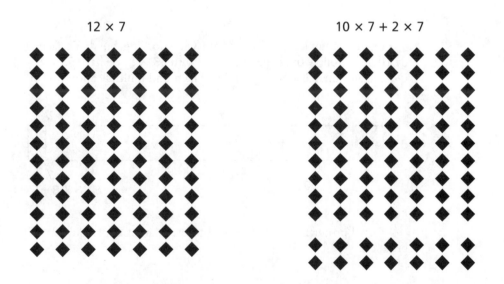

And, since $10 \times 7 = 70$, and $2 \times 7 = 14$, $12 \times 7 = 70 + 14 = 84$. In the same way, $36 \times 4 = 30 \times 4 + 6 \times 4$:

Note that 30 × 4 is a basic fact and a multiplication by 10, and 6 × 4 is a basic fact. So, we have broken 36 × 4 into two easy partial products:

$$36 \times 4 = 30 \times 4 + 6 \times 4 = 120 + 24 = 144$$

When the notion of *area of rectangles* has been developed, the array model for multiplication evolves into the area model. If the sides of a rectangle are 8 and 3, the area of that rectangle is 8 × 3 = 24:

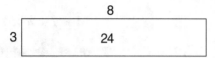

In the same way, 36 × 4 can be represented by a rectangle with sides of 36 and 4. The area of this rectangle is equal to 36 × 4:

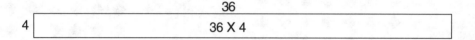

If we cut the rectangle into two parts, we see a representation of the two partial products:

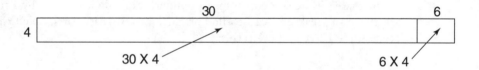

In this example, we also end up with nothing but basic facts and multiplication by 10. If we follow the same procedure with 53 × 8, we have 53 × 8 = 50 × 8 + 3 × 8. Once again, there is nothing but basic facts and multiplication by 10:

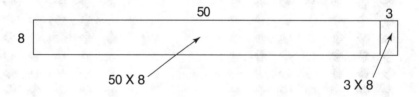

Partial products can also be used to break an example like 29 × 70 into easy partial products:

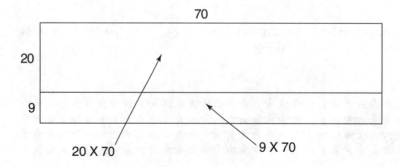

Notice that 20×70 is a basic fact and two multiplications by 10, whereas 9×70 is a basic fact and one multiplication by 10.

When we are multiplying two multidigit numbers, partial products still allow us to find the answer by using only basic multiplication facts and multiplication by 10. For example, consider 35×46 and 179×38:

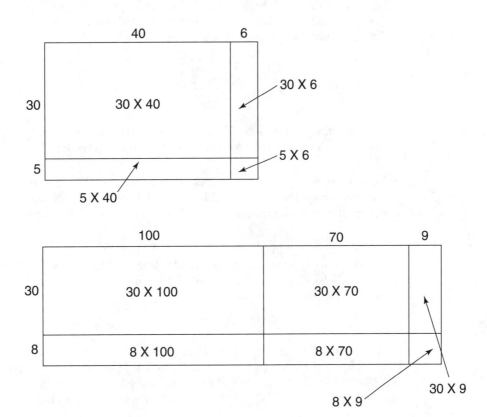

In every whole-number multiplication example, regardless of how large or small the numbers, partial products allow us to find the answer by using only basic facts and multiplication by 10. Once the partial products have been found, they are added to get the total product. We find then that the algorithm for multidigit multiplication consists of a series of easy steps.

When multiplying a three-digit number by another three-digit number, we have 9 partial products. When multiplying two four-digit numbers, we have 16 partial products. Keeping track of such a large number of partial products is a problem. So, to condense the recording of the algorithm, we must regroup as in addition. First, consider 54×7:

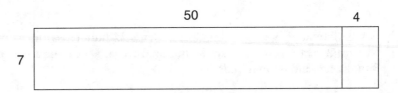

We can find the partial products separately and then add them to get the total product: 378.

$$
\begin{array}{ccc}
50 & 4 & 350 \\
\underline{\times 7} & \underline{\times 7} & \underline{+ 28} \\
350 & 28 & 378
\end{array}
$$

Or, we can do the two multiplications and use regrouping to find the answer. First, multiply 7 times 4. That's 28—or 2 tens and 8 ones. Record the 8 ones in the ones place and keep track of the 2 tens.

$$\begin{array}{r} \overset{2}{}54 \\ \times\ 7 \\ \hline 8 \end{array}$$

Next, we multiply 7 times 50. That's 7 times 5 tens, or 35 tens. But we already had 2 tens, so, altogether, we have 37 tens. That's the same as 3 hundreds and 7 tens.

$$\begin{array}{r} \overset{2}{}54 \\ \times\ 7 \\ \hline 378 \end{array}$$

We use regrouping in a similar fashion to multiply 3 × 486:

First, multiply 3 times 6. That's 18, or 1 ten and 8 ones. Record the 8 ones in the ones place and keep track of the ten.

$$\begin{array}{r} \overset{1}{}486 \\ \times\ 3 \\ \hline 8 \end{array}$$

Next, multiply 3 times the 8 tens. That's 24 tens. With the ten that we already had, we have 25 tens or 2 hundreds and 5 tens. Record the 5 tens in the tens place and keep track of the 2 hundreds.

$$\begin{array}{r} \overset{21}{}486 \\ \times\ 3 \\ \hline 58 \end{array}$$

Finally, multiply 3 times the 4 hundreds. That's 12 hundreds. But we already had 2 hundreds, so that's 14 hundreds, or 1 thousand and 4 hundreds. Record this.

$$\begin{array}{r} \overset{21}{}486 \\ \times\ 3 \\ \hline 1458 \end{array}$$

If the student can use regrouping to find 54 × 7 = 378, then 54 × 70 is the same, except there is also a multiplication by 10. If the student can use regrouping to find 483 × 6 = 2898, then 483 × 600 is the same, except there are also two multiplications by 10. To multiply 342 × 90, the student would think to herself or himself:

I know that I will multiply by 9 and also by 10. Since I can multiply in either order, I'll multiply by 10 first. I know to "add a zero" to the answer, so I'll go ahead and write the zero.

$$\begin{array}{r} 342 \\ \times\ 90 \\ \hline 0 \end{array}$$

Now, I'll multiply 9 times 2. That's 1 ten and 8 ones. I'll record the 8 ones and keep track of the ten.

$$\begin{array}{r} \overset{1}{}342 \\ \times\ 90 \\ \hline 80 \end{array}$$

Now, I'll multiply 9 times 4 tens. That's 36 tens. But we already had 1 ten, so that makes 37 tens. That's the same as 3 hundreds and 7 tens.

$$\begin{array}{r} \overset{31}{}342 \\ \times\ 90 \\ \hline 780 \end{array}$$

Now, I'll multiply 9 times 3 hundreds. That's 27 hundreds. But we already had 3, so that makes 30 hundreds. That's the same as 3 thousands and no hundreds.

$$\begin{array}{r} \overset{31}{}342 \\ \times\ 90 \\ \hline 30780 \end{array}$$

Similarly, the student can multiply 264 × 400:

There are two multiplications by 10. I'll do that first. I'll need to add two zeros.

$$\begin{array}{r} 264 \\ \times\ 400 \\ \hline 00 \end{array}$$

Then, I'll multiply 264 by 4.

$$\begin{array}{r} 21 \\ 264 \\ \times\ 400 \\ \hline 105600 \end{array}$$

We can now do any whole-number multiplication example by using an efficient, written algorithm. For example, consider 316 × 274:

First, multiply by 4.

$$\begin{array}{r} 316 \\ \times\ 274 \\ \hline 1264 \end{array}$$

Next, multiply by 70.

$$\begin{array}{r} 316 \\ \times\ 274 \\ \hline 1264 \\ 22120 \end{array}$$

Then, multiply by 200.

$$\begin{array}{r} 316 \\ \times\ 274 \\ \hline 1264 \\ 22120 \\ 63200 \end{array}$$

Finally, add the partial products.

$$\begin{array}{r} 316 \\ \times\ 274 \\ \hline 1264 \\ 22120 \\ 63200 \\ \hline 86584 \end{array}$$

The following activities illustrate how a teacher might introduce and have the students use partial products.

Activity 6.11 Pieces of the Problem

Show a graph-paper representation of a multiplication on a transparency. For example, you might use 8 × 23. Lay a piece of yarn across the transparency to separate the multiplication into two parts:

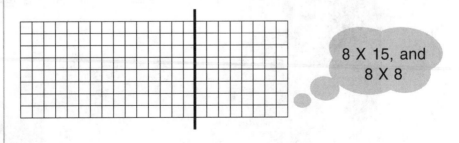

8 X 15, and
8 X 8

Repeat by placing the yarn in different places.

Activity 6.12 Use the Easy Tens

This is a continuation of activity 6.11. Show a graph-paper representation of another multiplication example on a transparency. For example, you might use 7 × 27. Lay a piece of yarn across the transparency to separate the multiplication into two parts. Have the children name the two parts:

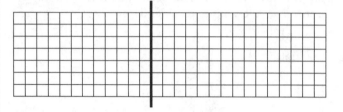

7 X 12, and
7 X 15

Then, move the yarn so that all the tens are in one piece. Have the children name the two parts:

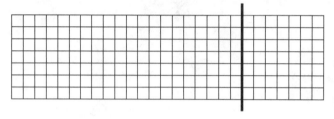

7 X 20, and
7 X 7

Ask, "Which would be easier to do: 7 × 12 and 7 × 15, or 7 × 20 and 7 × 7?"

Repeat the process with other multiplication examples.

Use of the Multiplication Algorithm.

So, we find that the two big ideas on which the multiplication algorithm is based are *multiplication by 10* and *partial products*. Multiplication by 10 is easy, and using partial products reduces the algorithm into a

series of steps that involve nothing but basic multiplication facts, multiplications by 10, and addition with regrouping.

Paper-and-pencil computations is an area that should have decreased emphasis. At the same time, mental arithmetic and the use of calculators should have increased emphasis. When teaching the two big ideas—*multiplication by 10* and *partial products*—as the basis of the multiplication algorithm, your goal is not to develop a high level of skill with the algorithm. The goal is, rather, to develop a high level of understanding of the algorithm and of how it simplifies multiplication with large numbers.

Summary of the Developmental Sequence for Multiplication

Establish the meaning of the operation	1. Associate multiplication with combining groups of the same size.
	2. Learn to use addition to find answers.
Develop the easy basic facts	1. Find the answers by using the meaning of multiplication.
	2. Discover relationships among the facts.
	3. Memorize the facts.
Develop thinking strategies for hard multiplication facts that	1. Are mental strategies.
	2. Use memorized facts to find answers for the hard facts.
Develop the hard basic facts	1. Find the answers by using the thinking strategies.
	2. Review relationships among the facts.
	3. Memorize the facts.
Develop the algorithm	1. Multiply by 10.
	2. Use partial products.

Adapting a Multiplication Lesson

Now we adapt a fourth-grade lesson on multiplication. As we have done before, we begin with a traditional plan, taken directly from suggestions like those that might appear in a teacher's guide of a published textbook program. You should note that this plan is a good one. However, its focus is to teach the textbook page. Notice also that the developmental part of the lesson consists of a detailed explanation of a single example, and that the lesson consists mainly of practice. (It was pointed out earlier that the most important thing a teacher can do to make a lesson appropriate for all students is to thoroughly develop the concepts and skills.)

LESSON OBJECTIVE

The student will multiply a two-digit number and a one-digit number.

Lesson Opener

Have students find each of the following products:

$$10 \times 5 \qquad 31 \times 3 \qquad 7 \times 34$$
$$2 \times 18 \qquad 42 \times 3 \qquad 26 \times 2$$

Ask students if they have estimated how many people are in a room by using multiplication. For example, they may have estimated by multiplying a row of 10 by 5 (the number of rows). Explain that this will help them to understand the multiplication of a two-digit number and a one-digit number.

Development

Direct the attention of the class to the example on the first page of the lesson: 4×34. Point out that 34 is between 30 and 40, so 4×34 will be between 4×30 and 4×40. Ask what 4×30 equals. [120] What does 4×40 equal? [160] So, the answer to 4×34 must be between 120 and 160.

Point out the picture of the base-10 blocks used to illustrate the example. Multiply the ones. Record it as 1 ten and 6 ones. Point out the second picture that shows the renaming. Multiply the tens. Add the extra ten. Write the tens.

Ask if this answer is reasonable. Is it between 120 and 160?

Monitoring Learning

Have the students do the *Check Understanding* examples. Watch for students who add the extra ten to the tens digit before multiplying.

Practice

Have students complete the practice exercises on the second page of the lesson. Students who had difficulty with the *Check Understanding* examples may be assigned the *Reteaching Worksheet* instead of the practice exercises.

This lesson will be adapted to make it more effective in meeting the needs in a diverse classroom. The adapted lesson plan that follows includes an increased amount of developmental instruction. Notice the shift in instructional emphasis from teaching the pages of the student book toward an emphasis on teaching the concept. We have also increased visual input, kinesthetic activity, student communication, and monitoring of learning.

LESSON OBJECTIVE

The student will multiply a two-digit number and a one-digit number.

Lesson Opener

Prepare pairs of cards. One card of each pair will show a multiplication example—for example, 30 × 7; the other card of the pair will show the answer to the multiplication:

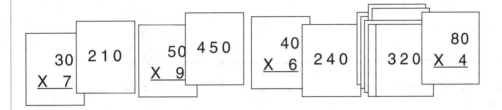

Shuffle the cards and give a card to each student. If there is an odd number of students, the teacher should keep a card and participate. Have the students find their partners. After everyone has found a partner, call on several students to tell how they were able to figure out the correct answers.

Monitor understanding. Observe the children carefully throughout this activity. Direct leading questions to children who are unable to find their partners. (For example, ask, "How many tens are you starting with? How many times do you have those tens?")

Write 4 × 90 on the board. Point out that this is an easy multiplication to do. Then, write 4 × 93 on the board and tell the students that today they will learn that multiplying these numbers is also easy.

Development

Show 6 × 8 as an array of squares. Draw a line through the array to show that 6 × 8 can be broken into two easy parts:

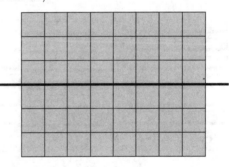

6 × 8 is the same as 3 × 8 + 3 × 8

Monitor understanding. Observe the children carefully throughout this activity. If a child seems not to understand, explain the two partial products by showing them in the pictorial model.

Next, use the same model to show that 6 × 14 is the same as 6 × 10 plus 6 × 4:

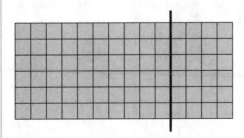

Then, show that 4 × 28 is the same as 4 × 20 + 4 × 8:

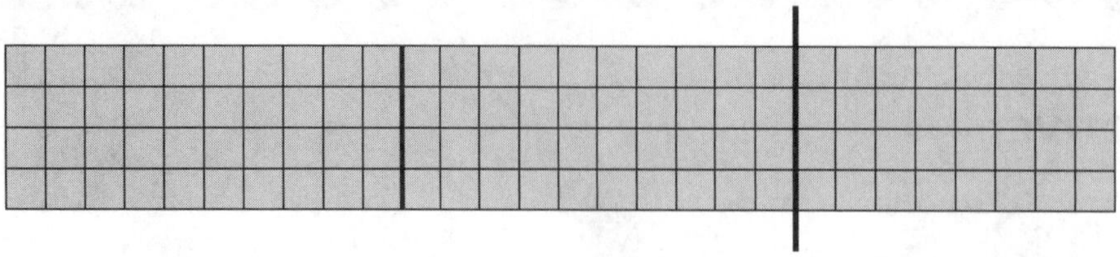

Monitor understanding. Continue to observe the students to see if they understand. Provide extra explanations as needed.

Next, use base-10 blocks to model similar examples. Show 4 × 36. Show the students that the 6 ones are there four times, and that the 3 tens are there four times:

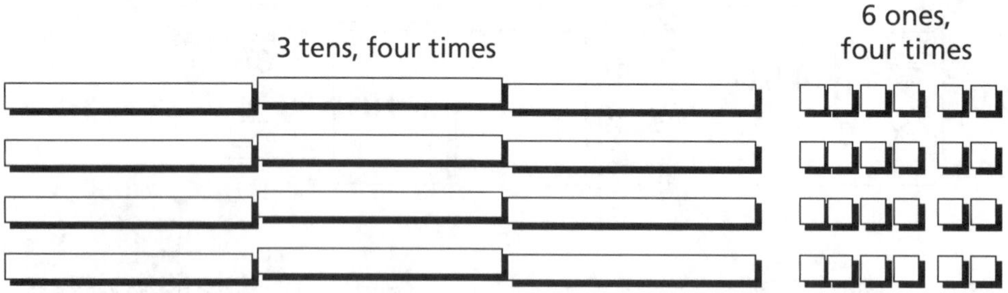

3 tens, four times

6 ones,
four times

Help the students see that these two parts show the two multiplications that must be completed to get the answer to the original problem: 4 × 30 and 4 × 6. Have the students find these two partial products and add them to get the final product.

Monitor understanding. Watch the students to be sure that they understand.

Also use the base-10 blocks to show the multiplication of 6 × 43:

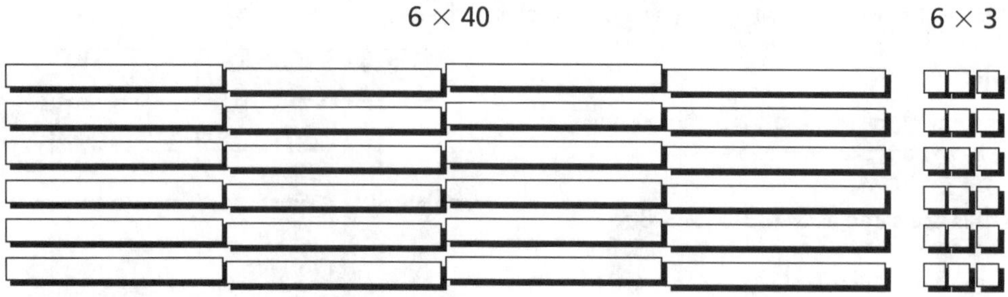

6 × 40

6 × 3

Once again, have the students find the two partial products and add them to get the final product.

Explain to the children that although it is necessary to do both multiplications, it is not really necessary to write the two partial products separately. Redo the two previous examples using base-10 blocks to illustrate how to use regrouping. Be sure to record each step so that the students can see the relationship between the written steps and the steps using the model. Show 4 × 36 and write it on the board in vertical form.

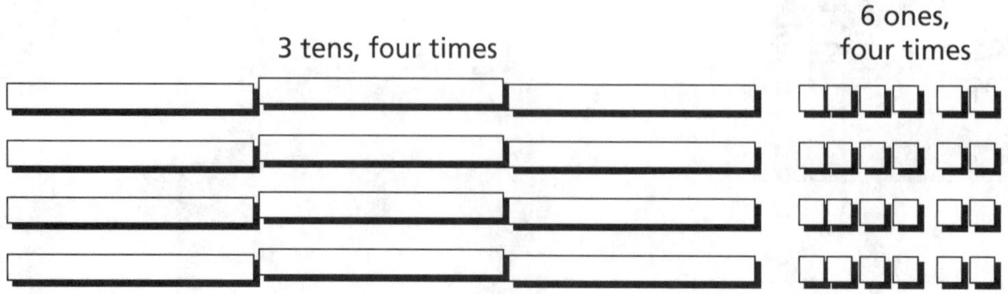

3 tens, four times

6 ones,
four times

Point out that there are some tens and some ones. The children should think first about how many ones there are. There are 6 ones, four times. That's 24 ones. But, as everyone learned in relationship to addition, that is too many to write, so they must make a trade—20 of the ones for 2 extra tens.

Monitor understanding. If students do not understand, a short review of regrouping in addition may be needed.

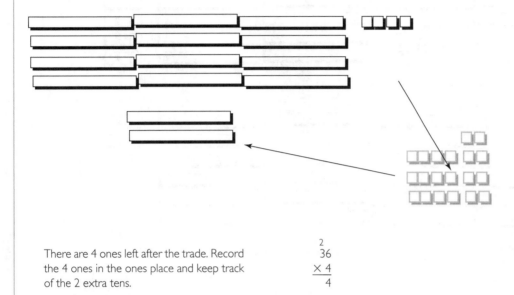

There are 4 ones left after the trade. Record the 4 ones in the ones place and keep track of the 2 extra tens.

$$\begin{array}{r} 2 \\ 36 \\ \times\ 4 \\ \hline 4 \end{array}$$

Next, ask the students to think about how many tens they have. There are 3 tens, four times. That's 12 tens. But they must also count the 2 extra tens that they traded for, so altogether there are 14 tens. But that's too many to write, so they trade 10 tens for a hundred:

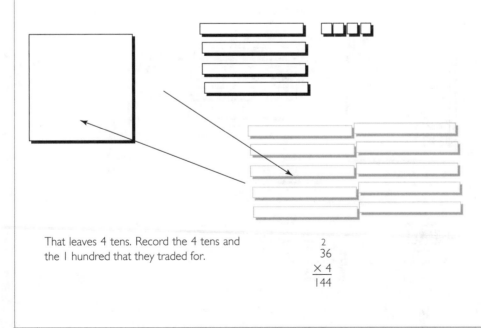

That leaves 4 tens. Record the 4 tens and the 1 hundred that they traded for.

$$\begin{array}{r} 2 \\ 36 \\ \times\ 4 \\ \hline 144 \end{array}$$

Use the base-10 blocks to show the multiplication of 6 × 43:

| 6 × 40 | | 6 × 3 |

There are 18 ones. That's too many to write, so we make a trade:

After the trade, the children are left with 8 ones and an extra ten. Record the 8 ones in the ones place and keep track of the extra ten.

$$\begin{array}{r} 1 \\ 43 \\ \times\ 6 \\ \hline 8 \end{array}$$

Monitor understanding. Be sure that the students realize that what they write is merely recording what they see.

There are 6 × 4, or 24, tens, plus the extra ten that they traded for, so altogether there are 25 tens. That's too many to write, so they must make a trade:

After the trade, the children have 2 hundreds and
5 tens, in addition to the 8 ones that they already
recorded. Record the tens and hundreds.

$$\begin{array}{r} 1 \\ 43 \\ \times\ 6 \\ \hline 258 \end{array}$$

Practice

Have the children work with partners to complete practice examples from a practice page in the child's textbook.

Closure

Ask the students what they learned today. Hand out papers with one multiplication example. Have the children take this example home and show a parent how to do it.

Teaching Division of Whole Numbers

The same developmental sequence used for addition, subtraction, and multiplication is used to teach whole-number division. As with the other operations, the first major instructional task is to establish the meaning of division.

Developing the Meaning of Division

There are several different ways that division can be approached. However, when division is introduced at the elementary school level, it is nearly always considered to be the separation of a quantity into equal-sized parts. Therefore, we want children to *associate division with separating a quantity into equal-sized parts.* The association should be so strong that when the children see the symbols 12 ÷ 4, they visualize a group of 12 things being separated into equal groups. When a child sees a situation where a quantity is being separated into equal parts, the child will think, "That's division!" After division has been mastered, the child will see problem settings where quantities are being separated into equal parts and will think, "I can use division to solve this problem."

There are two distinct kinds of division when a quantity is being separated into equal parts: measurement division and partition division. The easiest way to understand the difference between them is to consider an example of each.

Measurement Division.　Suppose in a game where players use chips, there are 20 chips and all 20 must be used. If the children know that each player must use 4 chips, how many players must there be in the game? To answer this question, set aside 4 chips (that's enough for one player), then set aside 4 more chips (that's enough for another player), and continue this process until all the chips have been set aside. Then count the groups of 4 chips to see how many players there would be. Since there are five groups of 4 chips, there would be five players:

In this example, the children know how many chips they are starting with and they know the size of the groups. The children want to find out how many groups there are. The division described is 20 ÷ 4 = 5:

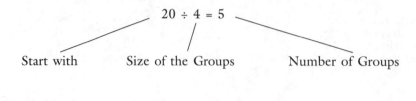

Start with   Size of the Groups   Number of Groups

This is called *measurement division. In measurement division, we know the beginning number, we know the size of the groups, and we want to find the number of groups.*

Partition Division.   Now, let's consider the other type of division. Suppose this time there is another game where the players use chips. In this game, there are also 20 chips and every chip must be used. However, there are four players and every player must have the same number of chips. This time, the students know that there are four groups of chips (one group of chips for each player), but they don't know how many chips are in each group. To find out how many chips each player gets, designate four players and give each of them a chip. Then give each of them another chip, and continue this process until all the chips have been passed out. Finally, count to see how many chips each of the four players has after all the chips have been passed out:

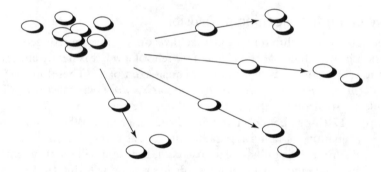

In this example, the children know how many chips they are starting with and they know the number of groups. The children want to find out how many chips are in each group. The division described is 20 ÷ 4 = 5:

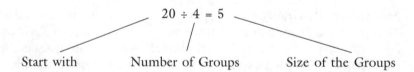

Start with   Number of Groups   Size of the Groups

This kind of division is called *partition division. In partition division, we know how many we are starting with, we know the number of groups, and we want to find out how many are in each group* (Moyer, 2000; Tucker, 1973).

Teaching Both Measurement Division and Partition Division.   The two kinds of division seem to be the same, but actually they are different in three ways. First, we know different information: in measurement division, we know the size of the groups, whereas in partition division, we know the number of groups. Second, we want to find different things: in measurement division, we want to find the number of groups; in partition division, the size of the groups. Third, we use different procedures to get the answer. In measurement division, we repeatedly remove (subtract) the same amount, but in partition division, we distribute (pass out) the objects equally.

Since the students encounter both kinds of division situations, it is important that they be exposed to both as they are learning the meaning of the operation. The following activities illustrate how a teacher might lead students to understand the meaning of division. The activities provided here illustrate only partition division. Development of similar activities for measurement division is left as an exercise for the reader.

Activity 6.13   Equal Sharing

Place a transparency on the overhead projector. Put 24 raisins in one corner. Use a marker to draw four 3-inch circles on the transparency.

Explain that you have four children to whom you want to give the raisins and that you want them all to have the same number. Tell the students that you want to put each child's raisins in one of the four circles.

Ask the students how to do it. Follow their directions exactly until there are the same number of raisins in each circle. If the students' directions do not lead to equal groups, let them figure out what to do. When the groups are all the same size, write the word *divide* on the board. Explain that when you separate a number of things into equal-sized groups, it is called *division*.

Repeat the activity, but this time, start with 36 raisins.

Activity 6.14   Equal Sharing—Write It

Follow the procedures of activity 6.13, but for the first two examples, write the division sentence.

Write 24 ÷ 4 = 6, and explain that 24 is the number that you start with (24 raisins), 4 is the number of equal groups (there are four children), and 6 is the number in each group (each child gets 6 raisins). Also explain the division sign and demonstrate how to read the division sentence.

On the third example, have a student read the division sentence. For the rest of the examples, ask a student to tell you what the division sentence is, and have another student write the division sentence.

Developing the Easy Basic Division Facts

To reinforce the meaning of division, the teacher should expose the children to a wide variety of division examples by using familiar objects. The students should use appropriate terminology to describe the division verbally and use the division sign and equal sign to write the division sentence. In each example, they should figure out the answer for themselves, and the teacher should continually say how easy it is. The teacher should emphasize that they can find the answers by themselves.

Discovering Relationships among the Easy Basic Division Facts.   After the meaning of division has been established and children can confidently find answers on their own, we focus on the easier basic division facts. For purposes of our discussion here, we consider division facts with divisors of 1 to 5 to be the easy ones. There are 50 of these easy basic division facts.

As these facts are discovered, organized, and reorganized, the students are led to discover as many relationships among them as possible. Many of these relationships, in effect, reduce the amount of memorization that is necessary. All of them contribute to improved retention of the facts that are memorized. It is always easier to remember things that are related to other things that are already known. Among the relationships that the teacher should be sure to emphasize are the following five:

1. When 0 is divided by any number, the answer will always be 0. (There are 5 of these facts among the 50 facts that we are considering easy basic division facts. That's *5 facts* but *only one thing to remember.*)

2. When any number is divided by 1, the answer will be the starting number. (In addition to $0 \div 1$, there are 9 of these facts among the 50 easy basic division facts. That's *9 facts* but *only one thing to learn.*)

3. When any number is divided by itself, the answer will always be 1. (In addition to $1 \div 1$, there are 4 of these facts among the 50 easy basic division facts. That's *4 facts* but *only one thing to learn.*)

4. There are several pairs of facts that are related:

$6 \div 2 = 3$ and	$6 \div 3 = 2$	$8 \div 2 = 4$ and	$8 \div 4 = 2$
$10 \div 2 = 5$ and	$10 \div 5 = 2$	$12 \div 4 = 3$ and	$12 \div 3 = 4$
$15 \div 3 = 5$ and	$15 \div 5 = 3$	$20 \div 4 = 5$ and	$20 \div 5 = 4$

   Each of these pairs has the same dividend, and the numbers that are the divisor and quotient in 1 fact of the pair are the quotient and divisor in the other fact of the pair. The 2 facts in a pair should be learned together. Then, each pair of facts becomes one thing to learn. (That's *12 facts* but *only six things to learn.*)

5. Every division fact is related to a multiplication fact. For example, consider these pairs of facts:

$12 \div 2 = 6$ and	$6 \times 2 = 12$	$18 \div 3 = 6$ and	$6 \times 3 = 18$
$21 \div 3 = 7$ and	$7 \times 3 = 21$	$24 \div 4 = 6$ and	$6 \times 4 = 24$
$30 \div 5 = 6$ and	$6 \times 5 = 30$	$36 \div 4 = 9$ and	$9 \times 4 = 36$

   Once this relationship is discovered, students can use it to find answers to division facts without counting objects. However, they are able to do this only if they already know the related multiplication facts.

Memorization of the Easy Basic Division Facts.

When the students have become familiar with the helpful relationships among the easy basic division facts, you can expect them to make fairly rapid progress toward memorizing these facts. The instructional activities that are selected to lead the children to memorizing the easy basic division facts should have certain characteristics. These are the same eight characteristics presented earlier in this chapter for multiplication facts:

1. Children should be aware that they are to memorize the facts.
2. The activities should use an interesting and fun format.
3. Activities should have a high level of involvement.
4. Activities should focus on a small number of unmemorized facts at any given time.
5. Some already-memorized facts should be mixed in with the target unmemorized facts. This will improve retention.
6. Children should be allowed enough time to figure out facts that they do not know.

7. To figure out answers, children should think about what they already know that will help them find this answer. What other facts or relationships do they already know that will help?

8. Accuracy, not speed, should be emphasized.

The following examples of memorization activities have these eight characteristics.

Activity 6.15   One Is Important!

Write the following problems on the board:

$$4 \div 1 = \qquad 8 \div 1 = \qquad 3 \div 1 =$$

Have the children figure out the answers. Ask them what the pattern is. When they are sure of the pattern, have them use it to find the answers to these examples:

$$7 \div 1 = \qquad 5 \div 1 = \qquad 6 \div 1 =$$

Erase the board and write these examples:

$$3 \div 3 = \qquad 9 \div 9 = \qquad 7 \div 7 =$$

Have the children figure out the answers. Ask them what the pattern is. Once they are sure of the pattern, have them use it to find the answers to these examples:

$$2 \div 2 = \qquad 8 \div 8 = \qquad 5 \div 5 =$$

Finally, use flash cards showing a mixture of the two types of division just illustrated. Show a flash card. Call on a child to answer. Ask the other students if the answer is correct. Ask how they know. What pattern are they using?

Activity 6.16   Related Pairs

Write the following pairs of problems on the board:

$$15 \div 3 = \qquad 20 \div 5 = \qquad 6 \div 3 =$$
$$15 \div 5 = \qquad 20 \div 4 = \qquad 6 \div 2 =$$

Have the children figure out the answers. Ask them what the pattern is. After they are sure of the pattern, write these facts on the board:

$$8 \div 2 = 4 \qquad 10 \div 5 = 2 \qquad 12 \div 3 = 4$$
$$15 \div 5 = 3 \qquad 6 \div 2 = 3 \qquad 20 \div 4 = 5$$

Use flash cards showing the facts $6 \div 3 =$, $8 \div 4 =$, $10 \div 2 =$, $12 \div 4 =$, $15 \div 3 =$, and $20 \div 5 =$, Show a card. Call on a student. Ask which of the facts on the board can help us with this one.

Developing the Hard Basic Division Facts

Thinking Strategies for the Hard Basic Division Facts.   Before beginning work on the harder basic division facts, the students must have learned to use an efficient thinking strategy to figure out answers. The most effective fact strategies have two characteristics: they are mental strategies and they require the student to use facts that are already memorized to figure out the ones that are not memorized. We consider two of those strategies.

Use Partial Quotients The *partial-quotients strategy* (Tucker, Singleton, & Weaver, 2002) for hard basic division facts is similar to the partial-products strategy that was used for hard basic multiplication facts. In this strategy, the student thinks about what easier division facts with the same divisor can help. For example, suppose the student needs to find 48 ÷ 6:

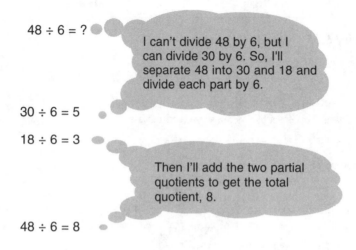

48 ÷ 6 = ?

I can't divide 48 by 6, but I can divide 30 by 6. So, I'll separate 48 into 30 and 18 and divide each part by 6.

30 ÷ 6 = 5

18 ÷ 6 = 3

Then I'll add the two partial quotients to get the total quotient, 8.

48 ÷ 6 = 8

If the student does not know the answer to 56 ÷ 8, he or she can break 56 into two easy parts and use partial quotients to find the answer:

56 ÷ 8 = ?

I can't divide 56 by 8, but I can divide 40 by 8. So, I'll separate 56 into 40 and 16 and divide each part by 8.

40 ÷ 8 = 5

16 ÷ 8 = 2

Then I'll add the two partial quotients to get the total quotient, 7.

56 ÷ 8 = 7

 In the same way, the children can find the answer to 28 ÷ 7. Separate 28 into 14 + 14. Divide each part by 7 and add the partial quotients to get the total quotient, 4. Using this strategy lays the groundwork for the algorithm that is taught later. However, partial quotients are seldom used in textbooks for basic division facts.

 Think of a Related Multiplication Fact The strategy that is most commonly taught in elementary school mathematics textbooks comes from one of the relationships that exists among the basic facts. Most commonly, the thinking strategy taught for hard basic division facts is: *think of a related multiplication fact*. For example, to find the answer to 36 ÷ 9, think, "What number times 9 will equal 36?"

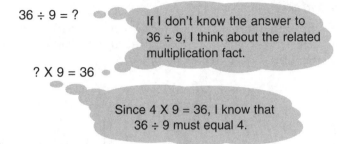

$36 \div 9 = ?$

If I don't know the answer to $36 \div 9$, I think about the related multiplication fact.

$? \times 9 = 36$

Since $4 \times 9 = 36$, I know that $36 \div 9$ must equal 4.

Similarly, if a student does not know the answer to $72 \div 8$, she or he can think about the related multiplication fact: "What number times 8 equals 72?" Since $9 \times 8 = 72$, the child knows that $72 \div 8 = 9$. This strategy works well if the students are thoroughly familiar with the relationship between division facts and multiplication facts and if they have mastered the required multiplication facts before they try to use them to find answers to division facts.

A Remediation Note   Students who have difficulty using related multiplication facts to find answers to the hard basic division facts often have that difficulty because they have not yet mastered the hard basic multiplication facts. *A student cannot use facts that he or she does not know.*

Teaching the Hard Basic Division Facts.   After students have developed an efficient thinking strategy to quickly and accurately find answers to the hard basic division facts, it is relatively easy for them to achieve mastery of those facts. The teacher should *revisit the relationships* that were discovered during development of the easy division facts to ensure that the students realize that the easy division facts also apply to the hard division facts. And the students should *work toward memorization* of those facts.

Teaching the Division Algorithm

After the basic division facts have been mastered, it is possible to develop the division algorithm very quickly. Rapid success depends, however, on the application of the same principles that were presented for each of the other operations:

- **Let them see what it looks like.** Carefully model the operation with an appropriate physical or pictorial model. Use a model that lets the students see what happens to the basic units—ones, tens, hundreds, and so on—when they divide.
- **Deemphasize rote rules.** You might end up with rules, but they should be meaningful. They should arise out of the modeling process.
- **Emphasize big ideas.** These are the important generalizations that describe the procedures. They also come from the modeling process.
- **Let the written algorithm simply be a recording of what happens when the algorithm is modeled.** Everything you write should match something you do.
- **Watch your language.** The language that you use should describe what you see when the operation is modeled, not language that describes what you write down.

Although the division algorithm can be developed by using measurement division, there are many points at which difficulties arise (Tucker, 1973). Consequently, since the early 1980s, textbook writers have used, almost without exception, partition division to develop the algorithm. We also use partition division in our development. We proceed by describing how a physical model can be used to clarify and give meaning to the algorithm. We see, too, how the entire algorithm is based on the application of two big ideas.

The First Big Idea

Divide One Unit at a Time This big idea is developed in the next two examples. Consider the example 48 ÷ 4. We want to divide 48 into four equal parts. To do this, begin by using bundled sticks to represent 48:

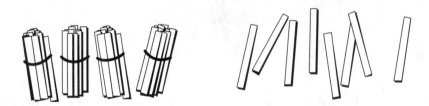

Next, write the division problem on the chalkboard:

$$4\overline{)48}$$

We want to separate 48 into four equal parts, so we designate four places to put those four equal parts. Begin by distributing the tens:

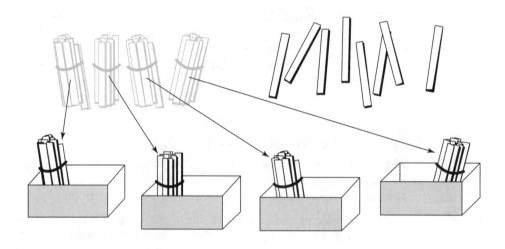

Record that 1 ten is placed in each of the equal parts:

$$\begin{array}{r} 1 \\ 4\overline{)48} \end{array}$$

Then record that 4 tens are taken away from the original number. After the subtraction, notice that there are still 8 ones to distribute:

$$\begin{array}{r} 1 \\ 4\overline{)48} \\ -4 \\ \hline 8 \end{array}$$

Next, we distribute the ones. We are able to place 2 ones in each of the equal parts:

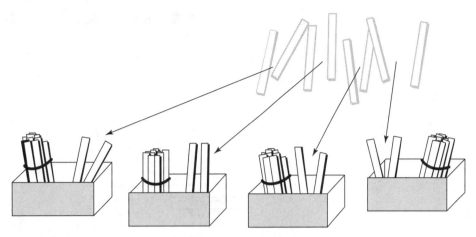

Finally, record the 2 ones that were placed in each of the equal groups, record that we took 8 ones away from what was left of the beginning number, and record that nothing is left of the original number to be distributed. We were able to place 1 ten and 2 ones (12) in each of the four equal parts.

$$\begin{array}{r} 12 \\ 4\overline{)48} \\ -4 \\ \hline 8 \\ -8 \\ \hline 0 \end{array}$$

One key to successfully teaching the division algorithm or any of the algorithms is to get the students to understand that the written algorithm is nothing more than an orderly recording of what is being done with the model. To accomplish this, the teacher must model the process one step at a time, and each step should be recorded immediately after it is completed. We look at one more example: 639 ÷ 3. This time we use base-10 blocks to model the process. Begin by writing the problem and representing the beginning number with the model:

$3\overline{)639}$

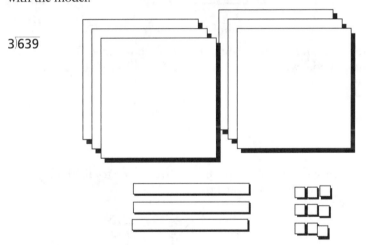

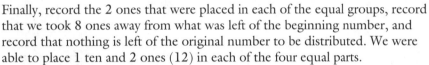

Then, designate three locations where we place the three equal parts:

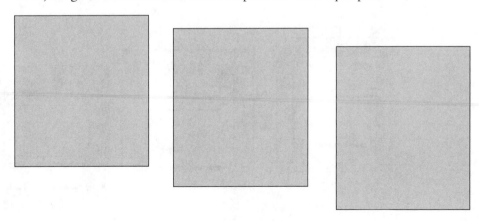

Distribute the hundreds first. We have 6 hundreds, so we can place 2 hundreds in each of the three equal parts:

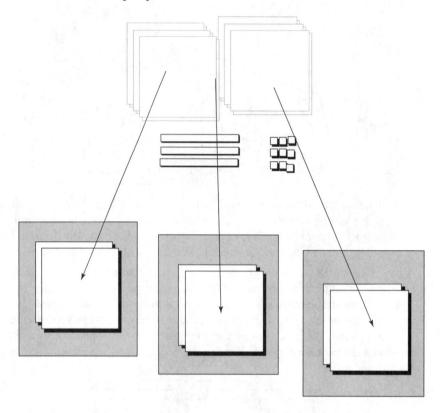

We took 6 hundreds away from the beginning number. We record that and see that after the subtraction, we still have 3 tens and 9 ones to distribute:

$$
\begin{array}{r}
2 \\
3\overline{)639} \\
-600 \\
\hline
39
\end{array}
$$

Next, we distribute the tens. We have 3 tens to distribute, so we are able to place 1 ten in each of the three equal parts:

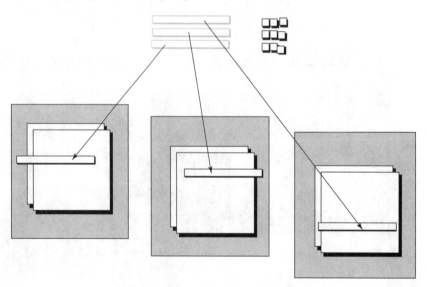

We took 3 tens away from what was left of the beginning number. We record that and find that there are still 9 ones to be distributed:

$$
\begin{array}{r}
21 \\
3\overline{)639} \\
-6 \\
\hline
39 \\
-3 \\
\hline
9
\end{array}
$$

Finally, we distribute the 9 ones. We are able to place 3 ones in each of the three equal parts:

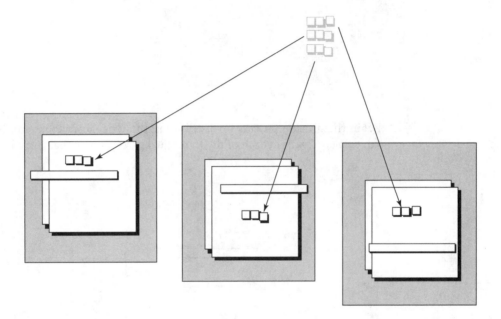

We record the 3 ones that we placed in each of the equal parts. In this step, we distributed 9 ones. These were taken away from what was left of the beginning number, so we record this subtraction. We have nothing left to distribute.

$$
\begin{array}{r}
213 \\
3\overline{)639} \\
-6 \\
\hline
39 \\
-3 \\
\hline
9 \\
-9 \\
\hline
0
\end{array}
$$

We were able to place 2 hundreds, 1 ten, and 3 ones in each of the three equal parts. The answer to the division problem is 213.

In the preceding two examples, we have seen the first of the two big ideas that are the basis of the division algorithm: *divide one unit at a time*. What we are really doing is using *partial quotients* in the same way that they were suggested for simplifying hard basic division facts.

The Second Big Idea

Trade Remainders for Smaller Units   The second big idea for the division algorithm also arises out of the modeling of division examples. This time, we begin with 92 ÷ 4. First, we write the division problem and represent 92 (the number that we start with) using base-10 blocks:

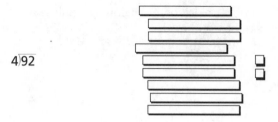

4)92

Designate four locations where we place the four equal parts:

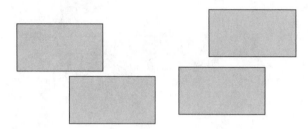

Begin the division process by distributing the tens. Since there are 9 tens, we have enough to place 2 tens in each of the four equal parts. Notice that there is 1 ten left over:

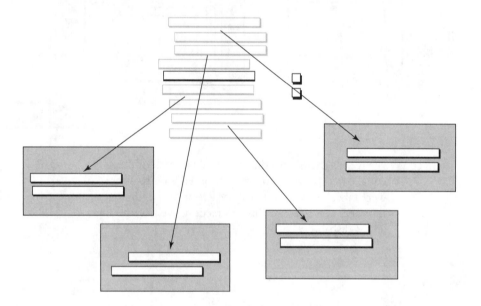

Place 2 tens in each of the four equal parts. We took 8 tens away from the starting number and are left with 1 ten and 2 ones:

$$
\begin{array}{r}
2 \\
4\overline{)92} \\
-8 \\
\hline
12
\end{array}
$$

Now we are faced with a problem that we have not seen before. What do we do with the ten that we were unable to distribute? Whenever we have "leftovers," we trade them for smaller units. So, in this case, we trade the leftover ten for 10 ones:

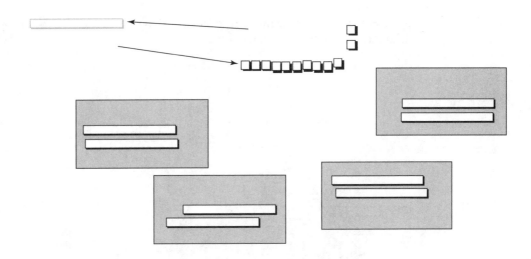

Before the trade, we had 1 ten and 2 ones. After the trade, we have 12 ones:

$$
\begin{array}{r}
2 \\
4\overline{)92} \\
-8 \\
\hline
12 \\
\end{array}
$$

These 12 ones need to be distributed to the four equal parts. We can place 3 ones in each of the four equal parts:

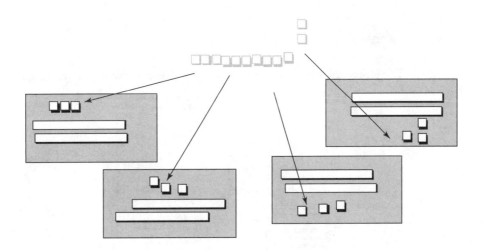

We record the 3 ones that were placed in each equal part. In this step, we took 12 ones from what was left of the beginning number. We record this subtraction and see that there is nothing left to be distributed.

$$
\begin{array}{r}
23 \\
4\overline{)92} \\
-8 \\
\hline
12 \\
-12 \\
\hline
0 \\
\end{array}
$$

The answer to the division problem is 23.

The preceding example illustrated the second big idea on which the division algorithm is based: *trade remainders for smaller units.* We next examine another example in which this big idea is used. To find the answer to 625 ÷ 5, we write the problem and represent the beginning number, 625, with base-10 blocks. We begin by distributing 1 hundred to each of five equal parts:

5)625

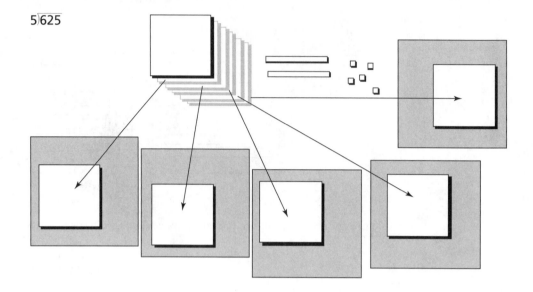

In this step, we took 5 hundreds away from our beginning number. After we record this subtraction, we have 1 hundred, 2 tens, and 5 ones that still need to be distributed:

$$
\begin{array}{r}
1 \\
5)\overline{625} \\
-5 \\
\hline
125
\end{array}
$$

The remaining hundred can be traded for 10 tens. We now have 12 tens:

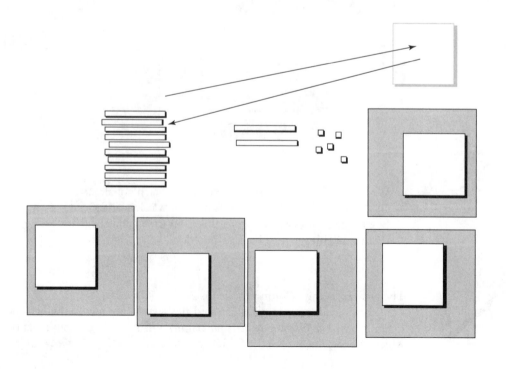

Now, we can place 2 tens in each of the five equal parts:

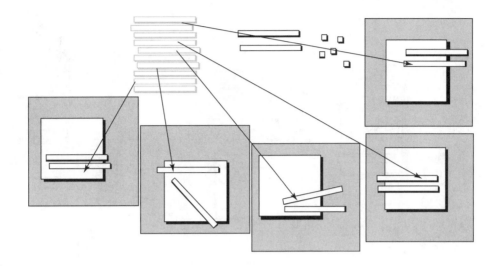

We record the 2 tens that we placed in
each of the equal parts. To do this, we take
10 tens away from what is left of our starting
number. We record this subtraction and we
have 2 tens and 5 ones left to distribute.

$$
\begin{array}{r}
12 \\
5\overline{)625} \\
-5 \\
\hline
12.5 \\
-10 \\
\hline
25 \\
\end{array}
$$

We then trade the remaining 2 tens for 20 ones. Now we have 25 ones to distribute:

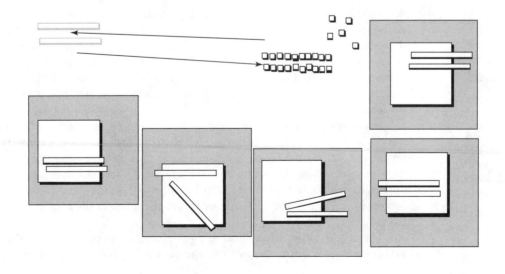

We place 5 ones in each of the five equal parts:

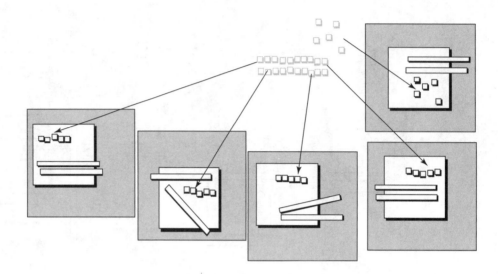

Finally, we complete the recording of the process. We record 5 in the ones place, and since we took 25 ones away from what was left of the beginning number, we record this subtraction. We see that there is nothing left to distribute: $625 \div 5 = 125$.

$$
\begin{array}{r}
125 \\
5\overline{)625} \\
-5 \\
\hline
125 \\
-10 \\
\hline
25 \\
-25 \\
\hline
0
\end{array}
$$

Use of the Division Algorithm.
Both big ideas for the division algorithm arise out of experiences as we model division examples: *divide one unit at a time* and *trade remainders for smaller units.* Regardless of what the numbers are, that's all there is to the division algorithm.

Notice that all the examples we examined had one-digit divisors. If we want students to be able to use pencil-and-paper computation to divide by large divisors, a great deal of time must be spent teaching them to estimate partial quotients. However, we should seriously question the practice of using pencil-and-paper computation for these examples. With the availability of calculators, we do not need to teach today's students to do complex, pencil-and-paper division computation. The time can be better spent on literally hundreds of other things—things that will be far more useful to the students.

In the spirit of the NCTM Standards, it is more important for students to understand how the algorithm works than for them to become proficient with long division involving multidigit divisors. It is more important that they can use the principles that are the basis of the algorithm to make quick and accurate estimates. It is also more important that they become able to intelligently decide whether it is appropriate to estimate the answer, use a calculator to get the exact answer, or use pencil-and-paper computation.

The following activities illustrate how a teacher might introduce the first big idea: *divide one unit at a time.* Notice that the early examples involve common objects.

Activity 6.17 Rocks and Blocks

Bring about 20 small rocks to class. Place 18 rocks into a box with 12 wooden blocks. Write "18 rocks and 12 blocks" on the board. Have six students come to the front of the room. Tell the class that you want to share the rocks and blocks equally among these six people, but that you want the class to tell how to do the sharing so it will be equal.

Call on other students to give directions. Do exactly as you are told, but keep asking, "Is that right?" "Now what do I need to do?" "Are we done yet?"

When the sharing is complete, repeat the process by sharing 20 rocks and 15 blocks among five students.

Activity 6.18 Pennies and Dimes

Share 9 dimes and 6 pennies among three people.

Record the results as a division example. Point out how the children can share the tens (the dimes) first and then share the ones (the pennies).

The next activity illustrates how a teacher might introduce the second big idea: *trade remainders for smaller units*. Once again, this example involves common objects.

Activity 6.19 More Pennies and Dimes

Share 9 dimes and 6 pennies among four people.

Record the results as a division example. Point out how the students can share the dimes first, trade the leftover dime for 10 pennies, and then share the 16 pennies.

The following activity illustrates how a teacher can encourage students to use the principles of the division algorithm to estimate division answers.

Activity 6.20 Guesstimation

Prepare cards with division examples on them. Some should have one-digit divisors and some should have two-digit divisors. Form a group of two or three students. Shuffle the cards and place the deck facedown on the table.

On each play, one card is turned over and the students estimate the answer and write down the estimate. Then they should use a calculator to find the answer. The student with the best estimate gets a point. If there is a tie, all who tied get a point. After each play, the one(s) with the best estimate must explain how the estimate was figured out.

When all the cards have been played, the one with the most points wins.

Adapting a Division Lesson

Now we adapt a fourth-grade lesson on division. As we have done before, we begin with a traditional plan that follows the kind of suggestions that would be found in a teacher's guide of a published textbook program. Note that this plan is a good one. As with previous textbook lessons that we examined, the focus is to teach the textbook page, the developmental part of the lesson consists of a detailed explanation of a single example, and the lesson consists mainly of practice.

LESSON OBJECTIVE

The student will record the steps in division computation.

Lesson Opener

Have students find each of the following quotients:

30 ÷ 3   60 ÷ 3   80 ÷ 4   40 ÷ 2

Have students separate 26 pennies into three equal parts. How much is in each part? How much is leftover?

Development

Direct the attention of the class to the example on the first page of the lesson. Forty-two cents (4 dimes and 2 pennies) is being separated into three equal parts. Refer to the pictures on the page. The dimes are separated first. One dime is placed in each part, and one dime remains. Point out the written steps that are shown on the page.

The next picture shows 10 pennies in place of the dime. Altogether, there are 12 pennies to be divided. Four pennies are placed in each part. Point out the written steps that are shown on the page.

Ask if the students understand that the written division is just the recording of the steps.

Monitor Learning

Have the students do the *Check Understanding* examples.

Practice

Have students complete the practice exercises on the second page of the lesson. Students who had difficulty with the *Check Understanding* examples can be assigned the *Reteaching Worksheet* instead of the practice exercises.

Closure

Ask students what they learned about recording division.

Next, we adapt this lesson to make it more effective in meeting the learning needs in a diverse classroom. We increase the amount of developmental instruction, visual input, kinesthetic activity, and student communication, and we make monitoring of learning a more integral part of the lesson. These adaptations make the lesson appropriate for almost all students. But, remember that some students with severe needs might require further instructional adaptations.

LESSON OBJECTIVE

The student will record the steps in division computation.

Lesson Opener

Make enough copies of each of the following division examples so that there will be enough for all the students:

30 ÷ 3	40 ÷ 2	40 ÷ 4	50 ÷ 5
60 ÷ 2	60 ÷ 3	60 ÷ 6	80 ÷ 2
80 ÷ 4	80 ÷ 8	90 ÷ 3	90 ÷ 9

Write the numbers 10, 20, 30, and 40 on pieces of paper and put the pieces of paper at different locations on the wall. Tell the students that the numbers on the wall are the answers. Have the students go stand by the answers to their problems.

Monitor understanding. Watch the students during this activity to be sure that they understand. Provide help as needed. Explain that today the class will divide two-digit numbers and will learn how to record the steps.

Development

Show the students seven strings of beads with 6 beads on each string and 9 beads not on strings. Ask the students to tell you how to separate the beads into three equal groups. Record the steps using a chart like this one. Begin by placing two strings of beads in each part. Record the two strings that were placed in each part and subtract the six strings that were distributed.

STRING	BEADS	
2		In each group
7	9	Starting amount
−6		
1	9	

Ask what to do with the leftover string of beads. [Take them off the string.] Record this result.

Monitor understanding. At each step, watch for students who do not understand. Provide extra explanation as needed.

STRING	BEADS	
2		In each group
7	9	Starting amount
−6		
1̶	9̶	
	15	

Distribute the 15 beads. Record the number placed in each group, and subtract the number that was used.

STRING	BEADS	
2	5	In each group
7	9	Starting amount
−6		
1̶	9̶	
	15	
	−15	
	0	

Using blocks to represent eggs, show the students five cartons of eggs and 8 eggs not in cartons. Tell them that you want to separate the eggs into four equal groups. Follow the steps outlined for the previous example and record the steps on a chart like this one:

	CARTONS	EGGS
In each group		
Starting amount	5	8

Monitor understanding. At each step, watch for students who do not understand. Provide extra explanation as needed. For example, you might need to remind some students that there are 12 eggs in each carton.

Show the students 75 cents (seven dimes and five pennies). Tell them that you want to separate the money into five equal parts. Follow the same procedures that were used in the previous two examples.

Record the steps on a chart like this one:

DIMES	PENNIES	
		In each group
7	5	Starting amount

Monitor understanding. Continue watching for students who do not understand. Provide help as needed.

Tell the students that you are now going to do this example again, but that you will record the steps a little bit differently. Point out that since each dime is equal to 10 pennies, we can think of the dimes and pennies as tens and ones. Write the division and record the steps using standard division notation:

Tens ─── Ones
15 ─── Amount in each group
Number of groups ─── 5)75 ─── Starting number
−5 ─── Amount distributed in first step
Amount left to distribute ─── 25 ─── (After the trade, 25 ones)
−25 ─── Amount distributed in second step
Nothing left to distribute ─── 0

Monitor understanding. Be sure that students understand that everything we write is a recording of something that we do.

Direct the attention of the class to the example on the first page of the lesson. Forty-two cents (four dimes and 2 pennies) is being separated into three equal parts. Refer to the pictures on the page. The dimes are separated first. One dime is placed in each part and one dime remains. Point out the written steps that are shown on the page.

The next picture shows 10 pennies in place of the dime. Now, there are 12 pennies to be divided. Four pennies are placed in each part. Point out the written steps that are shown.

Monitor understanding. Ask if the students understand that the written division is just the recording of the steps.

Form groups of four students. Give each group eight dimes and 16 pennies. Write the example 7)84 on the chalkboard and have each group use the dimes and pennies to find the answer to the division example. Have them record each step the way you have been doing it.

Monitor understanding. Move around to observe the work in the groups. If a group is having difficulty, ask leading questions to help them. Emphasize the recording of the steps.

Practice

When all the groups have finished, have the students do the *Check Understanding* examples for practice.

Monitor learning. Move around the room, checking the students' work. Catch the errors and misconceptions and get them corrected. If some students need reteaching, form a group and reteach the concepts and skills.

Closure

Pick one more example and ask for volunteers to come to the front to find the answer. Have a student separate the dimes and pennies. Have the other student record the steps.

Follow-Up

Assign one example for homework. Tell the students that they are to explain to a parent how to do the division and record the steps.

Teaching Problem Solving Using Multiplication and Division

The beginning of the ability to solve problems involving multiplication and division is found in the way that the meanings of those operations are developed. If the essence of the problem is that several equal-sized quantities are being combined, the student can look at the situation and tell that multiplication can be used to find the answer. If the essence of the problem situation is that a quantity is being separated into equal parts, the student can look at the situation and tell that division can be used to find the answer. Students should be led to analyze the problem situation, decide what "physical action" is taking place, and relate that physical action to the appropriate arithmetic problem.

All of the remarks in Chapter 5 about teaching students to solve problems using addition and subtraction also apply when teachers are teaching students how to use multiplication and division to solve problems. The students should experience *problems that they care about* and that involve *familiar objects*. They students should also experience *mixed examples and nonexamples* where they must decide when they can and cannot use each of the operations. And, finally, when solving word problems, the students should be led to focus not on key words, but on what is happening in the problem situation.

Exercises and Activities

1. Compare the two multiplication lesson plans in this chapter.
   a. Identify where the adapted plan provides more developmental work.
   b. Identify where the adapted plan provides more kinesthetic activity.
   c. Identify where the adapted plan provides more opportunity for communication from the children.
   d. Identify where the adapted plan provides more opportunity for communication among the children.
2. Adapt activities 6.13 and 6.14 so that measurement division is being developed and used.
3. Develop an instructional activity that uses a physical model to help children understand relationship 4 in the section titled "Discovering Relationships among the Easy Basic Division Facts."
4. Develop an instructional activity that uses a physical model to help children understand relationship 5 in the section titled "Discovering Relationships among the Easy Basic Division Facts."
5. Following the steps described in the "Divide One Unit at a Time" section, develop an instructional activity that has children use one, ten, and hundred dollar bills to divide 852 by 3.
6. Revise activity 6.13 to make it more kinesthetic.
7. Describe activities similar to activities 6.13 and 6.14 that will develop the concept of *measurement division*.
8. Develop an activity similar to activity 6.16 that will encourage students to think about related multiplication facts to find answers to division facts.
9. Choose a lesson on either multiplication or division of whole numbers from a published elementary school mathematics textbook series.
   a. Write a lesson plan that follows the teaching suggestions in the teacher's guide.
   b. Identify the parts of the lesson that provide visual information about the concept(s) or skill(s) being taught.

c. Expand the lesson by adding activities that provide more visual information about the concepts or skills being taught.

d. Identify all kinesthetic activity that is included in the lesson.

e. Add more kinesthetic activity to the lesson.

f. Identify parts of the lesson that include student communication about the concept(s) or skill(s) taught in the lesson.

g. Add more opportunities for communication from or among students to the lesson.

h. Identify the parts of the lesson designed to assess students' learning.

i. Add more continual assessment (monitoring of learning) to the lesson plan.

10. Read the discussion related to "Standard 7: Concepts of Whole Number Operations," which is found on pages 41–43 of *Curriculum and Evaluation Standards for School Mathematics*, published in 1989 by the NCTM. Relate the teaching suggestions in this chapter to Standard 7.

11. The following multiplication results illustrate an error pattern like the error patterns that were related by Robert Ashlock in his 2002 book, *Error Patterns in Computation: Using Error Patterns to Improve Instruction*:

$$
\begin{array}{cccc}
1 & 3 & 5 & 4 \\
14 & 34 & 47 & 68 \\
\underline{\times 4} & \underline{\times 9} & \underline{\times 8} & \underline{\times 5} \\
86 & 546 & 726 & 500
\end{array}
$$

a. What is this student's error pattern? What is the student doing to produce the incorrect answers?

b. Plan a mini-lesson to correct this student's error pattern.

12. The following division results illustrate an error pattern like the error patterns that were related by Robert Ashlock in his 2002 book, *Error Patterns in Computation: Using Error Patterns to Improve Instruction*:

$$
\begin{array}{cccc}
33 & 24 & 69 & 37 \\
2\overline{)66} & 4\overline{)168} & 3\overline{)288} & 5\overline{)365} \\
60 & 160 & 270 & 350 \\
\underline{6} & \underline{8} & \underline{18} & \underline{15} \\
6 & 8 & 18 & 15
\end{array}
$$

a. What is this student's error pattern? What is the student doing to produce the incorrect answers?

b. Plan a mini-lesson to correct this student's error pattern.

References and Related Readings

Allsopp, D. H. (1999). Using modeling, manipulatives, and mnemonics with eighth-grade children. *Teaching Exceptional Children, 32,* 74–81.

Ashlock, R. B. (2002). *Error patterns in computation: Using error patterns to improve instruction* (8th ed.). Upper Saddle River, NJ: Prentice Hall.

Moyer, P. (2000). A remainder of one: Exploring partitive division. *Teaching Children Mathematics, 6,* 517–521.

National Council of Teachers of Mathematics. (1989). *Curriculum and evaluation standards for school mathematics.* Reston, VA: Author.

National Council of Teachers of Mathematics. (2000). *Principles and standards for school mathematics.* Reston, VA: Author.

Tucker, B. F. (1973). The division algorithm. *The Arithmetic Teacher, 20*(8), 639–646.

Tucker, B. F., Singleton, A. H., & Weaver, T. L. (2002). Partial quotients: An optional thinking strategy for hard division facts. *The Illinois Mathematics Teacher, 53*(1), 23–30.

Websites

http://www.corestandards.org/the-standards/mathematics
The Common Core State Standards for Mathematics can be found at this site.

www.proteacher.com/100009.shtml
Lesson plans on multiplication and division, by teachers.

http://mathforum.org/
Math forum links to math discussions and ideas.

seven

FRACTIONS

Working with Units Smaller Than One

CHAPTER OUTLINE

Defining Fractions

There are three ways that a *fraction* can be interpreted. In other words, there are three distinct meanings for each fraction. For example, $\frac{2}{3}$ can be interpreted as 2 divided by 3:

Suppose we start with 2.

Now, we divide 2 by 3. That is, we divide 2 into three equal parts.

One of these three equal parts (the shaded part) is $\frac{2}{3}$. It is 2 divided by 3.

The fraction $\frac{2}{3}$ can also be interpreted as a ratio, which is a kind of comparison. Suppose we want to compare 2 and 3. The ratio is 2 to 3, which can be written as $\frac{2}{3}$. We can say that 2 is $\frac{2}{3}$ as big as 3:

Finally, the fraction $\frac{2}{3}$ can be interpreted as two of three equal parts. If we have a region (quantity) that is equal to 1 and divide that region into three equal parts, then two of those three equal parts would be written as $\frac{2}{3}$:

The shaded part is equal to $\frac{2}{3}$.

This last interpretation is typically used when children are first learning about fractions.

Three Sides of Fractions

Children should be able to achieve three goals with numbers (Thornton, Tucker, Dossey, & Bazik, 1983). First, they should be able to identify the quantity that is named by the number and they should be able to show how much it is. Second, they should be able to name the number and be able to say it. Third, they should be able to write the number clearly using standard notation that communicates the number unambiguously. Indeed, these goals imply that there are six tasks that the child should be able to complete. This is just as true when the numbers are fractions as when they are whole numbers:

1. If a student is shown some fractional quantity, he or she should be able to say the number (the fraction) that names that quantity.
2. If a student is shown some fractional quantity, he or she should be able to write the number (the fraction) that names that quantity.
3. If a student is shown a numeral (a fraction), he or she should be able to show that fractional quantity.
4. If a student is shown a numeral (a fraction), he or she should be able to say the number (the fraction).
5. If a student hears a number (a fraction) spoken, he or she should be able to show that fractional quantity.
6. If a student hears a number (a fraction) spoken, he or she should be able to write the student (the fraction).

Since we want children to be able to perform these tasks with fractions, our instruction must be designed so that these abilities are explicitly taught.

Fractional Units

Fractions are introduced to children very early (kindergarten or first grade). Although this early encounter with fractions is normally limited, it lays important groundwork for a later, more formal treatment of the topic. Usually, at this beginning level, children are introduced to only $\frac{1}{2}$ and $\frac{1}{3}$. The three big emphases at this level are that one of something is separated into *equal parts*, the number on the bottom (the *denominator*) *tells how many parts*, and the number on top (the *numerator*) indicates that we are considering *one of those equal parts*.

The equal parts are the *fractional* **units**. If the fraction is $\frac{1}{3}$, then the fractional unit is thirds. Since the numerator is 1, we are considering one of those fractional units (one third). Fractions with a numerator of 1 are called *unit fractions* because they name one fractional unit. One half is also a unit fraction, but the fractional unit is halves. When learning $\frac{1}{2}$, the children need to see many examples where objects are separated into two equal parts. The objects must be cut exactly in half. The children should see many nonexamples where objects are cut into more than two equal parts and other nonexamples where objects are cut into unequal parts. When learning $\frac{1}{3}$, the same procedure is used.

The children should also learn to identify the fractions, to say the fraction names, and to write the fractions. The following activities illustrate the way that the fraction $\frac{1}{2}$ can be taught. It is left as an exercise for the reader to develop similar activities for teaching other fractions.

Activity 7.01   Fair Sharing

Bring two apples and a knife to class. You also need three sheets of paper, three 1-foot lengths of yarn, and a pair of scissors.

Hold up one of the apples and tell the class that you want to cut the apple into two parts. Cut the apple into two parts that are unequal. Have two children come to the front of the class. Give each child one of the two parts of the apple. Have them hold their pieces so the class can see. Ask if they both got a fair share. [No.] Ask why not. [One got more. One didn't get as much. The two parts were not equal. They weren't the same size.] Hold up the second apple. Ask what to do so that both children will get a fair share. [Cut it into two equal parts.]

Cut the second apple into two equal parts and give each child one part. Ask if they both got a fair share. [Yes.] Write the fraction $\frac{1}{2}$ on the board. Tell the class that this is a *fraction*. It is one half. Point out the top number and the bottom number. Tell the class that the 2 tells us that there are two equal parts. Show the two equal apple parts. Hold up one of these parts and tell the class that this is one half of the apple. Hold up the other part and tell the class that this is also one half of the apple.

Show the class the two unequal apple parts. Ask if they are the same size. [No.] Hold up one of the unequal parts and tell the class that since the parts are not equal, this is not one half of the apple.

Repeat the activity using the three lengths of yarn. Cut one length of yarn into two equal parts to illustrate one half. Cut the second length of yarn into two unequal parts to illustrate a nonexample of one half. Cut the third length of yarn into three equal parts to illustrate another nonexample of one half. For each nonexample, ask why it is not one half.

Repeat the activity again using the three sheets of paper.

Activity 7.02 Putting Halves Together

Prepare a number of shapes. Cut each shape into two equal parts. Be sure that you make enough shapes so that there will be enough for all the children.

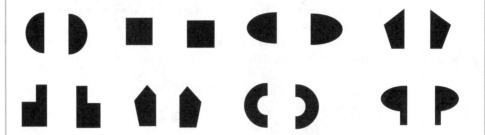

Give each child one of the pieces. If there is an odd number of children, keep one piece and participate in the activity so every child will have a partner. Tell the children that they each have one half of a shape. Have them find the person who has the other half of the shape. When they have all found their partners, have them put the two pieces together to see what the whole shape looks like.

Write $\frac{1}{2}$ on the board. Remind the class that this is the way to write one half. Point to the denominator. Ask what this number tells us. [The number of equal parts.]

Activity 7.03 Halves and Not Halves

Prepare a number of shapes like those used for activity 7.02. Cut some of them into two equal parts. Cut some into two unequal parts. Cut the rest into three parts. Use a piece of yarn to divide the bulletin board into two sections. Place a card showing the fraction $\frac{1}{2}$ in the middle of one section of the bulletin board.

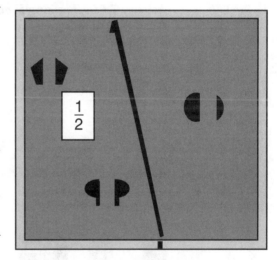

Show the children the parts of each shape. Let them children decide whether the shape was cut into halves. If it was cut into halves, place the two halves on the section of the bulletin board with the fraction $\frac{1}{2}$. If the children decide that the shape was not cut into halves, place the parts of the shape in the other section of the bulletin board.

Activity 7.04 Writing Fractions

Prepare a number of shapes like those used for activity 7.02. Cut some of them into two equal parts. Cut some into two unequal parts. Cut the rest into three parts. Tape the parts of each shape side by side on the board.

Show the children the parts of each shape. Let the children decide which shapes are cut into halves. If the children decide that a shape is cut into halves, have a child come forward and write $\frac{1}{2}$ below the parts of that shape. Draw an arrow from the fraction to one of the two equal parts.

Beyond Unit Fractions

After the children have had early experiences with unit fractions (usually $\frac{1}{2}$, $\frac{1}{3}$, and $\frac{1}{4}$), the fraction concepts are generalized to include fractions with numerators other than 1. This is usually accomplished by the end of second grade. The notion that the parts must be equal is revisited, and then the child learns to write a numerator to indicate how many equal parts are being considered and a denominator to indicate the total number of equal parts.

For example, when a shape is divided into four equal parts and three of the parts are shaded, then the fraction $\frac{3}{4}$ names the shaded part of the shape:

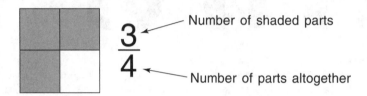

Once again, we want the children to be able to show the fractional quantity, name the fractional quantity using appropriate fraction terminology, and write the fraction name by using appropriate fraction notation.

Activity 7.05   Naming Fractions

Prepare cards showing pictures of fractional quantities.

Show the pictures to the children. Call on individuals to give the fraction name for the shaded part in the pictures. Ask how they can tell what the fraction name is.

Activity 7.06   Find the Fraction

Show the children a set of fraction circles:

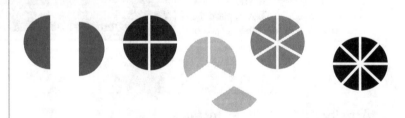

Write $\frac{2}{3}$ on the board. Point out the circle that is divided into thirds. Pick up two of those three parts and tell the class that this is two thirds of the circle.

Write other fractions on the board and call on the children to come to the front and use the fraction circles to show the fractions.

Fractions of a Set

Another way that fractions are used is to name a part of a set of objects. For example, consider the set of circles pictured next:

Since four out of six circles are black, we can name the part of the set consisting of black circles using the fraction $\frac{4}{6}$. We can find another fraction name by forming groups of two circles:

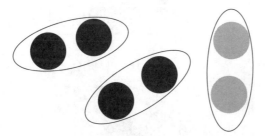

We can see that two out of three groups are black, so $\frac{2}{3}$ is another fraction name for the part of the set made up of black circles.

Now consider this set of shapes. Three of the five shapes are squares, so we can say that $\frac{3}{5}$ of the shapes are squares:

But, all the shapes are not the same size. This illustrates the primary difference between the way we use a fraction to name a part of a region and the way we use a fraction to name a part of a set. When we name a *fraction of a region*, all the *parts must be the same size*. But when we name a *fraction of a set*, all the *parts must have the same number of objects*.

In the following set of people, even though the men are not the same size as the women, $\frac{1}{2}$ of the set is men. There are the *same number* of men as women:

Equivalent Fractions

When two different fractions name the same quantity, the fractions are equal. We say that they are *equivalent fractions*. Consider this square, which has been divided by a vertical line into two equal parts. The shaded part is $\frac{1}{2}$ of the square.

Suppose we cut the square, with horizontal lines, into three equal parts. Notice that each of the two original parts has been cut into three equal parts, which leaves us with six equal parts. Three of those six parts are shaded, so another name for the shaded part of the square is $\frac{3}{6}$. The fractions $\frac{1}{2}$ and $\frac{3}{6}$ are equal. They are equivalent fractions. A similar procedure is illustrated next to show other pairs of equivalent fractions: $\frac{2}{3} = \frac{6}{9}$, $\frac{3}{4} = \frac{6}{8}$, and $\frac{2}{5} = \frac{4}{10}$:

$\frac{1}{2}$

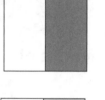

$\frac{3}{6}$

$\frac{2}{3}$  $\frac{6}{9}$

$\frac{3}{4}$ $\frac{6}{8}$

$\frac{2}{5}$ 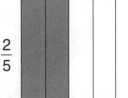 $\frac{4}{10}$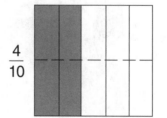

Fractions of sets can also be used to develop the idea of equivalent fractions. For example, in the following set of objects, 12 out of 18 are pentagons. One fraction name for the part of the set that is made up of pentagons is $\frac{12}{18}$:

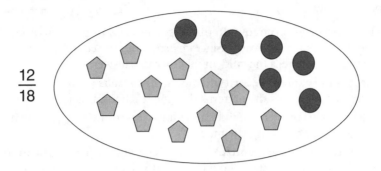

By grouping the objects, we can see other fraction names for the same part of the set:

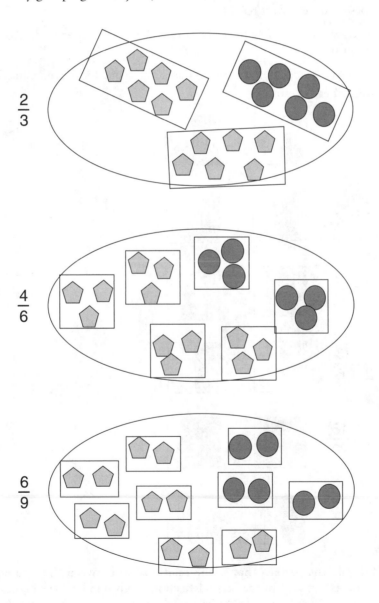

Using the Laboratory Approach

One effective way to teach equivalent fractions is to use the laboratory approach that was described in Chapter 2. Recall that in the laboratory approach, the students are led through a series of steps:

1. **Explore (or experiment).** In this step, a physical or pictorial model is used to find a variety of results (answers). Since the student can see where the answer came from, common sense tells the student whether the answer is correct.

2. **Keep an organized record of results.** The results are recorded in a way that facilitates recognition of the patterns that the teacher wants the student to notice.

3. **Identify patterns.** The children identify patterns that suggest ways to get the result (answer) without using the model.

4. **Hypothesize (or generalize) how to get results without the model.** In their own words, the children state the process that will produce the correct result.

5. **Test the hypothesis (the generalization).** Use the hypothesized procedure to get result(s). Then, do the same example(s) using the model to verify that the process does produce correct result(s).

Next, we examine how the laboratory process can be used to develop the concept of equivalent fractions:

1. **Explore.** Use fraction squares to find a new name for the same fractional quantity.

2. **Record each result.**

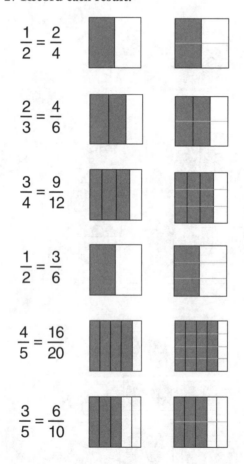

$$\frac{1}{2} = \frac{2}{4}$$

$$\frac{2}{3} = \frac{4}{6}$$

$$\frac{3}{4} = \frac{9}{12}$$

$$\frac{1}{2} = \frac{3}{6}$$

$$\frac{4}{5} = \frac{16}{20}$$

$$\frac{3}{5} = \frac{6}{10}$$

3. **Identify the pattern that is the relationship between the two equal fractions.** Students notice, "In the second fraction, both numbers are bigger." The teacher points to $\frac{3}{5} = \frac{6}{10}$ and asks, "How much bigger are they?" We want the students to

see that both numbers are twice as big. The numerator was multiplied by 2 and the denominator was multiplied by 2.

In another example, we find that $\frac{3}{4} = \frac{9}{12}$. In this case, the numbers in the second fraction are three times as big. The numerator and denominator were both multiplied by 3 to produce an equivalent fraction.

In still another example, $\frac{4}{5} = \frac{16}{20}$, the numerator and denominator were both multiplied by 4. Point out that the horizontal lines separate every part into four smaller parts. So, we have four times as many parts altogether. The horizontal lines also separate every shaded part into four smaller parts, so we have four times as many shaded parts:

$$\frac{4}{5} \times 4 = \frac{}{20}$$

$$\frac{4 \times 4}{5 \times 4} = \frac{16}{20}$$

4. **Generalize the pattern.** Help the students to see the same kind of pattern in all the other examples:

$$\frac{1 \times 2}{2 \times 2} = \frac{2}{4} \qquad \frac{2 \times 2}{3 \times 2} = \frac{4}{6}$$

$$\frac{3 \times 3}{4 \times 3} = \frac{9}{12} \qquad \frac{1 \times 3}{2 \times 3} = \frac{3}{6}$$

$$\frac{3 \times 2}{5 \times 2} = \frac{6}{10}$$

Ask the students if they think this always works. Can we always get an equivalent fraction if we multiply the numerator and denominator by the same number?

5. **Verify the generalization.** Write a fraction, such as $\frac{3}{4}$. Ask how to get an equivalent fraction. [Multiply the numerator and denominator by the same number.] Do this to get an equivalent fraction. Then, use the model to verify the result. For example, if the numerator and denominator were multiplied by 4 to find an equivalent fraction, the result would be:

$$\frac{3 \times 4}{4 \times 4} = \frac{12}{16}$$

To verify this result, start with a picture of $\frac{3}{4}$. To change from 4 equal parts to 16, cut each of the original parts into four pieces. When this is done, we can see that the shaded part of the square is 12 out of 16 equal parts:

So, we see that we obtain the correct result by multiplying the numerator and denominator by 4.

A natural extension of this idea is to find an equivalent fraction with a particular denominator. For example, we wish to find a fraction equivalent to $\frac{2}{3}$ that has a denominator of 15. It is left as an exercise for the reader to develop an instructional activity to teach this.

Comparison of Fractions

 When fractions are being compared, extra attention must be given to the development of strong mental imagery for the fractional units. Along with this mental imagery must come an awareness that if the denominator is greater, there are more parts. And, if an object is divided into more parts, the parts are smaller. A natural sequence is first to compare unit fractions, such as $\frac{1}{2}, \frac{1}{3}, \frac{1}{4}, \frac{1}{5}, \frac{1}{7}$, and $\frac{1}{15}$. After the students are able to correctly compare unit fractions, the second step is to teach them to compare nonunit fractions that have the same numerators. For example, they might compare $\frac{2}{7}$ and $\frac{2}{4}$. The third step is to teach students to compare fractions with the same denominators—$\frac{5}{8}$ and $\frac{7}{8}$, for example. Finally, the fourth step is to teach the students to compare fractions that have unlike numerators and unlike denominators. In this final step, the students encounter, and must learn to use, the one big idea of comparison: *compare like units*.

The following set of activities illustrates how a teacher can develop students' abilities to compare fractions.

Activity 7.07   Big and Little Pieces

Ask the students if they like candy. Ask if they would rather share a candy bar with two other people or with three other people. Ask why. What would be the difference? Show them two 2-inch by 6-inch rectangles of paper. Tell them to imagine that the two pieces of paper are two candy bars. Have the class tell you how to cut the first "candy bar" so it could be shared with two other people. [It needs to be cut into three equal pieces.] Have the class tell you how to cut the second candy bar so it could be shared with three other people. [It needs to be cut into four equal pieces.] Hold up a piece from each "candy bar" for the class to compare. Point out that the larger piece is $\frac{1}{3}$ and the smaller piece is $\frac{1}{4}$.

Point to the denominators and remind the students that when the denominator is bigger, the candy bar is cut into more pieces. So, the pieces are smaller.

Write $\frac{1}{3}$ and $\frac{1}{4}$ on the board, and ask which is more.

Activity 7.08   More Big and Little Pieces

Show the class a set of fraction circles:

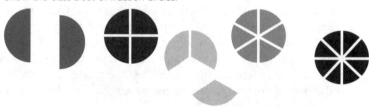

Write $\frac{1}{6}$ and $\frac{1}{4}$ on the board.

Ask which is greater. Have two children come forward and find the fraction piece that represents each of the fractions. Have them compare the two fraction pieces to verify which is greater. Repeat the activity with other pairs of unit fractions.

Emphasize repeatedly that a bigger denominator means smaller pieces.

Activity 7.09   When Three Pieces Is More Than Three Pieces

Tell the class to imagine that two people each have a candy bar. One cuts her candy bar into four equal parts. The other cuts hers into six equal parts. If both are willing to give you three pieces, who would be giving you more? Why?

Which is more, $\frac{3}{4}$ or $\frac{3}{6}$?

Show the class a set of fraction circles:

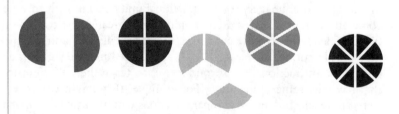

Write $\frac{3}{4}$ and $\frac{3}{6}$ on the board.

Ask which is greater. Have two children come forward and find the fraction pieces that represent each of the fractions. Have them compare the fraction pieces to verify which fraction is greater. Repeat the activity with other pairs of fractions. For example, you could use $\frac{2}{3}$ and $\frac{2}{6}$, $\frac{4}{6}$ and $\frac{4}{5}$, or $\frac{5}{8}$ and $\frac{5}{9}$.

Emphasize repeatedly that a bigger denominator means smaller pieces.

Activity 7.10   Fractions with Like Units

Show the class a set of fraction circles:

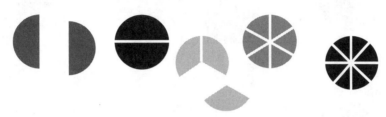

Write $\frac{5}{6}$ and $\frac{3}{6}$ on the board.

Ask which is greater. Have a child come forward and use the fraction circles to show the two fractions. Repeat the activity with other pairs of fractions with the same denominators. For example, you could use $\frac{3}{4}$ and $\frac{1}{4}$, $\frac{3}{8}$ and $\frac{5}{8}$, or $\frac{7}{9}$ and $\frac{8}{9}$.

Emphasize repeatedly that since the denominators are equal, the fractional units are the same. The numerator tells how many of those units you have. The fraction $\frac{8}{9}$ is greater than $\frac{7}{9}$ because eight of those units is more than seven of those units.

Adding Fractions

Recall that for whole numbers, two big ideas were identified for addition. The first of those big ideas was: *always add like units.* The same big idea holds for addition of fractions. Addition of fractions with the same units (like denominators) is easy. The most effective way to show students how easy it is to add like fractions is to use a physical model such as fraction circles. For example, suppose we want to add $\frac{3}{8}$ and $\frac{2}{8}$. We represent both fractions with the fraction pieces and then combine them. We have three of "these things" and two more of "these things." Altogether, there are five of "these things." "These things" are eighths, so $\frac{3}{8} + \frac{2}{8} = \frac{5}{8}$.

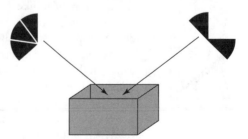

If we are adding like units (like fractions), we have to think about only how many of those units we have altogether. For $\frac{4}{7} + \frac{2}{7}$, we have 4 sevenths and 2 more sevenths. Altogether, we have 6 sevenths.

Addition of like fractions is easy if we use a physical model so the students can visualize combining the fractional units. If the fractions do not have the same fractional units (like denominators), then the students must be led to understand that the fractions can be renamed so that the fractional units are the same. That is, we change to equivalent fractions that have a *common denominator*. The students' previous work with equivalent fractions should have provided the needed understanding and skills, but rather than assuming that they remember, the teacher would be wise to redevelop the key ideas. It is not easy to add the fractions $\frac{3}{4}$ and $\frac{2}{3}$ because the fractional units are not the same. If we rename the two fractions so that both have the same denominator, 12, the addition becomes easy because we can *add like units*:

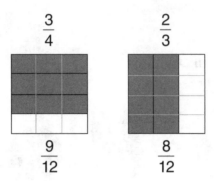

$$\frac{3}{4} \qquad \frac{2}{3}$$

$$\frac{9}{12} \qquad \frac{8}{12}$$

If we follow the same process for renaming fractions, it is easy to quickly rename the original fractions by using a common denominator. After seeing several examples completed by using the fraction-squares model, and after examining the results, the students notice that in every case, the product of the two given fractions can serve as a common denominator for the addition:

We can use 5×8 as the common denominator. $\qquad \frac{2}{5} + \frac{3}{8}$

In the first fraction, we multiplied the denominator by 8, so we must also multiply the numerator by 8. $\qquad \frac{2 \times 8}{5 \times 8} + \frac{}{5 \times 8}$

In the second fraction, we multiplied 5 times the denominator, so we must also multiply 5 times the numerator. $\qquad \frac{2 \times 8}{5 \times 8} + \frac{5 \times 3}{5 \times 8}$

This process for obtaining common denominators is simple and easily justified by using the pictorial fraction-squares model. Using the model, children can quickly master addition of unlike fractions. Some teachers are not comfortable with this process, however, because although the product of the two denominators is always a common denominator, it is not always the *least* common denominator.

When most teachers learned to add unlike fractions as elementary children, they were taught that the least common denominator must first be found. They have been convinced by their own training that the least common denominator must be used in adding unlike fractions.

So, then, does teaching children to find least common denominators not have any value? Of course least common denominators have value, and we should continue to teach children how to find them. However, it is actually much more difficult for children to find least common denominators than it is for them to add unlike fractions. It is recommended here to allow the children to first master addition of fractions and then, at a later time, to revisit the topic with a focus on least common denominators.

Subtracting Fractions

Developing understanding of subtraction of fractions exactly parallels the development of addition of fractions. Subtraction of fractions with like denominators is taught immediately after addition of like fractions. As with addition, subtraction of like fractions is most effectively taught by using a physical model. Select fraction pieces to represent the minuend, take away the pieces that represent the subtrahend, and recognize that the remaining fraction pieces represent the answer. It is good to point out how the process of subtracting fractions is like the process of subtracting whole numbers—we start with a number, take away a number, and see what number is left.

Immediately after addition of unlike fractions is taught, the children are taught subtraction of unlike fractions. The first of the big ideas for subtraction, *always subtract like units*, also applies to subtraction of fractions. So, subtraction of unlike fractions requires that we rename the two fractions by using the same fractional unit (a common denominator). Just as with addition, fraction squares are an excellent model for justifying the product of the two denominators as a common denominator. After the two fractions have been renamed with a common denominator, the children can easily apply their ability to subtract like fractions, as in this example:

$$\frac{6}{7} - \frac{3}{4} = \frac{6 \cdot 4}{7 \cdot 4} - \frac{7 \cdot 3}{7 \cdot 4} = \frac{6 \cdot 4 - 7 \cdot 3}{7 \cdot 4}$$

Addition and Subtraction Activities

The following sequence of activities illustrates how addition and subtraction of fractions can be taught.

Activity 7.11   Name the Rods

This activity uses colored number rods like Cuisenaire Rods (ETA/Cuisenaire, Vernon Hills, IL) or the older Colour-Factor system rods (originated by Seton Pollock in the 1960s). Choose any of the rods in the set and let its length be equal to 1:

1

Then, find fraction names for all the other rods:

1

Each of these is $\frac{1}{6}$.

Each of these is $\frac{1}{3}$.

See if the students can find more than one name for some of the rods:

$\frac{1}{3}$

$\frac{2}{6}$

Activity 7.12 What Fraction Is in the Box?—Addition

This is a partner activity. The participants must have a set of fraction circles:

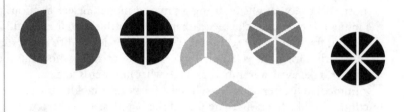

They should also be given a box and a set of cards showing examples of addition of like fractions:

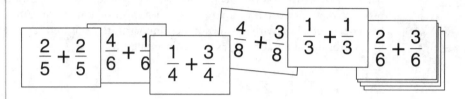

After choosing a card, one child should place the fraction pieces for the first fraction into the box. The other child should place the pieces for the second number into the box. Then they both write what they think the correct answer is. Finally, they look in the box to check their answers.

Activity 7.13 What Fraction Is in the Box?—Subtraction

This is a partner activity. The participants must have a set of fraction circles:

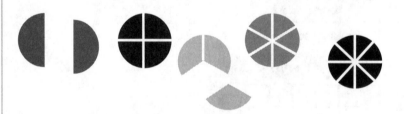

They should also be given a box and a set of cards showing examples of subtraction of like fractions:

$$\frac{2}{5} - \frac{2}{5} \qquad \frac{4}{6} - \frac{1}{6} \qquad \frac{3}{4} - \frac{1}{4} \qquad \frac{7}{8} - \frac{3}{8} \qquad \frac{1}{3} - \frac{1}{3} \qquad \frac{5}{6} - \frac{3}{6}$$

After choosing a card, one child should place the fraction pieces for the first fraction into the box. The other child should take the pieces for the second number out of the box. Then they both write what they think the correct answer is. Finally, they look in the box to check their answers.

Activity 7.14 Same-Size Units

Prepare several pairs of overhead transparencies showing fraction-square representations of two unlike fractions. One fraction square should be divided vertically and the other horizontally.

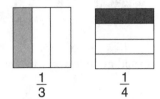

$\frac{1}{3}$ $\frac{1}{4}$

For example, one transparency could show $\frac{1}{3}$ and $\frac{1}{4}$.

Write $\frac{1}{3} + \frac{1}{4}$ on the board and show the transparency.

Explain that you want to have same-size pieces (like units) so that you can add the two fractions. Ask how you can cut up the pieces so that they will all be the same size. [Cut the first fraction horizontally into fourths and cut the second fraction vertically into thirds.]

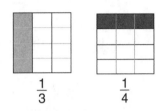

$\frac{1}{3}$ $\frac{1}{4}$

Write the addition using the new fraction names. Emphasize that you are still adding the same amounts:

$$\frac{1}{3} + \frac{1}{4} = \frac{4}{12} + \frac{3}{12}$$

Repeat the process with several other examples. After each example has been completed, write the new result under the previous one.

Ask the students if they can see what they might do in every example to get the new denominator (the common denominator). [The new denominator is the product of the two original denominators.]

Improper Fractions and Mixed Numbers

Fractions with numerators greater than their denominators are called *improper fractions*. Improper fractions are greater than 1. There is not really anything improper about such fractions. In fact, mathematicians generally prefer using improper fractions to mixed numbers, because an improper fraction is considered to be a simpler form of the number than the equivalent mixed number. However, there are situations when a mixed number is preferable to an improper fraction. For example, if you went into a fabric store and told the clerk that you would like to buy $\frac{17}{4}$ yards of cloth, the clerk would probably look at you as if you were crazy. If a price tag indicated the price of some piece of merchandise as $\frac{874}{100}$ dollars, the customer would probably say, "Just forget it."

In their first encounter with improper fractions and mixed numbers, children learn that these are merely two ways to name the same amount. The work focuses on finding mixed numbers equal to given improper fractions and finding improper fractions equal to given mixed numbers. Either physical models or pictorial models can be used effectively to develop the concepts and skills. Using the fraction circles, we can show that $1 + \frac{2}{6} = \frac{8}{6}$:

One and two sixths is the same amount as eight sixths.

And, using pictorial fraction squares, we can show that $1 + \frac{3}{4} = \frac{7}{4}$:

  One and three fourths is the same amount as seven fourths.

If we record the step where 1 is renamed as a fraction, we can see the steps that would be followed when a model is not being used:

$$1 + \frac{3}{4} = \frac{4}{4} + \frac{3}{4} + \frac{7}{4}$$

This is another name for 1.

We can then follow this same process for conversion of any mixed number to an improper fraction:

$$1\frac{5}{8} = \frac{8}{8} + \frac{5}{8} = \frac{13}{8} \qquad 3\frac{2}{3} = \frac{3}{3} + \frac{3}{3} + \frac{3}{3} + \frac{2}{3} = \frac{11}{3}$$

And we can follow a similar procedure to change an improper fraction to a mixed number:

$$\frac{14}{9} = \frac{9}{9} + \frac{5}{9} = 1\frac{5}{9} \qquad \frac{18}{7} = \frac{7}{7} + \frac{7}{7} + \frac{4}{7} = 2\frac{4}{7}$$

Addition and subtraction of mixed numbers is almost identical to addition and subtraction of whole numbers. For each operation, the procedures are based on the same two big ideas. First, when adding, *always add like units*:

$$
\begin{array}{r}
14\frac{1}{5} \\
+\ 32\frac{3}{5} \\
\hline
46\frac{4}{5}
\end{array}
$$

Add tens to tens ——— | | ——— Add fifths to fifths

Add ones to ones

We also apply the second big idea of addition: *when there are too many to write* in standard form or as a proper fraction, *make a trade*:

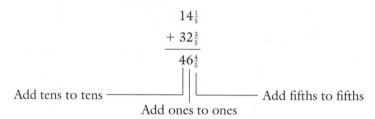

$$
\begin{array}{r}
\overset{1}{14\tfrac{4}{5}} \\
+\ 32\tfrac{3}{5} \\
\hline
\tfrac{2}{5}
\end{array}
$$

Altogether, there are 7 fifths. That's the same as 5 fifths and 2 fifths. Trade the 5 fifths for 1 one. Record the extra one, and record the 2 fifths.

$$
\begin{array}{r}
\overset{1}{14\tfrac{4}{5}} \\
+\ 32\tfrac{3}{5} \\
\hline
7\tfrac{2}{5}
\end{array}
$$

If we include the extra one that we traded for, we have 7 ones.

$$
\begin{array}{r}
\overset{1}{14\tfrac{4}{5}} \\
+\ 32\tfrac{3}{5} \\
\hline
47\tfrac{2}{5}
\end{array}
$$

And, we have 4 tens.

When subtracting, we *always subtract like units.*

$$57\tfrac{3}{5}$$
$$-\ 32\tfrac{1}{5}$$
$$25\tfrac{2}{5}$$

Subtract tens from tens ———————┐ └———— Subtract fifths from fifths
Subtract ones from ones

We also apply the second big idea of subtraction—*when there are not enough, make a trade*:

$$\overset{6}{4}\overset{7}{7}\tfrac{\cancel{1}}{5}$$
$$-\ 21\tfrac{4}{5}$$

We need to subtract 4 fifths. There are not enough, so we trade 1 one for more fifths. In the trade, we get 5 extra fifths. Record the trade.

$$\overset{6}{4}\overset{7}{7}\tfrac{\cancel{1}}{5}$$
$$-\ 21\tfrac{4}{5}$$
$$\tfrac{3}{5}$$

When we subtract 4 fifths, we are left with 3 fifths.

$$\overset{6}{4}\overset{7}{7}\tfrac{\cancel{1}}{5}$$
$$-\ 21\tfrac{4}{5}$$
$$25\tfrac{3}{5}$$

We then subtract the 1 one and the 2 tens.

A Remediation Note. The following incorrect computation illustrates what may be the most common error pattern among children who are subtracting mixed numbers:

$$\overset{6}{4}7\tfrac{\cancel{1}2}{5}$$
$$-\ 21\tfrac{4}{5}$$
$$25\tfrac{8}{5}$$

In this error pattern, the student is carrying over the rote borrowing procedure from whole-number subtraction. The student must be led to understand that the denominator tells how many pieces you get in the trade. Let them see it with a model.

Adapting a Lesson on Fractions

We consider now another lesson plan, beginning with a traditional lesson based on suggestions like those that would be found in the teacher's guide. This lesson, which teaches equivalent fractions, is similar to lessons found in fourth-grade textbooks.

LESSON OBJECTIVE

The student will write equal fractions using fraction models.

Lesson Opener

Have students name the fraction that is shaded:

 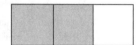

Development

Direct the attention of the class to the example on the first page of the lesson. Point out that the child in the picture is placing two fraction pieces for sixths on top of one fraction piece for thirds. Draw their attention to the fact that the 2 sixths fit exactly on top of the third, so two sixths is the same amount as one third. Write $\frac{2}{6} = \frac{1}{3}$.

Have the students look at the second picture on the page. Point out that the 6 eighths fit exactly on top of the 3 fourths. Ask what number should be placed in the box to make the fraction equation true.

Monitoring Learning

Have the students do the three examples in the *Checking Learning* section at the bottom of the page. Identify students who do not understand.

Practice

Assign the practice exercises on the second page of the lesson. Remind the students that they should look at the picture of the fraction strips if they have difficulty. Assign the *Reteaching Worksheet* to students who had difficulty with the examples in the *Checking Learning* section.

Closure

At the end of math time, remind the class that today they learned how to use the fraction model to find equal fractions. Tell the class that their homework is to complete the rest of the assigned exercises.

Following is a revised plan that expands the developmental portion of the lesson. The lesson provides more visual input, is more kinesthetic, and has more opportunities for communication from and among students. Learning will be monitored regularly throughout the lesson. These adaptations make the lesson appropriate for most students. But, remember that some students with severe needs may require further instructional adaptations.

LESSON OBJECTIVE

The student will write equal fractions using fraction models.

Lesson Opener

Have students name the fraction that is shaded:

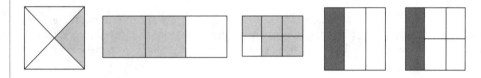

Direct the attention of the students to the last two examples. Ask if they can see how the two pictures are related. [The same amount is shaded.] If no one notices that the same amount is shaded, ask them what they would see if the shaded part of one picture were placed directly on top of the shaded part of the other picture. [They would fit exactly.]

After the students recognize that the same amount is shaded in both pictures, point out that the two fractions name the same amount. These two fractions are just two names for the same amount. Whenever two numbers name the same amount, they are equal.

Monitor understanding. Observe the students closely. If any appear not to understand, show an example using prepared overhead transparencies for $\frac{1}{2}$ and $\frac{2}{4}$. Place one transparency on top of the other to help the students see that exactly the same amount is shaded in both fractions.

Explain that in today's lesson, they will learn how to use this idea to find equal fractions.

Development

Tape the following pictorial models of fractions on the chalkboard. Leave about 10 inches of board space below them.

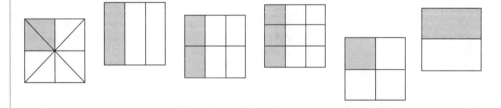

Point to the first fraction. Ask someone to name the fraction. Then have that student write the fraction on the board below its picture. Ask if anyone can find another fraction that has the same amount shaded. Have that person name that fraction and write it below the picture. Ask, "Since these two fractions name the same amount, what can we say about them?" [They are equal.] Write $\frac{2}{8} = \frac{1}{4}$.

Direct the attention of the students to the example on the first page of the lesson. Point out that the child in the picture is placing two fraction pieces for sixths on top of one fraction piece for thirds. Draw their attention to the fact that the 2 sixths fit exactly on top of the third, so two sixths is the same amount as one third. Write $\frac{2}{6} = \frac{1}{3}$.

Continue this process until all the equal fractions have been paired and identified as equal.

Monitor understanding. Continue observing to see that everyone understands. Give particular attention to students with a history of poor comprehension. Actively involve these students in the discussion of results.

Hand out cards showing pictorial models of fractions. Every fractional quantity used should be on two cards, each illustrating a different fraction name for the same quantity. Have each student locate the other person who has the same amount pictured.

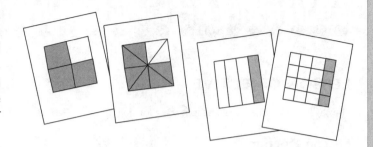

Monitor understanding. Notice if students are having trouble finding others with the same amount shaded. Provide individual help as needed.

When the students are paired correctly, call on them, one pair at a time, to write the equation on the board that says that their fractions are equal.

Monitor understanding. Provide help to students who are likely to have trouble so that they can complete this part of the activity correctly and avoid embarrassment.

Have the students look at the picture on the first page of the lesson in the textbook. Point out that the pictures show children using fraction pieces to do what we have been doing. Tell them to notice that, in the second picture, the 6 eighths fit exactly on top of the 3 fourths. Ask what number should be placed in the box to make the fraction equation true:

$$\frac{3}{4} = \frac{\Box}{8}$$

Pair the students with partners. Have the students complete the three examples in the *Checking Learning* section at the bottom of the page. When they are finished, they should compare answers with their partners. If their answers disagree, they are to discuss them and figure out together what the correct answers are.

Monitoring Understanding

Move around the room and observe student work. Identify students who do not understand. Provide assistance as needed.

Practice

Have the students continue to work with their partners to complete practice exercises 2, 3, 7, and 9 on the second page of the lesson. Remind the students that the pictures can help them if they have difficulty with any exercise.

Closure

When enough time has been allowed to complete the exercises, ask the students what they learned today about equal fractions. If necessary, ask these questions: "How can you tell that two fractions name the same amount? If two fractions name the same amount, what can we say about those two fractions?"

Follow-Up

Hand out copies of the *Extra Practice Worksheet*. Have the students take the sheet home and show a parent how to do exercise 6.

Solving Problems Using Fractions

There is little difference between problem solving using fractions and problem solving using whole numbers. It is still necessary to visualize what is happening to quantities, whether they are quantities named by whole numbers or quantities named by fractions. A single quantity can be measured, or it can be separated. If there is more than one quantity, those quantities can be combined, or they can be compared.

Suppose we start with a single quantity that is being separated. Subtraction can probably be used to solve the problem. Or, we might start with more than one quantity. If those quantities are being combined, addition can probably be used to solve the problem. If quantities are being compared to find a difference, subtraction can probably be used.

Exercises and Activities

1. Adapt activities 7.01 to 7.03 to develop the concept of *three fourths*.

2. Develop a learning activity that has children find other fractions equivalent to given fractions by using the first equivalent fractions procedure described in this chapter.

3. Develop a learning activity that has children find other fractions equivalent to given fractions by using the second equivalent fractions procedure (grouping the objects) described in this chapter.

4. Develop an instructional activity to teach children how to find a fraction with a particular denominator that is equivalent to a given fraction. The activity should use the fraction-squares pictorial model.

5. Choose a lesson on fractions or mixed numbers from a published elementary school mathematics textbook series.

    a. Write a lesson plan that follows the teaching suggestions in the teacher's guide.

    b. Identify the parts of the lesson that provide visual information about the concept(s) or skill(s) being taught.

    c. Expand the lesson by adding activities that provide more visual information about the concepts or skills being taught.

    d. Identify kinesthetic activity, if any is included in the lesson.

    e. Add more kinesthetic activity to the lesson.

    f. Identify parts of the lesson that include student communication about the concept(s) or skill(s) taught in the lesson.

    g. Add more opportunities for communication from or among students to the lesson.

    h. Identify the parts of the lesson designed to assess the learning of the students.

    i. Add more continual assessment (monitoring of learning) to the lesson plan.

6. In this chapter, a process for adding unlike fractions is presented that involves finding a common denominator. Develop a lesson using the laboratory approach to teach this process for adding unlike fractions.

References and Related Readings

National Council of Teachers of Mathematics. (1989). *Curriculum and evaluation standards for school mathematics*. Reston, VA: Author.

National Council of Teachers of Mathematics. (2000). *Principles and standards for school mathematics*. Reston, VA: Author.

Thornton, C. A., Tucker, B. F., Dossey, J. A., & Bazik, E. F. (1983). *Teaching mathematics to children with special needs*. Menlo Park, CA: Addison-Wesley.

Websites

http://www.corestandards.org/the-standards/mathematics
The Common Core State Standards for Mathematics can be found at this site.

http://mathforum.org/
Math forum links to math discussions and ideas.

http://mathforum.org/paths/fractions/
Links to fraction sites and lessons.

http://teachers.net/lessons/posts/262.html
Fractions of a set.

http://teachers.net/lessons/posts/17.html
Fractions of a region.

proteacher.com/100014.shtml
Lesson plans, by teachers, on fractions, decimals, and ratios.

eight

DECIMALS

Working with Base-Ten Units Smaller Than One

CHAPTER OUTLINE

Decimals

Decimals can be thought of as fractions and sometimes as mixed numbers. They are fractions or mixed numbers with denominators that are always equal to the base-10 whole-number units. The whole-number base-10 units are ones, tens, hundreds, thousands, ten thousands, and so on. The *decimal fraction units* are tenths, hundredths, thousandths, ten thousandths, and so on. The number 1 can be thought of as the denominator for the decimal units that are greater than or equal to 1. The properties that control what students can do with decimals are the same ones that govern the use of whole numbers and decimals.

As with other numbers that we have considered earlier, you want your students to recognize and name decimal quantities using appropriate terminology, to use appropriate models to show decimal quantities, and to write decimals using appropriate notation. These learning objectives require that you have effective models for decimals. The minimum requirement for a decimal model is the ability to represent the basic units. This means that the chosen model should allow for the representation of ones, tens, hundreds, and so on, as well as tenths, hundredths, thousandths, and so on, or at least the units from this list that are being used in the current lesson.

The *base-10 block set* is a model that fits this description. The large cube would represent 1, the flats (each one tenth of the large cube) would represent tenths. The longs, or the rods (each one tenth of a flat and one hundredth of a large cube), would represent hundredths. The small cubes (each equal to one tenth of a long, one hundredth of a flat, and one thousandth of a large cube) would represent thousandths. The following illustration uses base-10 blocks to represent the decimal 1.324:

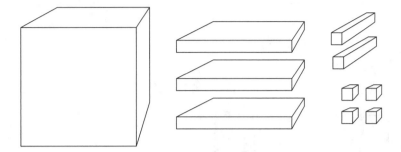

Another option is the *decimal square model*. This is a two-dimensional model that lends itself to the printed page, and it is frequently used in textbooks. A square represents 1. If the square is cut into 10 equal-sized strips, the strips represent tenths. If a strip is cut into 10 equal squares, these smaller squares represent hundredths. Sometimes the large square is divided into 100 smaller squares and part of the subdivided square is shaded to represent a decimal.

The number 2.47 is represented next by both models:

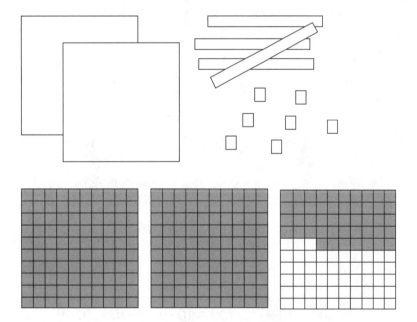

Another model that is sometimes used is the *metric-length model*. A meter represents 1, a decimeter represents 1 tenth, a centimeter represents 1 hundredth, and a millimeter represents 1 thousandth. This model is not often useful in instructional settings. In instructional settings, one of the other models is invariably more effective.

The *money model* is another model frequently used to represent decimals. Along with using one-, ten-, and hundred-dollar bills to represent ones, tens, and hundreds, this model also uses dimes to represent tenths and pennies to represent hundredths. Since the various pieces of money are capable of being combined, separated, and compared, this model is useful for teaching a wide variety of decimal topics.

The final model that we mention is the *pocket chart*, which is useful when the teacher is stressing place value. This model is relatively abstract and probably should not be used in the early introduction of decimals. Decimals are represented by markers placed in various positions, and the units associated with those positions must be identified in some way:

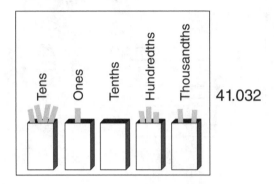

41.032

Place Value for Decimals

When decimal notation is used to write decimal fractions, the denominators are not written. Rather, they are indicated by the position of the number. One important task for the teacher, then, is to help students to be able to determine the decimal units from their position. *It is important to first communicate that decimal notation is really an extension of whole-number notation.* When moving from one position to another from right to left, the value of numbers in each position is 10 times the value of numbers in the previous position:

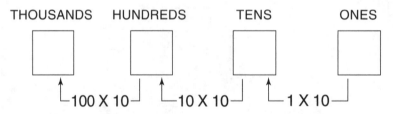

Similarly, moving from one position to another from left to right, the value of numbers in each position is the value of numbers in the previous position divided by 10:

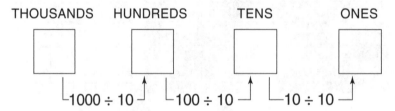

This pattern holds when adding the decimal units that are less than 1:

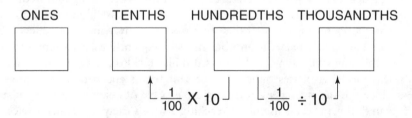

Students also need to understand that there is symmetry in the decimal numeration system (Thornton, Tucker, Dossey, & Bazik, 1983). A common misconception is that the system is symmetric around the decimal point. Actually, *the system is symmetric around the ones*.

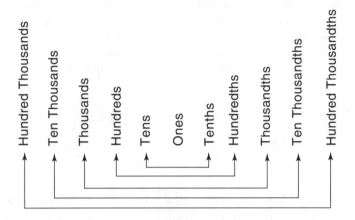

When the students are familiar with the nature of the symmetry, they have the ability to find the value of each place, starting from any known position. For example, if they know that the 7 is in the tens place of this number, they can figure out the value of the other places.

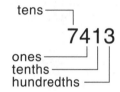

If the students know that the 2 in this number is in the tenths place, they can figure out the value of all the other places.

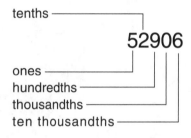

If the students know that the 8 in this number is in the ones place, they can figure out the value of every other place.

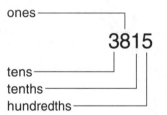

A device called the *decimal point* helps in identifying the place values. The decimal point is always placed to the right of the ones place. When the students know which position is the ones place, they use their knowledge of the symmetry of the system to identify the value of all the other positions:

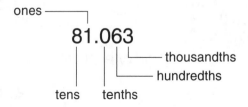

Children should be taught in a meaningful way to read decimals. If the instructional focus is on rote reading procedures, it might appear that the children gain fast results. However, because so much subsequent reteaching is necessary, the teacher should question the value of such fast results. Remember, it is always harder to remember things that are meaningless. There are, however, several connections that can be developed that improve retention of the rules for reading decimals in a standard way.

Let's begin by looking at two simple, related examples from our work with fractions and mixed numbers:

$4 + \frac{2}{3}$ is usually written as $4\frac{2}{3}$ and read as "4 and $\frac{2}{3}$."

$6 + \frac{1}{2} + \frac{1}{4}$ would usually be simplified by adding the two fractions together

to get $6 + \frac{3}{4}$. This would be read as "6 and $\frac{3}{4}$."

The decimal 5.27 literally means $5 + \frac{2}{10} + \frac{7}{100}$. This can be read as "5 and $\frac{2}{10}$ and $\frac{7}{100}$." The children can simplify the reading by adding the two fractions. Then they can just read it as a mixed number. To add the two fractions together, the children need to rewrite them using a common denominator:

$$5 + \frac{2}{10} + \frac{7}{100} = 5 + \frac{20}{100} + \frac{7}{100} = 5 + \frac{27}{100}$$

Then, they can read it as "5 and 27 hundredths." By looking at 5.27 using the decimal square model, the students can arrive at the same result:

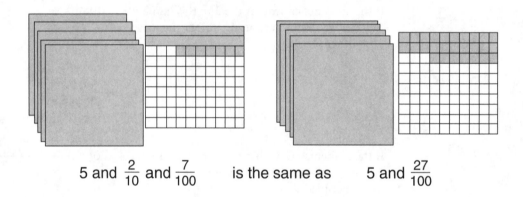

5 and $\frac{2}{10}$ and $\frac{7}{100}$ is the same as 5 and $\frac{27}{100}$

In the same way, you can show that 24.96, which is 24 and $\frac{9}{10}$ and $\frac{6}{100}$, is the same as "24 and $\frac{96}{100}$."

From examples like these, students can be led to understand why a decimal such as 207.435 is read as "207 and 435 thousandths." They understand that they are simply reading a mixed number:

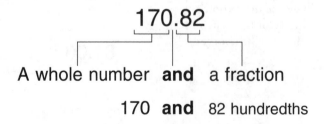

170.82

A whole number **and** a fraction

170 **and** 82 hundredths

When learning decimals, the students should be able to complete six tasks correctly:

1. When shown a decimal quantity (represented by a decimal model), the students should be able to name the decimal.
2. When shown a decimal quantity (represented by a decimal model), the students should be able to write the decimal.
3. When students hear a decimal named, they should be able to show the decimal quantity (using a decimal model).
4. When students hear a decimal named, they should be able to write the decimal.
5. When students see a written decimal, they should be able to name the decimal.
6. When students see a written decimal, they should be able to show the decimal quantity (using a decimal model).

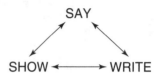

Instruction should include activities that help the students learn to do these tasks. The following activities illustrate how this can be done.

Activity 8.01   Show and Write

From a roll of receipt tape, cut nine strips that are 1 meter long, nine strips that are 10 centimeters long, and nine pieces that are 1 centimeter long. Explain that the 1-m strips each represent 1. The 10-cm strips each represent 1 tenth, and the 1-cm pieces each represent 1 hundredth.

Show the class some combination of strips of each size. Have each student write the decimal that is represented. Then ask someone to tell you how many of each unit is included. Write the correct decimal. Ask how many students got it right.

Repeat several times with different quantities.

Activity 8.02   I'll Tell; You Write and Show

Hand out copies of the decimal square worksheet shown at the right.

Read aloud a decimal (ones, tenths, and hundredths) and have the students color a representation of that decimal.

Then have the students write the decimal.

Repeat several times with different decimals.

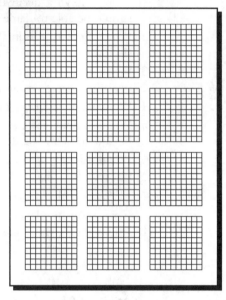

Activity 8.03   I'll Tell; You Write and Show Me the Money

Make 8 to 10 packages of play money. Include in each package 4 ten-dollar bills, 6 one-dollar bills, 5 dimes, and 9 pennies.

Form groups of three students, and give each group a package of money.

Explain that when you read a decimal, one person in the group will get the money to show that quantity, one person will write the decimal, and the third person will check the other two to see if they are right. Tell them that they are to take turns doing each job.

Read aloud a decimal (tens, ones, tenths, and hundredths). Be sure that there are no more than 4 tens, 6 ones, 5 tenths, or 9 hundredths.

Repeat several times with different decimals. Be sure to monitor the students' work to catch and correct misconceptions.

Comparing Decimals

Comparison of decimals is not difficult. Virtually every error pattern related to comparing fractions results directly from lack of appropriate mental imagery for the numbers being compared. The student who thinks .98 must surely be greater than 1.2 because 9 and 8 are both more than 1 or 2 is not visualizing the numbers. The student who thinks 6.21 must be greater than 7.3 because three-digit numbers are bigger than two-digit numbers is not visualizing the numbers.

Almost invariably, error patterns like these can be eliminated by providing mental imagery for the numbers. It seems reasonable, then, that development of appropriate mental imagery should be an integral part of the initial teaching of this topic. Experiences with models that allow the student to literally see when one decimal is greater than another can be used to develop meaningful rules and procedures for comparing decimals.

To compare .2 and .09, we begin by representing both decimals:

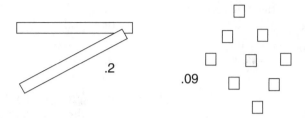

The student can easily see that 2 tenths is greater than 9 hundredths. If unsure, the student can place the hundredths pieces on top of one of the tenths pieces to determine that 9 hundredths is even less than 1 tenth. Then you could ask the student to figure out how many hundredths it would take to equal 2 tenths. This helps to reinforce the comparison.

We use the model to make a lot of comparisons. For example, we might compare 3 and .3, 7.2 and .72, and 1.2 and .98:

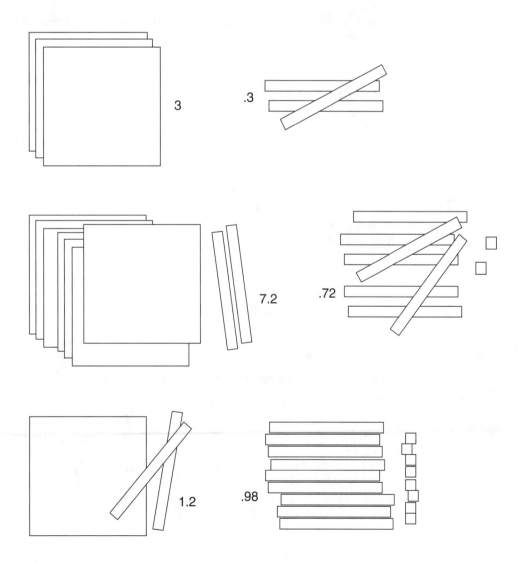

After recording these and other similar results, the teacher can lead the students to discover a number of helpful patterns:

The value of the number varies according to the position of the digits relative to the decimal point.

3 > .3
7.2 > .72
.06 < .60

The size of the digits is less important than the position of the digits relative to the decimal point.

.2 > .09
.086 < .34
1.2 > .98

Compare numbers by comparing the values of the first nonzero digit.

.206 > .094 (2 tenths is greater than 9 hundredths)
.061 > .059 (6 hundredths is greater than 5 hundredths)
6.93 < 20.1 (6 ones is less than 2 tens)

If the values of the first nonzero digits are equal, then compare the values of the next digits.

.519 < .523 (1 hundredth is less than 2 hundredths)
6.43 > 6.29 (4 tenths is greater than 2 tenths)
32.4 < 38.1 (2 ones is less than 8 ones)

These patterns can then be fashioned into meaningful rules and procedures for comparing decimals. The rules will be meaningful to the students because they are generalizations from the students' own discoveries rather than just "what the teacher said to do."

The following sequence of activities demonstrates how a teacher can develop decimal comparison concepts and skills.

Activity 8.04   Comparing Decimals

Write two decimals on the board. Have two students come forward. Have each student represent one of the numbers using squares, strips, and small squares like those illustrated at the right.

2.47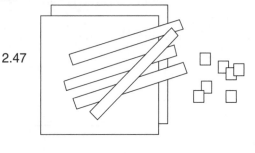

After the numbers have been represented with the model, have two other children come forward and check to make sure the numbers were represented correctly.

Then have another child come forward and look at the model representations and decide which number is greater. Have this child write < or > between the two numbers.

Repeat this activity with several pairs of decimals.

Activity 8.05   Comparison Prediction

Prepare a set of about 50 cards showing decimals.

Form a group of two to four students. Give the group a set of decimal pieces. Shuffle the deck and place it facedown on the table.

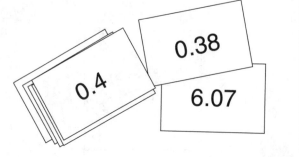

On each play, all the players take a card from the deck and place it faceup on the table. The player with the greatest decimal takes the cards from that play. They continue playing in this way until there are not enough cards for another play. The player who has taken the most cards is the winner.

If the players disagree about which decimal is greater, the disputing players explain their reasoning to try to convince the other players. If they cannot reach agreement, they should then represent the decimal with the model to check the comparison.

Adding and Subtracting Decimals

The teaching of addition and subtraction of decimals is almost identical to the teaching of addition and subtraction of whole numbers. The same big ideas that govern addition and subtraction of whole numbers are used for adding and subtracting decimals:

For addition: Always add like units.
                  When there are too many to write (in standard form), make a trade.

For subtraction: Always subtract like units.
                  When there are not enough, make a trade.

The only real difference between addition and subtraction of decimals and that of whole numbers is that with decimals, there are more units. We start the instruction by reestablishing the big ideas using a physical model. Using squares, strips, and small squares as a decimal model is an excellent way to illustrate addition and subtraction.

When adding, we model the two numbers, combine them, and record what is there after combining. When subtracting, we model the subtrahend, take away the minuend, and record the remainder:

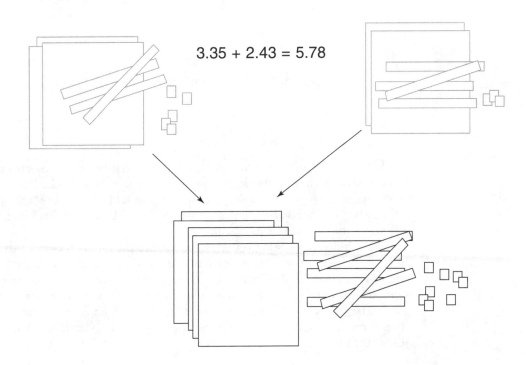

$$3.35 + 2.43 = 5.78$$

$$6.86 - 2.13 = 4.73$$

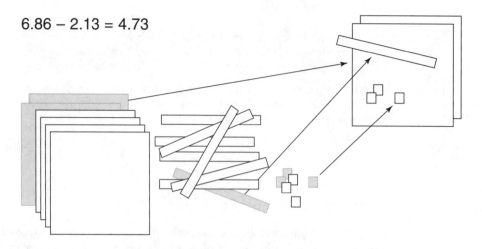

Another easy-to-use model for addition and subtraction of decimals is play money. When ten-dollar bills are used to represent tens, one-dollar bills to represent ones, dimes to represent tenths, and pennies to represent hundredths, this representation of decimals can be combined and separated, and, when necessary, equal trades can be made.

A Remediation Note. The most common error pattern in addition and subtraction of decimals comes from a rote rule learned when the students were working with whole numbers: the columns must be lined up. The problem with rote rules is that they are seldom true beyond certain narrow conditions. And students (even those who have memorized the rules correctly) tend to apply them in inappropriate circumstances. In particular, this rule, when correctly applied in whole-number addition, would not produce errors:

```
        ┌──── Line up the right side of the numbers
        ↓
     14                          Correct
 + 207
───────
```

However, when the rule is applied to addition of decimals, the computation is not correct:

```
        ┌──── Line up the right side of the numbers
        ↓
    .14                          Incorrect
 + 20.7
───────
```

When you identify this error pattern, it is important that the students not merely be given a new rule (line up the decimal points) to replace the old rule. Do not misinterpret this statement. We are not saying that students should not learn to line up the decimal points when they are adding or subtracting decimals. Lining up the decimal points actually makes the addition or subtraction easier.

What we are suggesting is that when you use the model to show that like units are lined up (remember that we *always add like units*), the result is that the decimal points will also be lined up. And, when the decimal points line up, it turns out that the like units are lined up. This is helpful because lining up like units makes it easier to *add like units*. The students still learn the same rule, but the rule is now meaningful. Not only does it make sense to the students, but the students also understand why they should follow the rule.

The activity sequence that follows can be used to develop the concepts related to addition and subtraction of decimals.

Activity 8.06 Adding Money

Using play hundred-, ten-, and one-dollar bills, have the students come to the front of the room and illustrate this addition. Be sure that everyone understands that they need to add like units and make a trade when there are too many to write.

$$\begin{array}{r} 628 \\ +\ 165 \\ \hline \end{array}$$

Then add some dimes and pennies to the money and have a student come forward and illustrate this addition. Emphasize that the students should add exactly the same way when they are adding decimals.

$$\begin{array}{r} 24.73 \\ +\ 3.84 \\ \hline \end{array}$$

Ask several other students come forward and use the money to illustrate other decimal addition examples.

Then write a decimal addition example on the board and have the students do the addition at their seats. When they are finished, have a student come forward and use the money to do the same example. Did everyone get it right?

Activity 8.07 Subtracting Money

Follow the procedures described for activity 8.06, except use subtraction examples.

Activity 8.08 Be Careful What You Add

Write 42.03 + 615.6 on the board in horizontal form. Tell the students that you want to do this addition. Ask what decimal units you will have in the answer. [Hundreds, tens, ones, tenths, and hundredths] Ask how many ones there will be in the answer. Write 7 on the board with a decimal point after it. Ask how many tens will be in the answer. Record the 5 tens. Ask how many tenths.

Record the 6 tenths. Ask how many hundredths. Record the 3 hundredths. Point out that to get the answer you must *add like units*. Model the same addition using play hundred-dollar bills, ten-dollar bills, one-dollar bills, dimes, and pennies to verify that the answer is correct.

Next, add 123.4 + 4.567 + 21.02 as a second example. After completing the addition, explain that even though decimal addition is easy, sometimes you really have to be careful to add only like units (ones to ones, hundredths to hundredths, and so on). Explain that it will be easier to add like units if the like units are written in columns. Rewrite the last example by lining up the like units. Add to demonstrate how much easier it is to add the like units when they are lined up.

Finally, do 107.64 + 5.193 as a third example, but this time line up the like units. When you have completed this example, point out that when you place the like units in columns, the decimal points are also lined up. Do another example by lining up the decimal points.

Activity 8.09   If There Aren't Any, Write Zero

Write 42.03 + 615.6 on the board in horizontal form. Ask what the smallest unit is in either number. [Hundredths] Ask how many hundredths there are in the second number. [There are none.] Ask how you could write the number to show that there are no hundredths. [Write a zero in the hundredths place.] Rewrite the addition example as 42.03 + 615.60 and add.

Write 123.4 + 4.567 + 21.02 as a second example. Ask what fractional decimal units there are. [Tenths, hundredths, and thousandths] Rewrite the addition example using 0 to indicate when a number has none of some unit. Then add. Emphasize that decimal addition is just like whole-number addition: *always add like units* and *when there are too many to write, make a trade*.

Write 107.64 + 5.193 as a third example. Ask the students to rewrite the numbers using zeros as they were used in the previous examples. Have the students add to get the answer.

Activity 8.10   If There Aren't Any, Write Zero—Subtraction

Write 38.2 − 5.78 in horizontal form on the board. Ask the children, "What units do we have to take away?" [Ones, tenths, and hundredths] Point to the subtrahend. Ask, "How many hundredths are we starting with?" [There are none.] Ask, "How can we rewrite the number to show that there are no hundredths?" [Use a zero.]

Rewrite the subtraction example as 38.20 − 5.78. Rewrite it again in vertical form and complete the example. Emphasize that decimal subtraction is just like whole-number subtraction: *always subtract like units* and *when there are not enough to subtract, make a trade*.

Adapting a Lesson on Decimals

Next, we examine a lesson plan that follows suggestions that might be found in the teacher's guide of an elementary school mathematics program. Note that it is a good plan. However, it does have some weaknesses that are typical of traditional lesson plans for teaching elementary school mathematics. Notice the following:

1. The focus is on teaching the textbook pages.
2. The developmental part of the lesson is minimal.
3. A large amount of practice using the rule for placement of the decimal point is recommended.

Note that when there is a minimum of development, a maximum of practice is always required.

LESSON OBJECTIVE

The student will subtract decimals through hundredths with regrouping.

Lesson Opener

Have the students complete the following examples:

23 – 11   648 – 127   296 – 105   806 – 304

After enough time has been allowed for the students to complete the examples, have four of them come to the front and write a completed example. Point out to the class that *we always subtract like units* (ones from ones, tens from tens, etc.).

Development

Direct the students' attention to the first page of the lesson in the students' textbook. Tell them to look at the first example. Talk through the steps needed to find the answer.

Line up the decimal points.

$$62.08$$
$$-\;1.5$$

Write 1.5 as 1.50.

$$62.08$$
$$-\;1.50$$

Subtract zero hundredths from 8 hundredths.

$$62.08$$
$$-\;1.50$$
$$\overline{8}$$

Rename to get 10 more tenths. Subtract 5 tenths from 10 tenths.

$$62.08$$
$$-\;1.50$$
$$\overline{.58}$$

Complete the subtraction of the ones and tens.

$$62.08$$
$$-\;1.50$$
$$\overline{60.58}$$

Talk the students through the steps needed to solve the second example. Then ask them to complete the third example without your direction.

Monitor Understanding

While the children are doing the last example, take note of any who need extra help.

Practice

Have the children complete the odd-numbered exercises on the practice page.

Closure

At the end of the lesson, remind the children that they have learned to subtract decimals.

Now, we will adapt this lesson to increase the amount and depth of the developmental part of the lesson. To do this, we will make the lesson more visual and more kinesthetic, make assessment a continual process that provides feedback about the effectiveness of instruction while that instruction is going on, and increase communication about what is being learned from the students and among the students. These adaptations make the lesson appropriate for almost all students. But, remember that some students with severe needs may require further instructional adaptations.

LESSON OBJECTIVE

The student will subtract decimals through hundredths with regrouping.

Lesson Opener

Prepare pairs of cards like the ones shown below with a subtraction example on one card and the answer to the example on the other. Make enough cards so that every child in the class will have either a subtraction card or an answer card.

| 367 − 104 = | and | 263 | 583 − 248 = | and | 335 | 326 − 59 = | and | 267 |
| 294 − 213 = | and | 81 | 744 − 666 = | and | 78 | 946 − 264 = | and | 682 |

Shuffle all the cards and give a card to each student. If there is a card left over, keep it for yourself and participate with the class.

Tell the children to find their partners so that partners will have a problem and the answer.

Explain to the students that they are to help one another to find their partners. When everyone has found his or her partner, ask the students how they found their partners.

Development

Direct the students' attention to the first page of the lesson in the students' textbook. Tell them to look at the first decimal subtraction example, 62.08 − 1.50. Explain that you are going to use play money to find the answer. Show them the ten-dollar bills, the one-dollar bills, the dimes, and the cents. Point out that in the first example they will start with 62.08.

Monitor understanding. Be alert to identify students who do not seem to understand. Do the students all seem to understand how to represent decimals with money? Emphasize that they *always subtract like units* (ones from ones, tens from tens, etc.). Also emphasize that when there are not enough, they need to make a trade.

Have a student come to the front to put $62.08 in a shoebox. Ask the students how many ten-dollar bills should be placed in the box. [6] Have your helper place the money in the box. Ask how many one-dollar bills go in the box. [2] Have your helper place the money in the box. Ask how many dimes go in the box. [none] Ask how many pennies go in the box. [8] Have your helper place the money in the box.

Monitor understanding. Do the children understand how to represent decimals with money?

Point out that they will take away $1.50 from the shoe box. The amount left in the box will be their answer.

Call on another child to help by taking the number out of the box. Ask the others how many pennies need to be taken out of the box. [none] Ask how many dimes they need to take out of the box. [5] Tell the class that there is a problem. Ask what the problem is. [There are not 5 dimes in the box.] Ask the class what to do. [Trade a one-dollar bill for 10 dimes.] Have your helper make the trade. Have your helper take 5 dimes out of the box.

Monitor understanding. Watch for students who do not seem to fully understand.

Ask how many one-dollar bills should be taken out of the box. [1] Ask how many 10-dollar bills should be taken out of the box. [none] Ask, "How much did we take from the box?" [1.50]. Ask, "How much is left in the box?" [60.58]

Write 62.08 − 1.5 = 60.58.

Talk the students through the same steps on the second example. Except this time, record each step as it is taken. Then have the students complete the third example with only minimal help from you.

Monitor understanding. Do the students all seem to understand? Make a note of those who may need individual help.

Using Decimals to Solve Problems

When teaching problem solving using decimals, teachers should apply the same basic principles as when they teach problem solving using other kinds of numbers (see Chapters 6 and 7). The teacher should emphasize that the choice of operation depends on what is happening to the quantities in the problem. For example, if quantities are being combined, then addition can probably be used. If the number names of the quantities are decimals, then those decimals should be added. If the quantities in the problem are being separated, then subtraction can probably be used.

We now examine a problem appropriate for children at about the fourth-grade level. The solution employs one of the strategies demonstrated in Chapter 7 (use a table), and it also uses three additional strategies: *solve a simpler problem, try and check* (sometimes called *trial and error*), and *list the possibilities*.

Exercises and Activities

1. Choose a lesson on decimals from a published elementary school mathematics textbook series.
    a. Write a lesson plan that follows the teaching suggestions in the teacher's guide.
    b. Identify parts of the lesson that include student communication about the concept(s) or skill(s) taught in the lesson.
    c. Add to the lesson more opportunities for communication from or among students.
    d. Identify the parts of the lesson designed to assess the learning of the students.
    e. Add more continual assessment (monitoring of learning) to the lesson plan.

2. Suppose a small store in the mall called "Nuts to You" sells nuts by the scoop. The price for one scoop of each kind of nuts is shown on the sign. This year Mrs. Garcia wants to give gift bags of mixed nut to her friends and neighbors for Christmas. However, she wants to customize the bags for each neighbor and keep the cost per bag around $3.00. Describe the contents of three possible gift bags of nuts.

Price per Scoop	
Peanuts	$ .25
Walnuts	.50
Almonds	.75
Cashews	1.00
Pecans	1.25

References and Related Readings

National Council of Teachers of Mathematics. (1989). *Curriculum and evaluation standards for school mathematics.* Reston, VA: Author.

National Council of Teachers of Mathematics. (2000). *Principles and standards for school mathematics.* Reston, VA: Author.

Thornton, C. A., Tucker, B. F., Dossey, J. A., & Bazik, E. F. (1983). *Teaching mathematics to children with special needs.* Menlo Park, CA: Addison-Wesley.

Websites

http://www.corestandards.org/the-standards/mathematics
The Common Core State Standards for Mathematics can be found at this site.

www.mathforum.org/
Math forum links to math discussions and ideas.

http://mathforum.org/library/topics/fractions/
Links to decimal and fraction sites.

nine

MEASUREMENT

Assigning a Number to a Quantity

CHAPTER OUTLINE

Measurement and Geometry

This text deals with measurement and geometry separately. However, the elementary school mathematics curriculum typically integrates these two content areas. In fact, elementary school geometry content can hardly be discussed without continual references to measurements of some sort. This chapter shows how measurement concepts are developed. More-advanced measurement concepts depend on understanding and using more-advanced geometric concepts.

Defining Measurement

Before discussing the teaching of measurement, we first consider the meaning of measurement. People measure many different kinds of things, including the size of a set of objects, the length of an object, the capacity of a container, the value of an object, or the likelihood of an occurrence. Not only are the things people measure different, but also the processes used to measure them vary from type to type. But, in every case, people are assigning a number to some quantity. In fact, this is precisely what measurement is: *measurement* is the process of assigning a number to a quantity.

For example, suppose there is a set of children consisting of Ann, Tyler, Jake, Rebecca, Henry, and Chloe. A set of children has many attributes that can be measured. We might be interested in how intelligent the group of children is. We might be interested in how long the group is if the individuals were laid end to end. We might be interested in how heavy the group is. We might be interested in how fast the group can run. We might be interested in how polite the children are. All of these things can be measured by assigning a number to the group that represents the attribute being measured. Frequently when a set of objects is being measured, the attribute that we are most interested in is the "numerousness" of the set: How many objects are in the set? In this case, how many children are in the group? If we count the children in the group, we find that there are six children. The number that tells how many is 6. We have measured the set.

An important idea in all measurement is the notion of *unit*. When we measure the set of children, the unit is *child*. To find the size of the set, we count to see how many units there are (that is, we count to see how many *children* there are) in the set. The unit of measurement used to measure the set of children is an example of a direct unit. In nonformal language, a *direct unit* is a piece of the attribute that is being measured. When measuring with direct units, we count how many of those units are contained in the thing being measured.

Measuring Length

Length is measured in direct units. For example, when we measure the length of a desk, we decide on a unit of length (a piece of length) and figure out how many of those units equals the length of the desk. If we decide to use a crayon as the unit of length, we lay crayons end to end on top of the desk to see how many crayons equals the length of the desk.

The length is 11, 11 crayons.

Before beginning to measure length, the children must have a sense of what length is. The meaning of the attribute *length* can be established through a series of gross comparison activities. As the students make these comparisons, the comparisons should be sequenced in order to isolate the attribute length from the other attributes possessed by the objects being measured:

Which is longer?
The black rectangle is longer.

Which is longer?
This time, the gray
rectangle is longer. (We are
not measuring the color.)

Which is longer?
The checkered rectangle is
longer. (The direction does
not make any difference.)

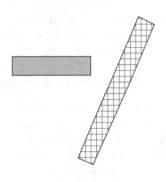

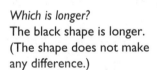

Which is longer?
The striped rectangle is
longer. (The thickness is
not what we are measuring.)

Which is longer?
The black shape is longer.
(The shape does not make
any difference.)

As the concept of *length* is developed through these comparisons, the teacher should introduce the vocabulary of length by using it correctly in appropriate contexts. Specifically, the students should become familiar with these terms: *long, longer, longest; short, shorter, shortest;* and *tall, taller, tallest.* Encourage the children to use this terminology as they talk about the comparisons being made.

At some point, students should be asked to compare the length of two objects that are nearly the same length but are arranged so that it is difficult to decide which is longer. For example, two strips of paper could be placed on the bulletin board as pictured here. The students should learn that when the two strips are moved side by side, we can easily tell which is longer.

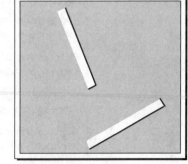

The next step is to present the students with a similar comparison task, but one in which the objects cannot be moved. For example, to compare the length of the chalk tray on a section of chalkboard with the length of a board in the floor, the students should discover that they can stretch a string along the board in the floor to see how long it is and then keep holding that length of string while moving it next to the chalk tray to see which is longer.

With the preceding example, the students used a unit of length; in this case, the length of string. The concept of *unit of length* can be expanded by making comparisons in settings where a unit of length is inherent in the setting. For example, if two objects are placed on a tile floor, students could make the comparison by counting the tiles. Or, the height of objects in the classroom could be compared by counting spelling books that are stacked next to the objects.

Other arbitrary units that are placed beside the objects can be used to make comparisons. Students can line up paper clips, new pencils, or paper strips that are cut the same length next to the objects being compared. When the students refer to the lengths as some number of paper clips or some number of pencils, they have actually measured those objects.

The following key ideas related to the measurement of length should be emphasized:

- **When a length is being communicated, the number is meaningless without the unit.** The length of an object might be 2 pencils long or it might be 8 paper clips long. If one object has a length of 3 and another object has a length of 7, we do not know which is longer unless we know which units were used to measure the two objects.

- **The number of units depends on the size of the unit.** If we use a short unit to measure the length of something, it will take more units than if we use a longer unit.

The following sequence of activities can be used to develop the concepts of *length*, *units of length*, and *measurement of length*.

Activity 9.01   Pick the Longest; Pick the Shortest

Tape strips of paper horizontally to the walls around the room. The strips should be of different colors and very different lengths. Some strips should be wider than others; some should be narrower than others.

Point out two strips and ask which is longer. Talk about the two strips, using appropriate length vocabulary. [This strip is *longer than* that one; that strip is *shorter than* this one; and so on.] Choose different pairs of strips and have the students decide which is longer and which is shorter. If the strips are too close in length for the students to decide, have them move the strips side by side so they can tell which is longer.

Point out three strips and decide which is longest. Talk about the strips, using appropriate vocabulary. [This strip is *shorter than* both of the other two strips; it is the *shortest*; that one is the *longest*; and so on.]

Activity 9.02   Long, Longer, and Longest

Bring a doll, a baseball bat, a screwdriver, and a necktie to class. Lay these objects on the table where the students can see them.

Choose two of the objects and place them side by side with one end of each object at the same edge of the table. Help the students to decide which one is longer and which one is shorter.

Next, have the children choose different pairs of objects and place the end of each object right at the edge of the table. Have the children use appropriate language to compare the objects.

Choose three objects and decide which is longest. Talk about the objects, using appropriate vocabulary. [The baseball bat is *longer than* both the doll and the screwdriver. It is the *longest*. The screwdriver is the *shortest*.]

Ask the children to choose three of the objects and compare them, using appropriate vocabulary.

Activity 9.03   Pick the Longest; Pick the Shortest (variation 2)

Tape strips of paper to the walls around the room. The strips should be of different colors and the lengths of the strips should be nearly, but not quite, the same. The strips should be taped to the wall so that they are not parallel.

Point out two strips and ask which is longer. Since they are about the same length, it is hard to determine which is longer. Ask for suggestions. If someone suggests that the strips be moved together, explain, "Well, yes, we could do that, but I want to try a different way."

Ask for two helpers to come help you. Give them some string and show them how to stretch it out along one of the strips and hold their fingers on the string to mark the length. Then have them save that length on the string and take it to the other strip to see which is longer.

Have the children choose two strips. Have everyone guess which is longer. Have two students use the string to show the class which is longer. How many students guessed correctly?

Repeat several times with other pairs of strips.

Activity 9.04   Up-and-Down Length

Stand several objects (for example, a vase, a statue, and a box) around the room.

Point to one of the objects. Explain that when you think about how long something is up and down, you are thinking about how tall it is. Use your hands to indicate the vertical length of the object and tell the students that the object is this tall.

Indicate a second object and ask the class which of the two is taller.

Choose other pairs of objects and ask which is taller. If the students cannot decide, have them move the objects together to decide. Encourage the students to use appropriate vocabulary (*tall, short, taller, shorter, tallest, shortest*).

Have the class look at two things outside (for example, a tree and a building). Which is taller? Which is shorter?

Activity 9.05   Tall, Taller, Tallest

Have the tallest student and the shortest student in the class stand up. Ask who is taller. Ask who is shorter. Then have the shorter student stand on a chair. Ask who is taller now. Be sure that the students understand that the one on the chair is not taller just because his or her head is higher.

Have two students that are about the same height stand up. Ask who is taller. Ask who is shorter. If the class is not sure, ask how the comparison can be made. [Move the two students together; use a string.] Allow the class to solve the problem of how to make the comparison.

Repeat the process with other pairs of students.

Have three students stand. Ask who is tallest and who is shortest.

Activity 9.06   How Long?

Lay two objects on a checkerboard. Ask the students if they can use the squares on the board to compare the two objects. Ask how many squares long each object is.

Have them take the checkerboard around the room and use it to see how long other selected objects are.

Activity 9.07   Units of Length

Show the class an object. Explain that you are going to measure its length. Use several new pencils to measure the length. Write the length on the chalkboard. Then measure the object using paper clips. Write the length on the chalkboard. Then measure the object using crayons and write the length.

Explain that what you use to measure an object is called the *unit of measurement*. Point out that the number of units will be a big number or a small number, depending on how long the unit is.

Have the students measure several objects and then measure them again using a different unit.

Activity 9.08   Who's Wrong?

You will need two sticks. One should be 11 inches long. The other should be 13 inches long.

Show the class how to measure a length when you have only one copy of the unit. For example, use one pencil to measure the length of a tabletop by moving it along the table and keeping track of how many times the pencil was used to reach the other end of the table.

Have the students measure several things using a pencil, a board eraser, and a shoe.

Then give a student the 13-inch stick and have her or him measure the length of the room. Before the student finishes, have a second student measure the length of the room to check the first student's measurement. But have the second student use the 11-inch stick.

When both students have reported their measurements, ask the class why their answers are different. After the class has discussed how one of the students might have made a mistake, hold the two sticks side by side so that the class can see that they are not the same length. Reemphasize that if the unit is smaller, it takes more units to make the measurement. If the unit is larger, it does not take as many.

When a measurement is communicated to another person, there must be agreement regarding the unit that is used to make the measurement. For example, suppose we are told that a length is 17 pencils. If the measurement is to be unambiguous, we must know how long the pencil is.

Suppose a tailor uses a new pencil to determine that she needs a length of wool cloth that is 26 pencils long. Her assistant cuts off a length of cloth that is 26 pencils long. He wants to do it correctly, so he measures very carefully. However, he uses his own pencil, which has been sharpened several times. The cloth will be too short because the tailor and her assistant had not agreed on which pencil to use.

Suppose a carpet layer who wears a size 14 shoe uses his foot to measure a piece of carpet for a room and finds that the carpet needs to be 12 shoes wide and 17 shoes long. Suppose that he sent his helper who wears a size 9 shoe to cut the carpet. The piece of carpet cut by the helper would be too short and too narrow because the carpet layer and his helper had not agreed on what shoe to use.

The process of agreeing on the length of the units is called *standardization of the units*. To arrive at a "standard foot," the parties must first agree on what foot to use. And since the person whose foot is to be used cannot be everywhere, everyone using that standard unit must have a copy of the standard foot. Then, length measurements can be communicated unambiguously. Five feet will mean the same thing to everyone, and 42 feet will mean the same to everyone.

Whatever system of standard units of length is to be used can be effectively taught by following these five steps:

1. **Justify the need for the system of standard units.** This is best accomplished by stressing the need for clear communication of measurements.
2. **Develop mental imagery for each unit.** Students should be able to show a reasonable approximation of each unit. This step is essential if they are to have any success in estimating lengths.
3. **Help students develop the ability to estimate lengths using each of the units.**
4. **Aid students in discovering, understanding, and learning the relationships among the units within the system.**
5. **Help students become familiar with and proficient in the use of measurement tools that make use of the units in the system.** Examples of such tools include 12-inch rulers, yardsticks, meter sticks, and tape measures.

The most common mistake made in teaching length measurement is to begin with the fifth step without spending sufficient time on the previous four steps. Emphasizing the first through fourth steps helps students become proficient (1) in using measurement both inside and outside the classroom, (2) in completing measurement exercises, and (3) in solving problems that involve measurement. This emphasis allows students to gain such proficiency in both common and unusual settings and both when the need to measure is anticipated and when unexpected needs require measurement.

The following activities illustrate how the preceding five steps of length measurement can be taught.

First, establish the need for standardized units.

Activity 9.09 The King's Foot

Have students work with partners to trace around their feet. They should cut out the foot tracings. As much as is possible, pair students with partners who are much taller or much shorter than they are.

Choose a pair of partners to measure the length of the room two times, once with each partner's foot tracing. Choose another pair of partners to measure the distance from the classroom door to the next door down the hall. Have other partners measure the length of the board, the width of the room, the distance from the teacher's desk to the corner of the room, and so on.

In most cases, the partners will get two different measurements because their feet are not the same size. Discuss why this could be a problem. Explain the need to agree on what foot to use. Choose a student to be the "captain." Tell the class that the captain has decided that everyone should use his or her foot. Make copies of the captain's foot for everyone.

Have the partners measure the same things again, using their copy of the captain's foot. Now their measurements should agree.

Hold up a copy of the king's foot (a 12-inch foot). Explain that a long time ago people all over the British Empire decided to use this foot to make measurements. Then, everyone knew how long 4 feet was. It was the same length all over the Empire.

Second, develop mental imagery for each unit.

Activity 9.10 Pick a Foot

Choose several objects that are 1 foot long. Choose an equal number of objects that are not 1 foot long. They should be either shorter than 10 inches or longer than 14 inches. Place the objects in pairs around the room. Each pair of objects should have one object that is a foot long and one object that is not a foot long.

Direct the attention of the class to one pair of objects. Ask which one is 1 foot long. Take a vote. Have someone bring a copy of the king's foot to check who was right and who was not.

Continue in this way until all the pairs of objects have been considered. After about five pairs of objects have been looked at and checked, almost everyone should be choosing the foot-long object.

Third, help students develop the ability to estimate lengths.

Activity 9.11 Best Guess

Prepare 10 cardboard strips ranging from 4 inches to 20 inches in length. Also prepare from colored paper 2 strips that are 10 inches long and 10 strips that are 1 inch long.

Place the cardboard strips under a box so that about 2 inches of each strip can be seen. Place the colored strips in the box.

Form a group of three or four students. They will each need a sheet of paper and a pencil. They take turns choosing a cardboard strip and pulling it out from under the box. Everyone looks at the strip and guesses how many inches long it is. They each write their guess on their paper.

After everyone has written a guess, the student who chose the strip uses the 10-inch colored strips and the 1-inch colored strips to measure the cardboard strip. The child with the best guess gets a point. If there is a tie for the best guess, everyone who tied gets a point.

Continue until all the cardboard strips have been used. The student with the most points wins.

Activity 9.12   Place and Guess

Form pairs of partners. Each pair of partners needs two paper clips, ten 10-centimeter rods, and ten 1-centimeter cubes.

Both partners close their eyes and place a paper clip on the table between them. Both look at the paper clips, guess how far apart they are, and write the guess on a sheet of paper. Then they use the 1-centimeter cubes and 10-centimeter rods to measure the distance between the paper clips. The partner with the best guess gets a point. If they tie, both get a point. The first one to get 10 points wins.

There is a great deal of similarity in the two estimation activities. In fact, they are really two versions of the same activity—the same idea packaged in two different ways:

An object is identified.

The measurement is estimated.

The length is measured to check the estimate.

Another object is identified.

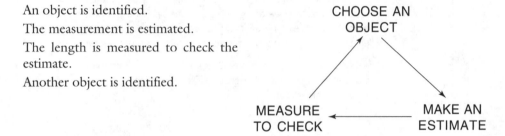

If measurements are made with measuring tools that provide clear imagery of the unit being used, that mental imagery can then be used to make subsequent estimates. The activity provides immediate feedback on the accuracy of each estimate, which allows students to make corrections in their mental imagery before making the next estimate. Accuracy of estimates typically improves dramatically.

We continue with the sample teaching activities.

Fourth, help students discover, understand, and learn the relationships among the units within the system.

Activity 9.13   Scavenger Hunt

Prepare four lists of six measurements as shown here:

8 feet	29 inches	5 feet 3 inches	37 inches
2 yards 14 inches	4 feet 7 inches	1 yard 18 inches	1 yard 25 inches
2 yards 4 feet	3 yards 2 feet	4 feet	2 feet 6 inches
14 inches	7 feet	2 yards 5 feet	4 yards 2 feet
6 feet 8 inches	1 yard 40 inches	20 inches	6 feet
4 yards	8 yards	5 yards	7 yards

Prepare 24 cards, each showing another name for a measurement on one of the lists. Tape these cards to the walls around the room.

Separate the class into four teams. Give one of the lists to each team. (You might want to provide a copy of the list for every member of the team.) Have the teams search for cards that give other names for the measurements on their list.

The first team to finish wins.

Activity 9.14   Order Three

Prepare sentence strips showing the measurements listed in activity 9.13.

Choose three strips and place them in the chalk tray where they can be seen by the class.

Have the class help you arrange them in order from the shortest length to the longest length. Keep asking the students how they can tell which is longer and which is shorter.

Choose other sets of three measurements to arrange in order. Also arrange sets of four or five measurements.

Activity 9.15   Line Up

Prepare sentence strips showing the measurements listed in activity 9.13.

Shuffle the strips and pass them out to the class. Separate the class into two groups that are about equal in number. Have one group go to one side of the room and have the other group go to the opposite side. Tell the class that you want each group to line up in order from shortest to longest length. Encourage the group members to talk to each other when they need help.

Have them hold their measurements so the students in the other group can see them. Each group should then check the other group to see if they are in the right order. Again, encourage them to talk when they are not sure.

Activity 9.16   Shuffle

Prepare cards showing measurements listed in activity 9.13.

Form a group of four students. Shuffle the cards and give the deck to the students. On each play, the dealer should give each player five cards facedown. When the dealer says "Go," the players turn their cards over and race to get them in order. The winner must explain why each of the cards is in the right position.

The winner then reshuffles the cards and starts a new play. The students continue until a player has won five rounds or until the teacher calls time.

Fifth, help students become proficient in the use of measurement tools.

Activity 9.17   Feet in a Row

The students will need to use their copies of the king's foot (cutouts of feet that are exactly 12 inches long). Tell the students that you are going to show them a faster way to measure lengths. Have several students bring their copies of the king's foot to the front. Tape the king's feet toe to heel in a row. Number the feet:

Use the row of feet like a tape measure to measure several things.

Activity 9.18 Make a Ruler

Give each student a strip of receipt paper and an inch unit. Show the students how to mark 1-inch intervals on their strip of receipt paper to make a ruler. Have them number the inches:

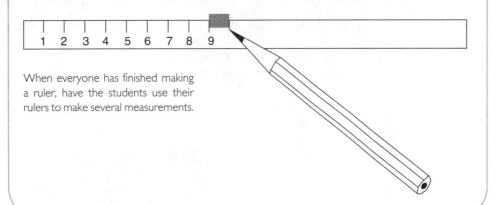

When everyone has finished making a ruler, have the students use their rulers to make several measurements.

Activity 9.19 To the Nearest Foot

Review rounding of numbers to the nearest ten. Use a number line to help the students visualize the process. Then use a tape measure that shows feet to measure something between 3 and 4 feet long. Show that the length is more than 3 feet but less than 4 feet. Explain to the children that they need to round to the nearest foot. Have the children decide if the length is nearer to 3 feet or 4 feet. Point out the halfway point between 3 feet and 4 feet. Show how to use this halfway point to make the judgment.

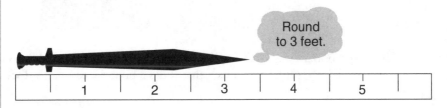

Measure some other things to the nearest foot.

Teaching Area Measurement

Area is different from length in that we do not, for the most part, actually measure area. In most cases, we measure some combination of lengths and use them in a formula to compute the area. So, the study of area can be separated into two parts. The first part consists of developing the concepts of *area* and *unit of area* and using the units to determine the area. The second part consists of the development of the area formulas. Problem solving, using the level of understanding and skill that has been developed, is found throughout.

The early part of instruction parallels some of the same ideas that were developed for measurement of length:

- The *concept of area* should be developed first by making gross comparisons of the areas of different objects.
- The *concept of a unit of area* as a piece of area should be developed.

- The *concept of measurement of area* as the number of units it takes to cover the area being measured should be developed. Mental imagery for the units should be developed. Students should be able to show a reasonable approximation of the unit.
- Students should develop the *ability to estimate areas* using each of the units.

Although we provide a brief development here, creating teaching and learning activities for developing area concepts is left as exercises for you, the reader.

Comparisons of area are more complex than comparisons of length. When comparing areas, you must take into account length, width, and shape. When the following shapes are compared, children have very little problem deciding which has the bigger area. Shape B is bigger in every way. Students would probably choose shape B even if they did not know what area is:

The next two shapes are considerably more difficult because one shape is longer but the other is wider. This forces the child to think beyond one dimension:

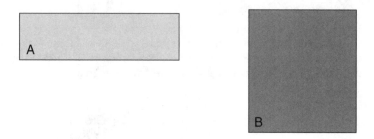

An appropriate way to check the comparison is to cut shape A into parts and rearrange them. Then it can easily be seen that B has a bigger area than A does:

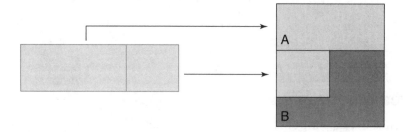

The next pair of figures is even more difficult because, in addition to length and width, the shapes of the figures have an impact on their areas:

Once again, by cutting and rearranging one of the figures, we can easily check the comparison. Figure C has the greater area:

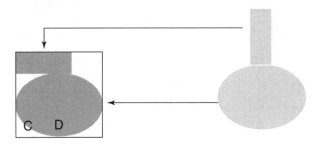

As figures get more complex in shape, look–see comparisons become more difficult, and so you need to introduce the use of units to help with the comparisons. A good way to start is to have students cover the shapes with some common objects, like pennies, in order to help with the comparisons. Tell the children to determine how many pennies can be placed inside each shape. They may not have any pennies go outside the boundary of the shape. Fourteen pennies are required to cover figure A, whereas 18 pennies are required for figure B. This can help the students to decide that figure B has the greater area:

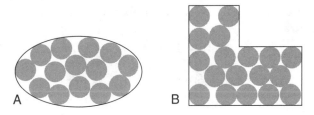

This process breaks down with complex shapes. Consider the following two figures. The students can place seven pennies on figure C but only six pennies on figure D. But does figure C really have the greater area?

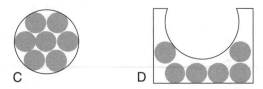

The students will quickly point out that more of the inside of D is left uncovered. The problem is that the pennies do not fit together well. There is space between them that does not get counted. We need to use a unit with a shape that *tessellates* (a shape that fits together with copies of itself without any space in between). Among the many shapes that tessellate are a triangle, a parallelogram, a hexagon, and a plus sign:

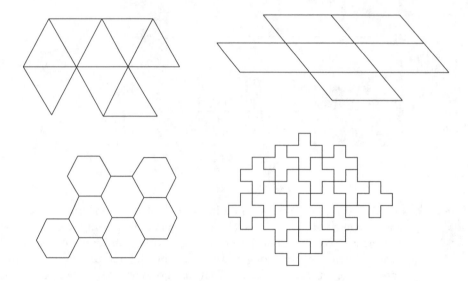

Although there is value in allowing students to explore the measurement of area with the tessellating units just illustrated, the majority of student time should be spent using *square units* of area. These are the units that are commonly used in area-computation formulas. When introducing students to the use of square units, emphasize that the area of a figure is the number of square units it takes to cover the inside of the figure:

The area of this figure is 12 square units.

To cover this area, we use 12 whole squares and 3 half squares. Altogether, the area is $13\frac{1}{2}$ square units.

After the students are comfortable measuring areas by placing and counting squares, area-computation formulas can be taught. The first of these is the area formula for rectangles. This formula can be developed from a series of discoveries made when the students are placing squares on rectangles and determining how many squares there are.

First, because rectangles are the same length from the bottom all the way to the top, every row of squares contains the same number of squares:

In this rectangle, every row has six squares. We can find the total number of squares by multiplying the number in each row times the number of rows.

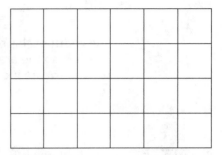

Area = 6 X 4 = 24 squares

In this rectangle, there are three rows of five squares. The area is $5 \times 3 = 15$ square units.

In this rectangle, there are six squares in the first row, so there must be six squares in every row. There are three rows. The area is $6 \times 3 = 18$ square units.

So, the children see that they can compute the area by multiplying the number of squares in each row times the number of rows:

Area of rectangle = Number of squares in each row × Number of rows

Second, if the length and width of the rectangle are given in inches and the area units are square inches, then the number of squares in the first row is the same as the length of the rectangle. The length of this rectangle is 8 inches, so 8 square inches fit in the first row:

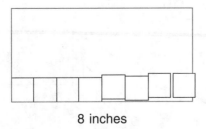

8 inches

Third, if the width is given in inches and the area units are square inches, then the number of rows is the same as the width:

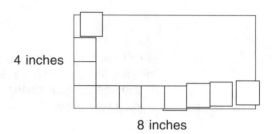

4 inches

8 inches

The width of this rectangle is 4 inches, so the area will be four rows of square inches.

The formula for the *area of a rectangle* can then be written as:

Area = Length of the rectangle × Width of the rectangle

or $\quad$ **A = L × W**

Teaching Volume Measurement

Strong parallels exist between area concepts and volume concepts. Units of area are pieces of area. Units of volume are pieces of volume. We measure area by finding how many units it takes to cover the interior of the shape. We measure volume by finding how many units it takes to fill the interior of the shape. We do not normally actually measure area; we measure linear dimensions and compute the area using formulas. We do not normally actually measure volume; we measure linear dimensions and compute the volume using formulas. The one big idea when we are developing area formulas is: *when we have a shape for which we do not have an area formula, we rearrange the area into a shape for which we do have a formula.* The one big idea when we are developing volume formulas is similar: *when we have a shape for which we do not have a volume formula, we rearrange the volume into a shape for which we do have a formula.*

We begin the development of volume concepts by establishing meaning for the term *volume*. We talk about the size of the inside of the shape and make gross comparisons. For example, we can see that box A will hold more than box B, so we say that the volume of box A is greater than the volume of box B:

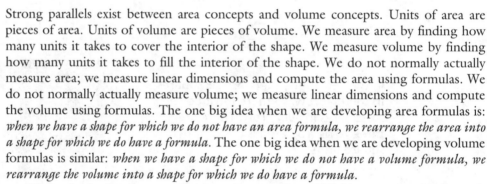

On the other hand, because they are shaped differently, it is harder to tell which of the following two boxes, C and D, would hold more:

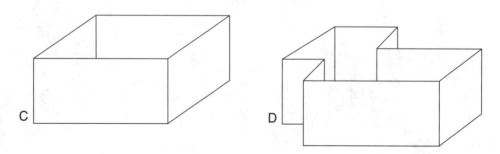

If we fill both shapes with marbles, we can count the marbles to see which shape holds more:

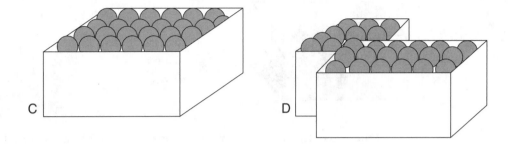

But, now we can see a problem similar to the one we saw when we used circular units of area. There is space between the marbles that is not being measured. So, we want to use a unit of volume that completely fills the shape without leaving space between the units. There are actually a lot of shapes that would work, but the volume-computation formulas require the use of units in the shape of a cube. We begin experimenting with *cubic units* to measure the volume of rectangular prisms (or boxes).

As students fill boxes with cubes and count the cubes, they learn that the measure of the volume of the box is the number of cubes it takes to fill the box:

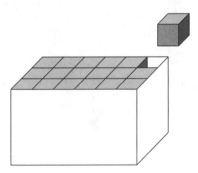

Students can also easily discover that since the box is the same size and shape from the bottom all the way to the top, every layer of cubes contains the same number:

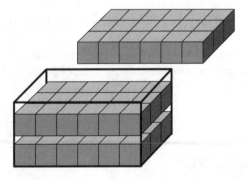

So, the volume will be the number in each layer times the number of layers:

Volume = Number of cubes in the first layer × Number of layers

In this transparent box, we see that the first layer contains 18 cubes and that there are three layers. The volume is 3×18, or 54 cubes:

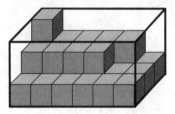

If the area of the base (bottom) of the box is marked off in squares, then in the first layer of cubes, a cube will be on top of every square. So, the number of cubes in the first layer is equal to the area of the base of the box:

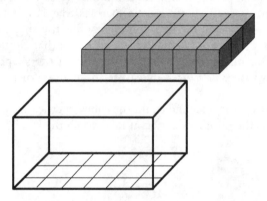

The number of layers is the same as the height of the box. In this example, the height is 3 units and there are three layers:

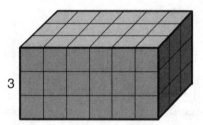

The volume is equal to the number of cubes in the first layer times the number of layers. But, since the number of cubes in the first layer is equal to the area of the base and the number of layers is equal to the height, we let B represent the area of the base, let h represent the height, and write the formula for the **volume of a box** (rectangular prism) as:

$$V = Bh$$

Activity 9.20 Pick the Big Box

Assemble a variety of boxes of different sizes and shapes.

Choose two of them and ask the students which will hold the most. Repeat this process with several pairs of boxes. If the students are unable to decide which of a pair of boxes is bigger, set that pair of boxes aside.

Activity 9.21　How to Decide?

Point out one of the pairs of boxes for which the students were unable to identify the biggest.

Conduct a brainstorming session, asking students to think of ways to decide which box is bigger. Remind them that the bigger box is the one that would hold more.

Write every suggestion on the board, regardless of how good or how practical it is. Then ask the students to decide which methods are most reasonable (make the most sense, are easy to use).

Try some of the suggested methods to see how they work.

Activity 9.22　How Can You Fill It Full If There Aren't Enough Cubes?

Construct six small boxes that have the following interior dimensions:

5 in. by 8 in. by 3 in.	6 in. by 6 in. by 4 in.
5 in. by 7 in. by 6 in.	4 in. by 9 in. by 7 in.
7 in. by 6 in. by 5 in.	4 in. by 8 in. by 5 in.

Form six groups of students. Give each group one of the boxes and about 300 1-inch cubes. Have each group fill its box with cubes to see how many cubes are needed.

Take away all but 60 cubes from each group. Then have the groups exchange boxes. Point out that the students no longer have enough cubes to fill the boxes. Tell them that you want each group to try to use the cubes that they have to figure out how many cubes it would take to fill the box.

Have each group of students report to the class how they were able to complete the task. Emphasize that every layer of cubes will contain the same number of cubes.

Activity 9.23　Even Fewer Cubes

Form six groups of students. Give each group one of the boxes prepared for activity 9.22. (Be sure that no group has a box that it previously worked with.) This time, give each group just 22 cubes. Have the group members see if they can figure out the number of cubes needed to completely fill the box when they have only 22 cubes.

After each group is finished, have the groups of students report how they figured out the answer. During the discussion, ask how they figured out how many cubes would be in the first layer. Also ask how they figured out how many layers there would be.

Activity 9.24　The Bottom of the Box

Cut a piece of white paper to fit exactly on the bottom of the inside of each of the boxes prepared for activity 9.22. Draw lines to make 1-inch squares on each piece. Place the papers inside the boxes.

Form six groups of students and give a box to each group. Also give each group about 50 1-inch cubes.

Point out that the students can look at the paper on the bottom of the box and see the area of the bottom. Ask each group to figure out the area of the bottom of its box.

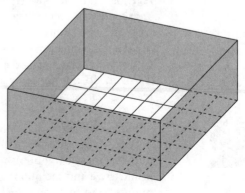

Next, have the students place a cube on top of every square in the area. Ask how the area of the bottom is related to the number of cubes it takes to make one layer.

Collect all but 10 cubes from all the groups and have the groups exchange boxes. Tell the groups of students to use what they have to find how many cubes will fit in their boxes.

When they are finished, ask how to find how many cubes it takes to fill the box. Emphasize that the number of cubes in the first layer times the number of layers is the number needed to fill the box.

Activity 9.25   Using a Ruler

Form six groups of students. Give each group one of the boxes prepared for activity 9.22. (Be sure that no group has a box that it previously worked with.) This time, give each group a ruler. Tell the students that you want each group to see if it can use the ruler to figure out how many 1-inch cubes will fit in the box.

After each group is finished, have the students report how they figured out the answer. Ask how they figured out how many cubes would be in the first layer. Also ask how they knew how many layers there would be.

Write the formula for the volume of a box on the board:

$$V = lwh$$

Place parentheses around the *lw*:

$$V = (lw)h$$

Explain that when the students multiply these numbers, they have the area of the bottom of the box. Remind them that this area is the same as the number of cubes in the first layer. Also remind them that the height tells how many layers of cubes there are.

Also remind students that a ruler can be used to obtain the measurements (length, width, and height).

Measuring Time

Time is not measured with units that are pieces of time. We use mechanical devices called *clocks* to measure time. Reading clocks seems a simple task to adults, who have had a great deal of experience with clocks. But to the child just learning to tell time, clocks are complex devices.

They consist of two "hands" (sometimes three) that move at different speeds and point to two different sets of numbers (one set of numbers is usually not there). We tell the children that the hands are moving, but when they look at the clock, both hands appear to be standing still. We never let the children see us figure out the time. When adults read clocks, it seems as if they are able to just look and know the time. A typical reaction from the child is "Wow! How did she do that?" Children often think that they are supposed to memorize all the different positions of the hands and the times that go with those positions.

To teach children to read clocks meaningfully, accurately, and quickly, teachers need to do two things. First, the clock-reading process must be simplified, so that the child learns to do one thing at a time. Second, the teacher must always model the clock-reading *process* and not just give the time.

The easiest way to simplify the clock-reading process is to *teach one hand at a time* (Thompson & Van de Walle, 1981; Thornton, Tucker, Dossey, & Bazik, 1983). First, obtain two inexpensive clocks that are identical and have large, easily read numbers. The numbers for the minutes should be indicated on the clock. The hours should be on the inside circle and the minutes should be on the outside circle. Then carefully remove the minute hand from one clock, and remove the hour hand from the other clock.

First, Teach the Hour Hand.   Explain that the hour hand is like a spinner that is moving very slowly, so slowly that we cannot see it move. Explain that the number that the hour hand points to is the hour. Sometimes it points right at a number, and that is the hour. Sometimes it does not point directly to a number. It might be a little bit before an hour or a little bit after an hour. Show the hour hand in several different positions. Have the children read the hour that is shown.

When they are comfortable reading the hour from the clock, explain to the children that when the hour hand points between two numbers, we are usually interested in what hour it is after. Show the hour hand in several different positions and have the children tell what hour it is when the hand points directly to a number and what hour it is after when the hand does not point directly to a number.

Second, Teach the Minute Hand.   The minute hand is more difficult because the numbers are often missing or partly missing. Create a large spinner with the numbers from 0 to 59. Spin the pointer several times and have the children read the "minutes."

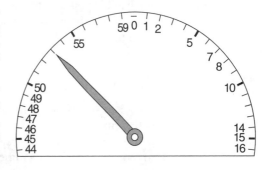

Then remove the numbers 3, 4, 6, 9, 11, 12, 13, 18, 22, 23, 24, 26, 37, 38, 39, 41, 42, 51, 52, 53, 54, 56, 57, and 58, but leave the marks showing where the numbers were.

Spin the pointer and have the children read the "minutes." When the pointer points to a missing number, have the children figure out what the minute is by counting forward or backward from a number that is given. When the children become comfortable with figuring out the missing numbers, remove all the numbers but multiples of 5. Next, remove all the numbers except 0, 15, 30, and 45, and have the children practice figuring out the minutes.

Then use the clock with the minute hands. Set the hand in different positions and have the children figure out the minutes. Emphasize that if the hand is pointing to a number that is not indicated, start with a number that is indicated and figure it out from there.

Use both clocks to find the time. Explain that we use the hour clock to see "what hour it is after" and use the minute hand to see "how many minutes after the hour." Demonstrate how to write the time:

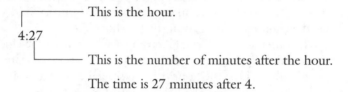

The time is 27 minutes after 4.

Finally, after the children are able to use the two clocks to find the time, show them a clock with both the hour hand and the minute hand on the same face. Lead them through the process of reading the time from this clock. First, read the hour. Then, read the minutes.

Whenever reading the time from a clock, the teacher should model this same process. First, see what hour the hour hand is pointing to. Then, see what minute the minute hand is pointing to. If the minute hand is not pointing at a number that you know, go through the process of starting with a minute that you are sure of and figure it out from there. Model the process that the children must use. Have the children help.

Measuring Weight

Weight is not typically measured with direct units. Rather, we usually measure weight with a spring scale. The object being weighed is placed on the scale. Gravity pulls down on the object, which causes the spring to stretch. The stretching spring causes a pointer to move along a number line (which is often curved around a circle). We read the number to get the weight in pounds, ounces, kilograms, grams, or some other measurement.

Students need to weigh many things to gain a "sense of heaviness." They need to estimate weights of objects and then weigh those objects to check their estimates. They should experience weight measurement in many situations to learn when and how weight is used.

Note that the mass of an object can be measured with direct units of mass and a balance scale. When the mass of an object is being measured, the object is placed on one side of the scale. Weights are placed on the other side of the scale until the object is balanced. By adding up the weights, we can find the mass of the object.

Measuring Temperature

Temperature is also measured with indirect units. A thermometer consists of a tube of mercury or another substance that reacts to heat and cold by expanding and contracting. As it expands and contracts, the top surface of the mercury reaches higher or falls lower. The numbers beside the tube of mercury indicate how hot or how cold it is.

Students need to measure the temperature of many things to gain a "sense of heat." They need to estimate temperatures and then use thermometers to check their estimates. They should experience temperature measurement in many situations to learn when and how measurement of temperature is used.

Measuring Value

The value of things is also measured with indirect units. When we use money to determine what something is worth, we are measuring the value of that thing. The same 20 pieces of paper ($20) can be traded for bread, for meat, for a taxi ride, for a haircut, or for any number of things. We can buy things with money because we agree with others to let money represent the value of those things.

The concept that money has certain value because we have agreed to let it have that value must be developed. Without an acceptance of this agreement about the value of money, many things do not make sense to a child. Why are five pennies worth the same amount as one nickel? Only because we have agreed that they should be. Why is a nickel worth less than a dime even though it is much bigger than the dime? Only because we have agreed that it is. Why is one dollar bill worth more than three nice shiny quarters? Only because we have agreed that it should be.

Help the child to accept this agreement about the value of coins. Then the value of coins and of different denominations of paper money, and the use of money as a measurement of the value of things, are easy concepts for the child to grasp.

When teaching students the value of individual coins, teach each coin separately, emphasizing the way the coin looks and the way it feels. Using real money is a good way to ensure that students have an accurate knowledge of the coins. As each coin is identified, state how much the coin is worth. When students can identify the coin and understand its worth, give students the opportunity to count several of the same coins. After students have mastered counting the same coins, have students count different coins using coins that they have already learned. Remember, when counting a group of coins, always start with the coin of the greatest value and then continue with the coin of the next largest value until all coins have been counted.

Because coins are small, round, and roll easily, some teachers package each student's coins using small clear sealable plastic bags. A permanent marker can be used to draw a large circle on the bag indentifying a space for students to use when moving the coin(s) requested during the learning activity. Using this approach to organize the coins makes their distribution easy and offers a more secure process for receiving the same amount when coins are returned.

Adapting a Lesson on Volume

The following lesson plan is similar to one that might be taken from the third-grade teachers' book of a published elementary school mathematics textbook series.

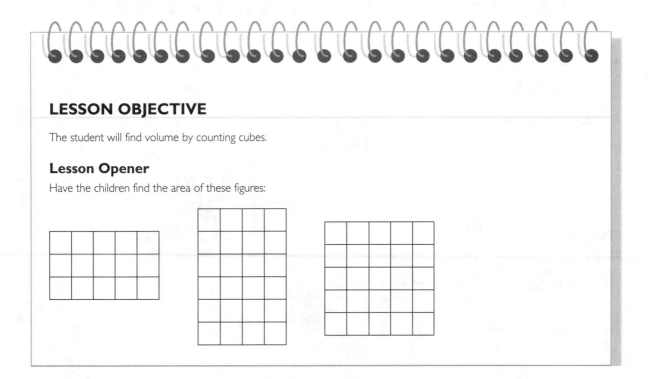

LESSON OBJECTIVE

The student will find volume by counting cubes.

Lesson Opener

Have the children find the area of these figures:

Development

Direct the attention of the children to the picture on the first page of the lesson in the student book. Point out that the child in the picture is filling the box with cubes. Explain that the number of cubic units something holds is called its *volume*. Ask how many cubes the box in the picture will hold. [8] Ask what the volume of the box is. [8 cubic units]

Monitoring Learning

Direct the attention of the class to the second example on the page. Have everyone find the number of cubes needed to fill the box. Ask how many cubes are needed. [9] Ask what the volume of the box is. [9 cubic units] Observe to identify children who do not understand.

Practice

Have children who had difficulties with the teaching examples complete the *Extra Practice Worksheet*. Have the rest of the children complete exercises 1 to 20.

Closure

At the end of the lesson, remind the children that the volume of a figure is the number of cubes needed to fill the figure.

This lesson focuses on completion of the textbook pages. There is very little development—only two examples. The nature of the lesson requires the children to be still, listen to the teacher, and do "seatwork." There is little active involvement in learning.

We adapt the lesson by increasing the amount of developmental work and reducing the amount of practice. We increase the visual input in the lesson and include a substantial amount of kinesthetic learning activity. We have the children communicate about the lesson, and we monitor learning throughout every part of the lesson.

LESSON OBJECTIVE

The student will find volume by counting cubes.

Lesson Opener

Prepare pairs of cards like these:

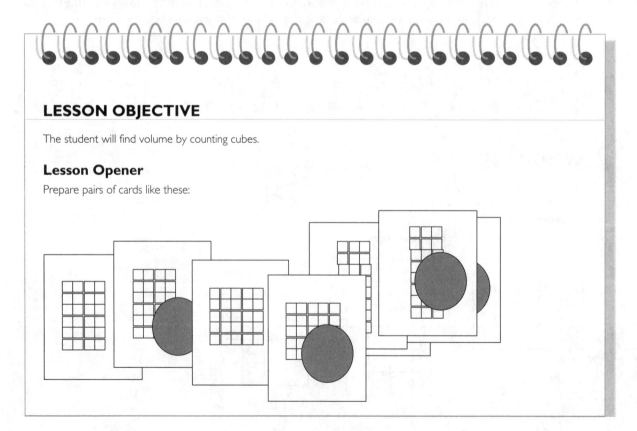

Shuffle the cards and give one to each child. Point out that some of the rectangles have part of the squares hidden. Have the children find partners whose rectangles are the same as theirs. One partner will have a rectangle with some squares hidden. The other partner will have an identical rectangle with no squares hidden.

Monitor understanding. Pay particular attention to children who might have difficulty with this activity. Provide assistance as needed.

When everyone has found a partner, have the partners figure out how many squares are in their rectangles. Ask them how they could have figured out how many squares if they had only the rectangle with some squares hidden. Choose one of the cards that has some of the squares hidden. With the class telling you how to do it, figure out how many squares are in the rectangle. Emphasize that every row of squares has the same number. They can multiply the number of squares in one row times the number of rows.

Development

Have the partners from the previous activity stay together. Give each pair of partners a small box and some centimeter-cubes. Tell them to fill the boxes completely full of cubes and figure out how many cubes their boxes will hold.

Monitor understanding. Observe to be sure that all the partners are stacking the cubes into the boxes so that there are no spaces between the cubes.

When everyone is finished, ask two or three students how many cubes fit in their boxes. Explain that the amount that a box can hold is called the *volume* of the box. The centimeter-cubes are the units used to measure volume. Choose one of the boxes. Ask how many cubes fit in that box. Write the volume of the box on the board. [For example, the volume might be 12 cubic centimeters.] Have each pair of partners write the volume of their box.

Monitor understanding. Observe to be sure that all the students are writing the volume correctly. If any students are having difficulty, provide assistance as needed.

Ask which box has the greatest volume. Which has the least? Choose four boxes. Have the class help you line them up in order from least to greatest volume.

Monitor understanding. Observe to be sure that all the students correctly understand volume.

Direct the attention of the children to the picture on the first page of the lesson in the student book. Point out that the child in the picture is filling the box with cubes. Remind the class that the child in the picture is doing exactly what they were doing, except that the cubes are bigger. Ask how many cubes the box in the picture will hold. [8] Ask what the volume of the box is. [8 cubic units] Write the volume on the board.

Direct the attention of the class to the second example on the page. Have everyone find the number of cubes needed to fill the box. Ask how many cubes are needed. [9] Have all the students write down the volume of the box. [9 cubic units]

Monitor understanding. Check what the students have written to be sure they understand how to write the volume.

Practice

Have the students work with their partners to complete exercises 1 to 5 in the student book. Tell them to do one exercise at a time. Each student is to find the answer, then check with his or her partner to see if they agree. If their answers are not the same, they should do the exercise together.

Monitor understanding. Move around the room, observing the students' work. Identify students who are having difficulty and provide assistance where needed.

Closure

After everyone is finished, ask the students what they learned today. Ask how to find the number of cubes that a box will hold. Ask what *volume* is.

Follow-Up

Tell the students that they are to take their books home and explain to their parents what volume is. Then they are to show their parents how to find the volume in exercise 6 on the practice page.

Using Measurement to Solve Problems

Remember that measurement is simply a process by which people assign a number to a quantity. When measurement is used in problem solving, computation is usually performed on those numbers (measurements). When teaching problem solving using measurements, the teacher should apply the same basic principles used when he or she is teaching problem solving using other kinds of numbers (see Chapters 6, 7, and 8). The teacher should emphasize that the choice of operation depends on what is happening to the quantities in the problem. If quantities are being combined, then addition of the measurements can probably be used. If the measurements in the problem are being separated, then subtraction can probably be used.

The second step of Polya's (1957) 4-Step Problem-Solving Process involves choosing a problem-solving strategy. At the elementary level, strategies like the following might be used:

Solve part of the problem.

Separate the problem into easier parts.

Work backward.

Use a picture or diagram.

Use a table.

Solve a simpler problem.

Try and check.

List the possibilities.

Exercises and Activities

1. Develop a learning activity that develops the concept of *area* by having the students make gross comparisons of the areas of different shapes.
2. Develop a learning activity that develops the concept of a *unit of area* as a piece of area. Use units of area that are not squares.
3. Develop a learning activity that develops the concept of *measurement of area* as the number of units it takes to cover the area being measured. Use square units.
4. Develop a learning activity that develops the *ability to estimate areas* by using some standard unit. For example, you might use square centimeters or square inches.
5. Write a sequence of developmental activities that can be used to teach the *area formula for rectangles*.
6. Choose a lesson on measurement from a published elementary school mathematics textbook series.
   a. Write a lesson plan that follows the teaching suggestions in the teacher's guide.
   b. Identify parts of the lesson that provide visual imagery for the concept(s) or skill(s) taught in the lesson.
   c. Add more activities to the lesson that will develop visual imagery for the concept(s) or skill(s) taught in the lesson.
   d. Identify the parts of the lesson that develop the concept(s) or skill(s) taught in the lesson.
   e. Add more developmental activity to the lesson plan.
7. Read "Standard 10: Measurement" on pages 51–53 of *Curriculum and Evaluation Standards for School Mathematics*, published in 1989 by the NCTM. In what ways are the suggestions for teaching problem solving presented in this text consistent with or inconsistent with those presented in the Standards?
8. Read the discussions related to "The Measurement Standard" on pages 44–47, 102–106, 170–175, and 240–247 of *Principles and Standards for School Mathematics*,

published in 2000 by the NCTM. In what ways are the suggestions for teaching measurement presented in this text consistent with or inconsistent with those presented in *Principles and Standards*?

9. The following subtraction results illustrate an error pattern like the error patterns related by Robert Ashlock in his 2002 book, *Error Patterns in Computation: Using Error Patterns to Improve Instruction*:

$$
\begin{array}{ll}
\overset{7}{8}\text{ yards, } {}^{1}1 \text{ foot} & \overset{8}{9}\text{ meters, } {}^{1}4 \text{ decimeters} \\
-5 \text{ yards, } 2 \text{ feet} & -4 \text{ meters, } 8 \text{ decimeters} \\
\hline
2 \text{ yards, } 9 \text{ feet} & 4 \text{ meters, } 6 \text{ decimeters}
\end{array}
$$

$$
\begin{array}{ll}
\overset{5}{6}\text{ feet, } {}^{1}7 \text{ inches} & \overset{5}{6}\text{ gallons, } {}^{1}2 \text{ quarts} \\
-2 \text{ feet, } 9 \text{ inches} & -2 \text{ gallons, } 3 \text{ quarts} \\
\hline
3 \text{ feet, } 8 \text{ inches} & 3 \text{ gallons, } 9 \text{ quarts}
\end{array}
$$

a. What is this student's error pattern? What is the student doing to produce the incorrect answers?

b. Plan a mini-lesson to correct this student's error pattern.

10. Choose a lesson on measurement from a published elementary school mathematics textbook and identify the objective(s) that the students are to learn during the lesson.

a. Write an objective test item that can be used to determine whether the students have learned the lesson objective(s).

b. Design a small-group activity that you could observe to determine which children have learned the lesson objective(s) and which students have not.

References and Related Readings

Ashlock, R. B. (2002). *Error patterns in computation: Using error patterns to improve instruction* (8th ed.). Upper Saddle River, NJ: Prentice Hall.

National Council of Teachers of Mathematics. (1989). *Curriculum and evaluation standards for school mathematics.* Reston, VA: Author.

National Council of Teachers of Mathematics. (2000). *Principles and standards for school mathematics.* Reston, VA: Author.

Polya, G. (1957). *How to solve it: A new aspect of mathematical method* (2nd ed.). Princeton, NJ: Princeton University Press.

Thompson, C. S., & Van de Walle, J. A. (1981). A single-handed approach to telling time. *Arithmetic Teacher, 28*(8), 4–9.

Thornton, C. A., Tucker, B. F., Dossey, J. A., & Bazik, E. F. (1983). *Teaching mathematics to children with special needs.* Menlo Park, CA: Addison-Wesley.

Van de Walle, J. A. (2004). *Elementary and middle school mathematics: Teaching developmentally* (5th ed.). Boston: Allyn & Bacon.

Wilson, P. S., & Adams, V. M. (1992). A dynamic way to teach angle and angle measure. *Arithmetic Teacher, 39*, 6–13.

Websites

http://www.corestandards.org/the-standards/mathematics
The Common Core State Standards for Mathematics can be found at this site.

www.iit.edu/
Measurement activities can be located on this site.

www.proteacher.com/
Activities and lesson plans on measurement can be located on this site.

ten

GEOMETRY

Learning the Names and Characteristics of Shapes

CHAPTER OUTLINE

For purposes of our discussion in this chapter, we consider *geometry* to be the naming of shapes and the study of their characteristics. This view of geometry is fairly limited. It departs somewhat from the more mathematical approach, which might be a study of points in space, or perhaps a logical development of a system of theorems from a beginning set of assumptions. However, the naming of shapes and the study of their characteristics is, more or less, what is done in elementary school geometry. As noted at the beginning of Chapter 9, geometry is closely related to measurement. The study of characteristics of geometric shapes frequently calls for the application of skills that were developed in measurement lessons.

The Big Ideas of Elementary School Geometry

The ability to identify and name shapes depends almost entirely on having a working understanding of some combination of geometric relationships (Clements & Sarama, 2000). When studying a geometric shape, we find that each of these relationships either exists or does not exist in that shape. Therefore, these relationships can be thought of as the big ideas of elementary school geometry: straightness, congruence, similarity, parallelism, perpendicularity, and symmetry (Lerch, 1981; Thornton, Tucker, Dossey, & Bazik, 1983). If we teach children to look for these big ideas, it is easier for them to classify, name, and use geometric shapes.

Straightness

The first big idea is the notion of *straightness*. It is important to know whether lines or line segments, or edges, or surfaces are straight when we are studying geometric shapes. For example, one of the following shapes is not a triangle. Why not? Figure C is not a triangle because all the sides of a triangle must be straight:

Knowing whether an object is straight is important, and children need simple methods for testing straightness. One simple way to check is to pick up the shape and look along the edge to see if the edge is straight. Another way to test straightness is to use a straightedge. Rather than using a ruler, children can be taught to fold a sheet of paper and use the folded edge as a straightedge. Chapter 3 includes a more complete discussion of straightness, along with examples of activities that can be used to develop this concept.

The notion of straightness has a three-dimensional extension—*flatness*. A surface is flat if and only if it is "straight in all directions." The simplest way to test a surface to see if it is flat is to lay a straightedge on the surface in a lot of directions. If the straightedge always coincides with the surface, then the surface is flat:

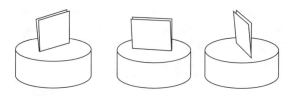

Congruence

The second of the big ideas of elementary school geometry is *congruence*. Two geometric figures are congruent if and only if they are exactly the same size and shape. In elementary school geometry, we study congruence of simple figures such as line segments and angles. We also consider congruence of more-complex figures such as triangles and prisms. When we are classifying geometric figures, congruence is always important. For example, why is one of the following figures not a rectangle? Figure K is not a rectangle because the opposite sides of rectangles are always congruent:

Consider the following two figures. Figure M is a prism, but figure P is not. How can you tell? The two bases of a prism are always congruent:

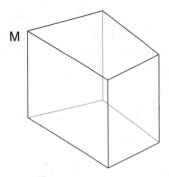
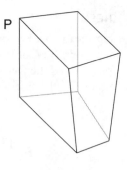

One of the following figures is a circle and one is not. How can you tell? Figure Y is not a circle. Every line segment from the center to the circle (all the radii) must be congruent:

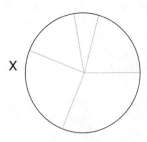
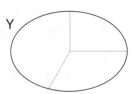

The easiest method for testing two plane figures for congruence arises from the fact that congruence is a transitive relation. Children can easily use the following procedure: The child traces one figure and then moves the tracing onto the second figure. If the tracing is an exact match for the second figure, then the two original figures are congruent. Children can understand that the two figures are congruent because they are both congruent to the tracing.

Similarity

The third of the big ideas for elementary school geometry is the notion of *similarity*. Two figures are similar if they are the same shape. Whenever two figures are the same shape, two important relationships are present: First, every angle of one shape is congruent to the corresponding angle of the second shape. Second, the lengths of one figure are proportional to the corresponding lengths of the second figure. Another description of proportionality is that the ratio of a length in the first figure to the corresponding length in the second figure is always the same. However, young children can grasp the notion of "same shape" without understanding the precise definition of similarity. For example, in the figures below, the two squares are the same shape, the two circles are the same shape, and the two equilateral triangles are the same shape.

Parallelism

The fourth big idea of elementary school geometry is *parallelism*. If two lines are parallel, we know that the lines do not intersect, no matter how far they are extended. We also know that the lines go in the same direction. The two lines also are the same distance apart, no matter where we measure the distance. The third of these characteristics of parallel lines offers a way to test for parallelism. Consider lines *j* and *k* in the following illustration. If we place a sheet of paper with its edge on line *j*, we can use a pencil to mark the distance between the two lines. By sliding the paper along the line, we can check to see if the distance is the same everywhere:

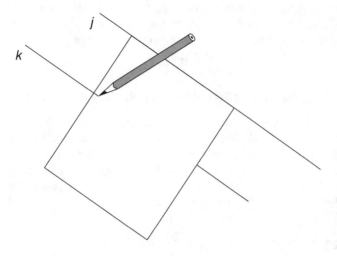

Whether lines are parallel can be used to identify and classify many figures. For example, one pair of opposite sides of a trapezoid is always parallel, but the other pair of opposite sides is not. On the other hand, both pairs of opposite sides of a parallelogram are parallel.

Perpendicularity

The fifth big idea of elementary school geometry is *perpendicularity* (square corners). Children are able to look for square corners to help them recognize certain shapes. For example, a square has four square corners, and every vertical edge of a right prism is perpendicular to the bases. For children, the simplest test of perpendicularity is to create a square corner by folding a sheet of paper and then laying that square corner on top of other corners that are being checked:

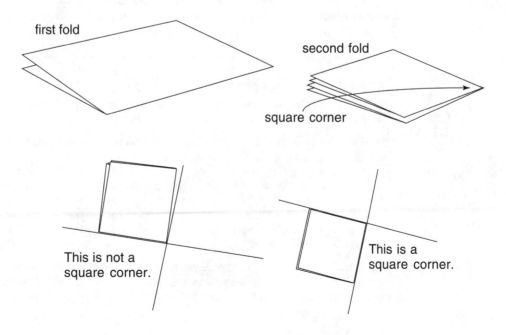

Symmetry

The sixth big idea of elementary school geometry is the notion of *symmetry*. There are actually several kinds of symmetry (line symmetry, slide symmetry, and rotational symmetry), but in elementary school geometry, we are primarily concerned with line symmetry. Therefore, we limit the discussion here to line symmetry.

A great number of shapes studied by elementary children are symmetric. Many important characteristics of those shapes arise from that symmetry. Children need to be able to check figures to determine if they are symmetric. The simplest test for line symmetry and the easiest for children to use is to fold the figure along the line of symmetry to see if the two halves are an exact match.

Using the Big Ideas to Study Geometric Shapes

We now trace the development of four geometric shapes as they might be developed in grades K–4 within an elementary textbook series. The four shapes that we examine are rectangles, circles, angles, and prisms. As we look at the development of these four shapes, take note of how the six big ideas identified earlier are used, either informally or formally, to characterize or classify the shapes. Keep in mind, also, that other geometric shapes are being developed at the same time.

Rectangles in Elementary School

Rectangles in Kindergarten.
Typically, children are first exposed to rectangles in kindergarten. They learn that rectangles have four sides that are *straight*. They are asked to identify examples of rectangles and recognize that other shapes are not rectangles (that they are nonexamples). Usually, the variety of shapes from which they must choose include circles, triangles, squares, and rectangles. They are asked to explain informally why examples are rectangles and why nonexamples are not rectangles.

Often, during the treatment of rectangles in kindergarten, a serious misconception develops that must be corrected later (Fuys & Lebov, 1997). The children are often taught that squares and rectangles are different shapes, when, in fact, a square is a special kind of rectangle in which all the sides are the same length (they are *congruent*). Certainly, it is true that rectangles are not necessarily squares. However, it is absolutely false to say that a square is not a rectangle.

The following sequence of activities illustrates how a kindergarten teacher could develop the concept of rectangles. Notice how the examples and nonexamples are limited so that the child can focus on one necessary attribute of rectangles at a time.

Activity 10.01   Straight Lines

For this activity, it may be necessary to place some things around the room that have straight lines and some other things that have lines that are not quite straight.

Show the class an oddly shaped piece of paper. Fold the paper and point out to the children that the folded edge is straight. Explain that this paper can be used to check if lines are straight. Show two lines, one straight and the other slightly curved, on the overhead projector. Use the folded paper to check each line for straightness. Use the folded paper to show something in the room that has a straight line. Then find something that has a line that is not quite straight. Use the folded paper to show that it is not straight. Ask the class to identify another straight line somewhere in the room. Have a child use the folded paper to check the line for straightness. Repeat with other lines around the room.

Form groups of two or three children. Give each group an oddly shaped piece of paper. Have the groups fold the paper to make a straightedge. Have them use their folded papers to find some straight lines and some lines that are not straight.

Activity 10.02 Straight Sides

Cut out several large shapes from construction paper. Some of the shapes should have only straight sides and some should have at least one side that is not quite straight. Place these shapes on the walls around the room where they will be within the children's reach.

Show the class two shapes on the overhead projector. One of the shapes should have all straight sides and the other should have one side that is slightly curved. Use a folded paper to show that one shape has all straight sides while the other one does not. Point out the construction-paper shapes. Use the folded paper to check all the sides of one shape to see if they are straight.

Form groups of two or three children. Have each group of students use their folded paper to identify a shape that has all straight sides and another shape that has a side that is not straight.

Activity 10.03 Rectangles Have Straight Sides

Cut out several large shapes from construction paper like the ones pictured:

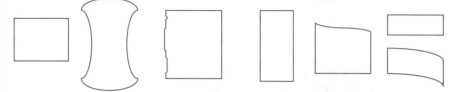

Explain that some of the shapes are rectangles and some are not. Show the class the first two examples. Tell the children which one is a rectangle and which is not. Repeat this process with another rectangle and nonrectangle. Continue until you have identified every rectangle and every nonrectangle.

Ask the class what the difference is between the shapes that are rectangles and the shapes that are not rectangles. [Rectangles have all straight sides.]

Show another shape that is not a rectangle. Ask if it is a rectangle. [No.] Ask why it is not a rectangle. [All its sides are not straight.]

Activity 10.04 Rectangles Have Four Sides

Cut out several large shapes from construction paper like the ones pictured:

Show several of the shapes to the class. Explain that some of the shapes are rectangles and some are not. Pick out a rectangle and tell the class that this one is a rectangle. Then choose one that is not a rectangle and tell the class that it is not a rectangle. Repeat this process with another rectangle and nonrectangle. Continue until you have identified every rectangle and every nonrectangle.

Ask the class what the difference is between the shapes that are rectangles and the shapes that are not rectangles. [Rectangles have four sides.]

Show another shape that is not a rectangle. Ask if it is a rectangle. [No.] Ask why it is not a rectangle. [It doesn't have four sides.]

Activity 10.05 Rectangle Search

Point to the door and say, "Look! The door is a rectangle!" Ask the class to look around the room and find other things that are shaped like rectangles.

Activity 10.06 Shape Sort

After the children have been introduced to circles and triangles, prepare cutouts of different-sized circles, different-shaped rectangles, and different-shaped triangles. Tape a rectangle to the front of one box, a circle to the front of the second box, and a triangle to the front of the third box. Place the shapes in a pile on the table in front of the three boxes.

Have the children take turns coming to the front and placing the top shape in the pile into the correct box. When all the shapes have been sorted, ask the children how they can decide if a shape is a rectangle, or a circle, or a triangle.

Rectangles in First Grade.   Children also identify rectangles in grade 1. However, a broader range of nonexamples can be used. That is, the shapes that are not examples of rectangles should be more varied.

This shape is not a rectangle because rectangles must have *four sides*.

This shape is not a rectangle because rectangles must have *straight sides*.

This shape is not a rectangle because rectangles must have *square corners* (adjacent sides must be *perpendicular*).

Consideration of these nonexamples, as shown in the following sequence of instructional activities, allows children to focus on the essential characteristics of rectangles and begins to formalize their understanding.

Activity 10.07 Finding Square Corners

Show the children an oddly shaped piece of paper and how to fold it twice to make a square corner. Explain that they can use the folded paper to check to see if a corner is a square corner. Place the folded paper on the corner of the board to show that it is a square corner. Use the folded paper to show that a window has a square corner.

Show a figure like the one pictured at the right on the overhead projector. Use the folded paper to show that it has two square corners and two corners that are not square.

Show the class several shapes with straight sides. Some corners should be square corners and some should not be square corners. Have children come to the front and use the folded paper to check the corners to see if they are square.

Activity 10.08 Rectangles Have Square Corners

Using construction paper, cut out several large shapes with four sides like the ones pictured:

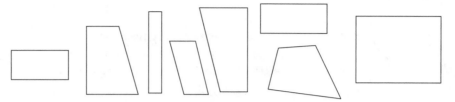

Show some of the shapes to the class. Explain that some of the shapes are rectangles and some are not. Pick out a rectangle and tell the class that this is a rectangle. Then choose one that is not a rectangle and tell the class that it is not a rectangle. Repeat this process with another rectangle and nonrectangle. Continue until you have identified every rectangle and every nonrectangle.

Ask the class what the difference is between the shapes that are rectangles and the shapes that are not rectangles. [Rectangles have square corners.]

Show another shape that is not a rectangle. Ask if it is a rectangle. [No.] Ask why it is not a rectangle. [It does not have square corners.]

Activity 10.09 Rectangles: Why or Why Not?

Cut out several large shapes from construction paper. Some of the shapes should be rectangles, some should have more than or fewer than four sides, some should have at least one side that is not straight, and some should have corners that are not square. Place these shapes on the walls around the room where they will be within the children's reach.

Point out one of the shapes to the children. Ask if it is a rectangle. If it is a rectangle, ask why it is. [It has four straight sides and square corners.] If it is not a rectangle, ask why it is not. [The children should identify the required attribute that the shape does not have.]

Form groups of two or three children. Have each group choose one of the shapes and stand by it. Have each group tell why its shape is a rectangle or why its shape is not a rectangle.

Activity 10.10 Rubber Rectangles

Pair the children with partners. Give each pair a nail board.

Stretch a rubber band on a nail board to form a parallelogram that does not have square corners. Show it to the children. Ask if it is a rectangle. Ask why not. [Rectangles must have square corners.] Have a child come to the front and change the shape to make it a rectangle.

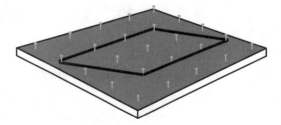

Have every pair of children make a shape on their nail board that is not a rectangle. Ask each pair to explain why their shape is not a rectangle.

Then have them form a shape that is a rectangle.

Rectangles in Second Grade.   In second grade, children review that rectangles have four sides, and they recognize that rectangles have four corners (an informal reference to the angles). They also learn that rectangles always have two lines of symmetry.

Square rectangles (squares) have four lines of symmetry. Children are also asked to recognize the faces of some three-dimensional objects as rectangles.

The instructional activity that follows illustrates how a teacher could build understanding of the symmetry that exists in rectangles.

Activity 10.11 Rectangles Are Symmetric

Using waxed paper, cut out four rectangles: two different-sized rectangles, one parallelogram, and one isosceles trapezoid (a trapezoid with base angles that are equal).

Show the shapes to the students. Ask which of the shapes are rectangles and which are not rectangles. Ask how they know. [Rectangles have four straight sides and square corners.] Take one of the rectangles and fold it in half vertically. Run your thumbnail down the fold so that the crease can be seen.

Show the students how the two sides of the rectangle are a perfect match. Open the rectangle and show them the crease. Explain that when you can fold a shape so that the two sides are a perfect match, we say that the shape is *symmetric*, and the fold line is called the *line of symmetry*.

Explain that the rectangle has a second line of symmetry by folding the rectangle along a horizontal fold. Show the class that the top half folds down onto the bottom half so that the two halves are a perfect match. Fold the other rectangle to show that it also has two lines of symmetry.

Hold up the parallelogram and ask the children if they think it is symmetric. Demonstrate that the parallelogram cannot be folded so that the two halves match. Hold up the trapezoid and ask the children if they think it is symmetric. Demonstrate that this shape can be folded along a vertical line so that the two halves match. It is symmetric. The fold line is the line of symmetry. Show that the trapezoid does not have another line of symmetry.

Rectangles in Third Grade.

By third grade, children can be asked to recognize rectangles in a variety of "real-life" settings—in flags, in the classroom (walls, doors, ceiling tiles, sections of the board, bulletin boards), in the sides of a box, in the pages of a book, in picture frames, in tabletops, and so on. They learn that the corners of rectangles are angles. They might also learn that the square corners are called *right angles*. (Adjacent sides are *perpendicular*.) They could also learn that rectangles are parallelograms. The opposite sides are *parallel*.

The following activities illustrate how a teacher could lead an exploration of the parallelism of the opposite sides of a rectangle.

Activity 10.12 Parallel Lines Go the Same Direction

Using an overhead projector, show the children a pair of parallel lines that go to the edge of the transparency, but do not tell them yet that the lines are parallel.

Trace the angle that one of the lines makes with the edge of the transparency. Explain that this angle shows the direction of the line across the transparency. Move the tracing of the angle down the edge of the transparency to show that the other line goes in the same direction. Explain that whenever two lines go in the same direction like this, they are parallel lines.

Using a second transparency with nonparallel lines, show that the lines do not go in the same direction. Explain that when lines do not go in the same direction, they are not parallel lines.

Have children come forward and help you check several other pairs of lines to see if they are parallel.

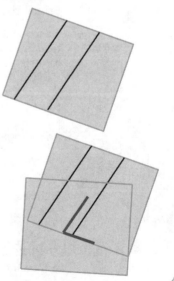

Activity 10.13   Opposite Sides Are Parallel

Using an overhead projector, show the children a parallelogram.

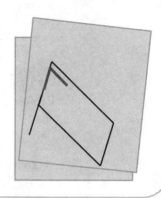

Extend one of the sides as illustrated. Trace one of the angles on the extended side onto another transparency sheet. Move the tracing of the angle down the extended side to show that the two opposite sides are parallel. Follow the same procedures to show that the opposite sides are also parallel.

With another transparency, show that the opposite sides of a second parallelogram are parallel. Explain that when both pairs of opposite sides of a four-sided shape are parallel, that shape is called a *parallelogram*.

Activity 10.14   Parallelograms or Not?

Form groups of two or three children. Give each group a sheet of paper with two shapes drawn on it. One shape should be a parallelogram. In the second shape, one pair of opposite sides should be parallel and the other pair should be almost, but not quite, parallel.

Have the groups test the opposite sides of both figures to see if they are parallelograms.

Activity 10.15   Rectangles Are Parallelograms

Tape a rectangle cut from construction paper to the chalkboard. Be sure that it has straight sides and square corners. Ask the class what they know about rectangles. [Four straight sides, square corners, two lines of symmetry]

Extend one of the horizontal sides of the rectangle as illustrated. Check these two angles to show that the two vertical sides go in the same direction. Point out that those sides are parallel.

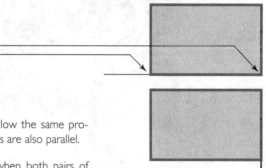

Extend one of the vertical sides and follow the same procedures to show that the horizontal sides are also parallel.

Ask what we call a four-sided shape when both pairs of opposite sides are parallel. [A parallelogram]

Repeat this process with two other rectangles to show that they are also parallelograms. Emphasize that the opposite sides of rectangles are always parallel, so rectangles are a special kind of parallelogram. *Rectangles are parallelograms with right angles.*

Circles in Elementary School

Circles in Kindergarten.   At the kindergarten level, children are introduced to circles informally. They identify shapes that are the same as circles (shapes that match). These shapes are *similar*. They identify shapes that are not the same as circles (for example, the shape that does not belong). They might identify the biggest circle, the smallest circle, and the circle that is the same size.

Kindergartners typically learn the name for circles. They learn to recognize circles in everyday objects like bicycle wheels, the shape of a clock, jar lids, and coins. They make and talk about patterns that use circles and other shapes. They use informal ways of describing circles, such as: circles are round, circles are smooth, circles are curved (there is no *straight* side), and circles are the same size in all directions (all diameters are *congruent*).

The following activities illustrate how a kindergarten teacher can develop the children's informal understanding of circles.

Activity 10.16   Same Shape or Not?

Cut out two copies of a triangle, a square, and a nonstandard shape like the one pictured. Also, cut out four copies of a circle.

Place three of the circles in a paper bag with a copy of two other shapes. Show the children the fourth circle and tell them that you want them to help you choose the shapes that are the same. Remove the shapes from the bag, one at a time. As each shape is removed from the bag, have the children decide if it is the same as the shape that you started with. If the children say that a shape is not the same, ask them why it is not.

Repeat the activity using a different combination of shapes. Be sure to include at least two circles in the bag. Repeat the activity, but this time ask them to choose shapes that are the same as one of the noncircle shapes. Include the second copy of the noncircle shape in the bag so there will be one match.

Activity 10.17   Which Doesn't Belong?

Cut out three circles of different sizes, each less than 2 inches across. Also cut out a square, a triangle, an oval, and an irregular shape, each less than 2 inches across.

Arrange the three circles and one of the other shapes on the overhead projector. Ask the children which shape does not belong. Whether or not you get the expected answer, ask why that one does not belong.

Repeat the activity using the three circles and a different noncircle shape.

Activity 10.18   All about Circles

Display several circles in front of the class. Explain that shapes like these are called *circles*. Ask the children to tell about the circles in their own words. Accept all descriptions that they offer. However, if a description is obviously not correct, ask the child to explain why he or she thinks the circles are like that. Ask what the other children think.

Activity 10.19   Circles, Circles, Everywhere

If necessary, place a variety of circular objects in sight around the room. Examples of objects that you might have in the room are a Hula Hoop, a Frisbee, a bicycle (for its wheels), a round-faced clock, a paper plate, a wastebasket (for its top and bottom), an oatmeal box, a drinking glass, a round picture frame, a pencil sharpener (circular holes for the pencils), a computer CD, or assorted circles cut from colored paper.

Point out one of those objects—for example, a clock with a circular face. Ask the children to tell you the shape of the clock. Do the same with a second round object. Then have them look around and identify other objects that have the shape of a circle.

Circles in the First and Second Grades.   During the first-grade and second-grade years, children continue to learn about circles informally. They choose circles from among other shapes like rectangles, squares, and triangles (from shapes that are *not similar*). They continue to use informal language to describe circles and to explain why other shapes are not circles. The following activity illustrates how a teacher can continue the development of the children's understanding of circles.

Activity 10.20   Circles: Why or Why Not?

Point out a circle. Ask the children what the shape is. Then ask how they can tell. Get a variety of responses and discuss them. Let the children decide what makes a circle a circle. Point out another shape. If it is a circle, ask again how they can tell. If it is not a circle, ask how they can tell it is not a circle. Continue this process, including several examples and several nonexamples.

Circles in the Third and Fourth Grades.   During the third and fourth grades, children will typically identify circles in three-dimensional shapes such as cylinders, cones, and spheres. They also learn that circles are *symmetric*. The activity that follows illustrates how the symmetry of circles can be taught.

Activity 10.21   The Halves Match

Cut several symmetric shapes (including at least one circle) in half along their lines of symmetry. Show the two halves of one shape to the children. Explain that they are the two halves of a shape. Put them together so the children can see what the whole shape looks like.

Pass out the shape halves to the children. Have them each find a partner so that together they have both halves of the shape. Have each pair of partners hold their shape halves together to show what the whole shape looks like.

Explain that shapes like these, in which the two halves are a perfect match, are called *symmetric shapes*. Write the word *symmetric* on the board.

Show other shapes, including circles, and have the children decide if they are symmetric shapes. Show the children how to fold the shapes to see if they are symmetric.

Angles in Elementary School

Angles in Kindergarten through Second Grade.   In the early primary grades, angles are encountered and used for the classification of shapes. However, in these grades the treatment of angles is informal. They are usually called *corners* by the children and by the teachers. The children recognize that some shapes have corners and some do not. They recognize that shapes with *straight* sides have corners and that shapes without straight sides do not have corners.

The children recognize that squares and other rectangles have four corners, and triangles have three. They notice that some corners are more "pointed" than other corners. This information (the number of corners and the "sharpness" of the corners) helps them to classify shapes.

The following activities illustrate how K–2 teachers can help children develop an informal understanding of angles.

Activity 10.22   Corners or Not?

Display several different shapes like the ones pictured here:

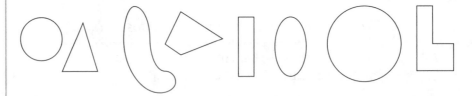

Ask the children if they see any shapes with corners. Ask if they see any shapes that do not have any corners. Have them help you sort the shapes into those with corners and those without corners.

Activity 10.23   I Have a Shape …

Cut out several circles, squares, and triangles. Place a cardboard box on its side on the teacher's desk with the open side facing away from the children. Mix up the cutout shapes and place them inside the box where you can see them but the children cannot.

Look at one of the shapes (for example, a triangle) and say, "I have a shape that has three corners. What is it?" After the children decide what they think the shape is, hold it up so they can see it.

Repeat this procedure until you have used each shape in the box.

Activity 10.24 Corners and Sharper Corners

Cut out several shapes like these:

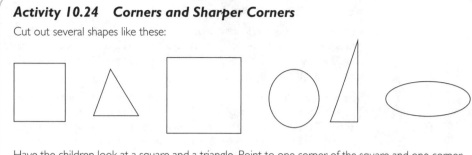

Have the children look at a square and a triangle. Point to one corner of the square and one corner of the triangle. Ask which corner is the "sharpest."

Ask if all the shapes have corners. Have someone identify a shape without a corner. Have someone else identify a shape that has corners. Point to a corner of that shape. Ask if any shape has a corner that is not this sharp. If the children identify such a shape, have someone come forward and point to that corner.

Ask someone else to choose a shape that has corners. Point to a corner of that shape and ask if any shape has a corner that is sharper than that corner. If the children identify such a shape, have someone come forward and point to that corner.

Repeat the activity until all the children have been included.

Angles in the Third and Fourth Grades. In the third and fourth grades, the study of angles continues as before, except corners of shapes begin to be referred to as *angles.* Square corners are called *right angles* (they are formed by *perpendicular* lines). Angles and right angles are identified as attributes of shapes. For example, rectangles, including square rectangles, have four angles, and all four of those angles are right angles. Triangles have three angles, and all three of them might be less than right angles. Triangles might have one right angle, but the other two angles must then be less than right angles.

In these grades, we expect the children to draw angles. They should be able to compare angles and identify the one that is greater or the one that is less. They learn about perpendicular lines and become aware that the sides of a right angle are perpendicular. The children classify angles as right angles, greater than right angles, or less than right angles.

The following activities illustrate how some of these concepts might be developed.

Activity 10.25 Make It Right

Have each child fold a sheet of paper in half and then fold it again to form a square corner. Explain that the angle in a square corner is called a *right angle.*

Have the children compare their right angles with those of several other children by laying one directly on top of the other. Ask them what they found out. [They are all the same size.]

Have two children place their right angles together as pictured. Ask them what they see. [The sides of the angle make a straight line.]

Have them unfold their papers and look at the folds. How many right angles do they see? [There are four right angles.]

Have the children refold their papers to show right angles. Tell them to hold up their right angles.

Activity 10.26 Right Angle Search

Cut sheets of paper into fourths and draw angles on them. There should be 20 right angles, 8 angles that are very close to but not quite right angles, 10 angles that are obviously less than right angles, and 10 angles that are obviously more than right angles. Mix up the angles and tape them to the walls around the room.

Separate the children into four teams. Have each team find 5 angles that are right angles and find 5 angles that are not right angles. The children are to use the right angles that they made by folding a sheet of paper to decide whether or not the angles are right angles. Each team is to take its 10 angles back to its table. Every team member is to check every angle to be sure that the team has 5 right angles and 5 angles that are not right angles.

Activity 10.27 Angle Sort

Prepare one-fourth sheets of paper with angles drawn on them. Some should be right angles, some should be greater than right angles, and some less than right angles. Some of the non–right angles should be very close to right angles. Tape the angles to the front wall of the classroom. Place three boxes on the desk. Label them "Right angles," "More than right angles," and "Less than right angles."

Choose two children to come to the front of the room. One child should choose an angle and indicate which box it should go into. The second child should use his or her right angle (made from folded paper) to see if the first child was correct. When they agree, they should remove the angle from the wall and place it in the correct box.

Repeat this procedure with other pairs of children until all the angles are sorted into the correct boxes.

Prisms in Elementary School

Prisms in Kindergarten through Second Grade. The study of prisms begins in kindergarten, where informal, nonmathematical language is used to describe them. Children at this age usually identify and describe prisms as box-shaped objects. They might notice that the corners of the box are square corners (are formed by *perpendicular* edges and *perpendicular* faces). They notice that the opposite sides of the box are the same size and shape (are *congruent*). They distinguish the prism-shaped (box-shaped) objects from other everyday three-dimensional objects like balls, ice cream cones, and cans. Even though boxes actually come in a wide variety of other shapes, curriculum materials generally assume that those other box shapes do not exist, and this assumption seldom conflicts with children's personal experiences.

By first grade, we expect the children to develop more formal mathematical language for prisms. They learn that certain box shapes (those with all edges *congruent*) are called *cubes*. By the end of second grade, the children learn the name for rectangular prisms:

Boxes are PRISMS

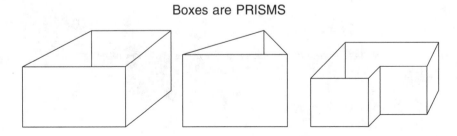

Unfortunately, the treatment of cubes and rectangular prisms often develops into the misconception that cubes are not rectangular prisms. Furthermore, from the limited variety of examples of rectangular prisms that they see in these early grades, children often think incorrectly that all rectangular prisms are right rectangular prisms, and that every face of a rectangular prism must be a rectangle.

The following activity develops the rectangular-prism concepts.

Activity 10.28   Tell Me about Boxes

Bring a variety of boxes to the classroom: big boxes, little boxes, cube-shaped boxes, boxes that are not rectangular. Place them at the front of the room where they are visible to the children.

Tell the children that you have brought some boxes for them to look at. Ask them to tell you all about the boxes that they see. Ask them how the boxes are alike and how they are different. Ask them what boxes are used for.

Select a cube-shaped box and another rectangular box and ask the children to tell you how these boxes are alike and how they are different.

Gather all the cube-shaped and rectangular-shaped boxes together. Have the children tell how all these boxes are alike.

Prisms in the Third and Fourth Grades.   In the third and fourth grades, the children learn the mathematical names for the faces and edges of cubes and other rectangular prisms, and before fifth grade, they have learned that a corner of a rectangular prism is called a *vertex*. They can also identify everyday objects that are in the shape of cubes or rectangular prisms.

In these grades, the children learn to find the volume of a rectangular prism by counting cubes, and later they compute the volume by multiplying length times width times height.

The following activity can be used by third- and fourth-grade teachers when the children are learning about rectangular prisms.

Activity 10.29   Describe These Shapes

Assign children to work with one or two partners. Have one set of partners complete the activity at a time.

Give the partners three shapes: a cube, a rectangular prism that is not a cube, and a triangular prism. Tell them to find out everything that they can about the three shapes and write down everything that they discover. Allow them to use any measurement tools that are appropriate.

After all sets of partners have completed the activity, have the children in the classroom discuss what they found out about the three shapes. Compile a list for each shape.

Adapting a Geometry Lesson

Earlier, in Chapter 2, we adapted a lesson on symmetry. We now adapt another geometry lesson, one that would likely be found in grade 1. The lesson plan uses teaching procedures typical of those suggested in current first-grade teacher's guides. The lesson is an acceptable one. However, as is all too common, there is a minimal amount of concept development before the practice.

LESSON OBJECTIVE

Children will learn to classify shapes using the attributes of circles, squares, rectangles, and triangles.

Lesson Opener

Display everyday objects in the classroom that are shaped like circles, squares, rectangles, and triangles. Draw a rectangle, a circle, a triangle, and a square on the board and ask the children to name each shape. Then ask the children to find something in the room that has the shape of a square, the shape of a triangle, the shape of a circle, and the shape of a rectangle.

Development

Direct the attention of the class to the picture at the top of the first student page. Explain that in this picture, there are a circle and a square. Point out the square and explain that a square has four square corners and four straight sides that are all the same length. Then point out the circle and explain that circles are round and do not have any straight sides.

Next, direct the class's attention to the second picture on the first student page. Tell the children that this picture has a rectangle and a triangle. Point out the rectangle and explain that rectangles have four square corners and four straight sides, but the sides do not have to be the same length. Point out the triangle and explain that all triangles have three straight sides.

Monitoring Learning

Direct the children's attention to the shapes in the *Check Understanding* part of the lesson. Tell them to color the circles red. Then tell them to color the squares green. Then tell them to color the rectangles blue. Finally, tell them to color the triangles yellow. Move around the room while the children are working, to check their understanding. Provide additional explanation to any children who need it.

Practice

Explain to the children how to identify the circles, squares, rectangles, and triangles on the practice page by coloring the shapes. Have the children complete the practice page of the lesson.

Closure

Remind the children that today they have learned to identify circles, squares, rectangles, and triangles.

We now adapt this lesson as we have adapted other lessons. We increase the amount of time spent developing the concepts and make the lesson more complete. Although, by the very nature of the concepts being developed, the lesson is essentially visual, we increase the amount of visual information. We make the lesson much more kinesthetic and plan for increased communication about the lesson concepts from and among the children. We also plan for more constant monitoring of learning throughout the lesson. These adaptations make the lesson appropriate for almost all students. But, remember that some students with severe needs may require further instructional adaptations.

LESSON OBJECTIVE

Children will learn to classify shapes using the attributes of circles, squares, rectangles, and triangles.

Lesson Opener

Cut out a variety of circles, squares, rectangles, and triangles, being sure that there are more shapes than children. Mix up the shapes and lay them in a circle on the floor with the shapes about 2 feet apart. Have the children march around the outside of the circle of shapes. Have the children stop and stand by a shape. Ask the children who are by triangles to raise their hands. Then have the children who are by squares raise their hands. Next, ask the children who are by circles to raise their hands. And, finally, have the children who are by rectangles raise their hands.

Have the children move around the circle of shapes and stop at a different shape.

Monitor understanding. Observe carefully to see if any children are confused about these shapes. Remember that it is correct if a child standing by a square identifies it as a rectangle. Use this activity as an opportunity to identify children who may need extra help during the lesson, but do not call undue attention to those who do not identify every shape correctly.

Development

Cut out several triangles, all different, from colored paper. Also cut out several rectangles, squares, and circles, all different. There needs to be enough of each shape for all sets of partners to have one during a partner activity.

Form sets of partners. Give each set of partners a triangle. Ask them what the shape is. Explain that each set of partners has a triangle that is different from all the others. Call on someone to tell the class something that is true about the triangle that he or she has. Ask if that is true about all the other triangles. For example, the child might say that his or her triangle has three corners. This is true of all triangles. Or, the child might say that his or her triangle is blue. That is *not* true of all triangles.

Monitor understanding. Pay particular attention to any children who had difficulty during the opening activity. Make a special effort to include those children in the discussion and give them confidence by praising correct responses.

Continue until the children have identified these attributes of triangles:

All triangles have   three corners.
                                     three sides.
                                     straight sides.

Next, draw the first of these shapes on the board:

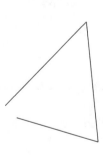
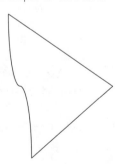
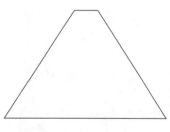

Ask if it is a triangle. [No.] Ask why not. [All triangles have three corners. The sides of triangles are connected to make those corners.]

Monitor understanding. Direct questions to children who do not participate.

Draw the second shape. Ask if it is a triangle. [No.] Ask why not. [All triangles have straight sides.]

Monitor understanding. Watch for difficulties among children who have a history of poor achievement.

Draw the third shape. Ask if it is a triangle. [No.] Ask why not. [All triangles have three corners. All triangles have three sides.]

Monitor understanding. Watch the eyes of children who do not respond for unspoken questions or indications of confusion.

Give each set of partners a rectangle. Be sure that some of the rectangles are squares. Ask the students what the shape is. Explain that each set of partners has a rectangle that is different from all the others. Call on someone to tell the class something that is true about the rectangle that he or she has. Ask if that is true about all the other rectangles. Continue like this until the children have identified these attributes of rectangles:

All rectangles have   four corners.
four sides.
square corners.
straight sides.

Next, draw the first of these shapes on the board:

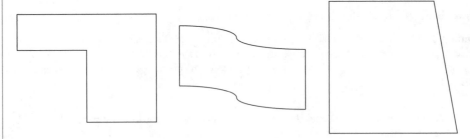

Ask if it is a rectangle. [No.] Ask why not. [All rectangles have four corners. All rectangles have four sides.]

Draw the second shape. Ask if it is a rectangle. [No.] Ask why not. [All rectangles have straight sides.]

Draw the third shape. Ask if it is a rectangle. [No.] Ask why not. [All rectangles have square corners.]

Monitor understanding. Throughout the entire development of rectangle attributes, watch for children who do not understand.

Repeat this same process with the circles and then with the squares. Lead the children to identify that all circles are curved, are the same size in all directions, and have no straight sides. Use the following nonexamples to reinforce those attributes:

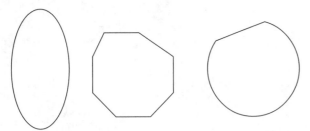

Lead the children to identify that all squares have four sides, four corners, straight sides, square corners, and sides that are equal. Use the following nonexamples to reinforce those attributes.

Monitor understanding. Ask further questions of children who do not understand. Provide additional explanations as needed.

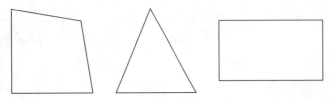

Direct the attention of the class to the picture at the top of the first student page. Explain that in this picture, there are a circle and a square. Have the children place a finger on top of the square.

Monitor understanding. Move around the room, checking that all the children have correctly identified the square.

Ask for someone to tell the class what he or she knows about squares. Ask for further help until all the necessary attributes of squares have been described. Repeat this process with the circle. Have the children place a finger on the circle and then have them tell about circles.

Monitor understanding. Listen carefully to ensure that all the children correctly understand the attributes of squares and circles.

Direct the children's attention to the second picture on the first student page. Have the children identify and then give the characteristics of rectangles and triangles.

Monitor understanding. Listen carefully to ensure that all the children correctly understand the attributes of rectangles and triangles.

Practice

Direct the children's attention to the shapes in the *Check Understanding* part of the lesson. Tell them to color the circles red. Then tell them to color the squares green. Next, tell them to color the rectangles blue. Finally, tell them to color the triangles yellow.

Monitor understanding. Move around the room while the children are working, to check their understanding. Provide additional explanation to any children who need it.

Closure

Ask the children to tell you what they have learned about circles, squares, rectangles, and triangles.

Follow-Up

Have the children take the practice page home with them and use it to explain to their parents what they know about circles, squares, rectangles, and triangles.

Exercises and Activities

1. Consider the topic *parallelograms*. Create a list of ways that each of the six big ideas of geometry (straightness, congruency, similarity, parallelism, perpendicularity, and symmetry) relates to parallelograms.
2. Consider the capital letter *W*:

Create a list of ways that each of the six big ideas of geometry (straightness, congruency, similarity, parallelism, perpendicularity, and symmetry) relates to the letter.
3. Choose a lesson on geometry from a published elementary school mathematics textbook series.
   a. Write a lesson plan that follows the teaching suggestions in the teacher's guide.
   b. Identify the parts of the lesson that develop the concept(s) of the lesson.

c. Expand the lesson by adding more development of the concepts being taught. Use the big ideas of geometry and the ways that those big ideas relate to the lesson concepts to build understanding of those concepts.

d. Identify kinesthetic activity that is included in the lesson.

e. Add more kinesthetic activity to the lesson.

f. Identify parts of the lesson that include student communication about the concept(s) taught in the lesson.

g. Plan more opportunities for communication about the lesson concepts from or among the children.

h. Identify the parts of the lesson designed to monitor the learning of the students.

i. Add more continual monitoring of learning to the lesson plan.

4. Read "Standard 9: Geometry and Spatial Sense" on pages 48–50 of *Curriculum and Evaluation Standards for School Mathematics*, published in 1989 by the NCTM. Then read the discussions of "The Geometry Standard" on pages 41–43, 96–101, 164–169, and 232–239 of *Principles and Standards for School Mathematics*, published in 2000 by the NCTM. Identify what you believe to be the most important and useful information provided in the Standards about the teaching of geometry.

References and Related Readings

Clements, D. H., & Sarama, J. (2000). Young children's ideas about geometric shapes. *Teaching Children Mathematics, 6*, 482–487.

Fuys, D. J., & Lebov, A. K. (1997). Concept learning in geometry. *Teaching Children Mathematics, 3*, 248–251.

Lerch, H. H. (1981). *Teaching elementary school mathematics: An active learning approach.* Boston: Houghton Mifflin.

National Council of Teachers of Mathematics. (1989). *Curriculum and evaluation standards for school mathematics.* Reston, VA: Author.

National Council of Teachers of Mathematics. (2000). *Principles and standards for school mathematics.* Reston, VA: Author.

Thornton, C. A., Tucker, B. F., Dossey, J. A., & Bazik, E. F. (1983). *Teaching mathematics to children with special needs.* Menlo Park, CA: Addison-Wesley.

Websites

http://www.corestandards.org/the-standards/mathematics
The Common Core State Standards for Mathematics can be found at this site.

http://mathcentral.uregina.ca/
Lessons and activities on geometry can be located on this site.

www.proteacher.com/
Activities and lesson plans on geometry can be located on this site.

www.sedl.org/
Construction and geometry with a link to standards-based activities.

eleven

DATA ANALYSIS AND PROBABILITY

Getting Information from Data and Measuring Likelihood

CHAPTER OUTLINE

Data Analysis and Probability—Two Distinct but Related Areas of Mathematics
Data Analysis
    Emphasizing the Big Ideas of Data Analysis
    From Exploratory Experiences toward
    Conceptual Understanding: A Typical K–4
    Development of Data Analysis
    Adapting a Data Analysis Lesson
    Using Data Analysis to Solve Problems

Probability
    Emphasizing the Big Ideas of Probability
    From Exploratory Experiences toward
    Conceptual Understanding: A Typical
    K–4 Development of Probability
    Using Probability to Solve Problems
Exercises and Activities

Data Analysis and Probability—Two Distinct but Related Areas of Mathematics

Statistics (or *data analysis*, as it is sometimes called) and *probability* are two distinct areas of mathematics, but the two fields are related. *Inferential statistics*—procedures used to make inferences about populations from representative data sets—is a field of study that is very dependent on probability. However, statistics in elementary school is mostly descriptive, dealing with ways to gather, organize, describe, and present sets of data. The field of *descriptive statistics* relies very little on probability.

In elementary school, probability and data analysis are normally developed independently. Although the elementary school mathematics textbook may present data analysis and probability in the same chapter, the two topics will generally appear as two distinct sections of the chapter. We will, therefore, follow the same pattern in this chapter. We will first examine data analysis (statistics), and then we will examine probability. We will emphasize the content and the approach to this content that one would expect to find in elementary school mathematics.

Data Analysis

Emphasizing the Big Ideas of Data Analysis

As was done in the earlier chapters of this book, we attempt in this chapter to identify big ideas—in this case, the big ideas of data analysis and probability. These big ideas are constantly recurring and can serve as a basis for developing students understanding of data analysis and probability. Of course, the language used when the teacher is discussing the big ideas with children should be developmentally appropriate for those children. With young children, the language should be informal and relate to specific situations that the children are experiencing. The language used with older children should be more formal and more precise.

The first big idea of data analysis is: *when appropriate data are gathered from a particular source, these data can inform you about that source.* With young children, data produced by counting might be used to describe the class or the children's families. Older children might gather data from a sample that has been selected from some larger group of people and then use those data to describe the larger group. At every level, however, this big idea should be emphasized. If someone collects *appropriate* data, then those data are *useful information* and can be used to *answer questions.*

The second big idea of data analysis that we have chosen to emphasize is: *well-organized data are more informative than data that are not well organized.* At every level, when data are gathered, students should be encouraged—and sometimes even required—to organize these data. As the children progress, they should learn to create tables to present the organized data. As this big idea is emphasized, students should learn to automatically think about *how data should be organized* to make it more useful for answering the questions that they wish to answer.

The third big idea of data analysis is: *appropriate graphic representation can make data more understandable.* As students progress through the elementary school mathematics program, they learn to use a wide variety of graphs, each of which has advantages in particular situations. The simplest graphs are merely visual representations of organized data, while the more-complex graphs provide visual representations that use statistics that are descriptive of the data set. However, throughout the development, the emphasis should be on *which graph is most appropriate* to present the information that we wish to convey.

The fourth big idea of data analysis is: *descriptive statistics (numbers) can be used to describe a set of data.* The notion of *descriptive statistics* begins with simple descriptors such as the number of items in the set of data and the greatest or least number in the set of data. Older students should learn to use averages to describe sets of data. Still older students should use a variety of *measures of central tendency* (means, medians, and modes) and *measures of spread* (range and possibly even standard deviation).

From Exploratory Experiences toward Conceptual Understanding:

A Typical K–4 Development of Data Analysis

Data Analysis in Kindergarten and First Grade.　In kindergarten and first grade, children's exposure to data analysis is generally limited to the simplest kind of data gathering and data organization. Often, the learning activity is a counting exercise. For example, after children have made various choices, the class might count the number of children who have made each choice and then write (record) those numbers. Or, the children might observe an experiment, count the times some outcome happens, and record the results. Their exposure to data organization might be a part of a classification activity, where they group objects by type, color, size, or function, then count the objects in each group and record the results. Often, these activities may be introduced by asking a question, and the activity—the counting, the grouping, or whatever the children do—is designed to answer the question.

In first grade, a class activity might be to survey a group of people (maybe the members of the class), organize the data, and then use that information to answer questions about the group that was surveyed. During the early years, the data-gathering and -organizing activities will look like counting and classification activities, but these early experiences provide a foundation for later learning of data analysis. The following sequence of activities illustrates how kindergarten and first-grade teachers might begin to develop children's understanding of data analysis.

Activity 11.01   Guess and Check

Place two white counting chips, four red counting chips, and three blue counting chips in a cap.

Hold the cap in front of the class. Have the children guess what is in the cap. Then take out a red chip. Hold it up so the children can see it, and tell the class that there are some red chips in the cap. Take out a white chip, hold it up, and tell the class that there are some white chips in the cap. Take out a blue chip, hold it up, and tell the class that there are some blue chips in the cap. Have the children guess whether there are more red, white, or blue chips. Write on the board the number of children who guessed each color.

Ask how we could find out what guess was correct. [Look in the cap.]

Empty the cap onto a desk and have children come to the front and count how many chips of each color were in the cap.

Activity 11.02   Guess and Survey to Check

Begin the activity by leading the children in a discussion of different kinds of pets people might have. Some pets live indoors; some live outside. Some pets are very small (some people even have ant farms), and some pets are very large (horses). Some people do not have pets. Others may have many pets.

To get the children thinking about the number of pets people might have, ask questions such as, "If I had a cat, a fish, and a dog, how many pets would I have?" "If Lily had a black cat and a black-and-white spotted cat, how many pets would she have?" "If Chad had a mother dog with two puppies, how many pets would Chad have?"

Tell the children that you want everyone to guess the answers to a question. Then ask, "What is the largest number of pets anyone in the class has?" Use tally marks to record the children's responses. Keep the tally marks on the board.

Ask if anyone knows how the class can check to see whose guess is correct. Explain that we can ask all the children in the class how many pets they have. Tell them that this is called a *survey*.

Write the numbers 0 to 10 in a column on the board. Then ask each class member, "How many pets do you have at your house?" Use tally marks beside the numbers to record the children's responses.

After the survey is complete, ask the children if anyone's guess was correct. Ask other questions: "What is the smallest number of pets that anyone has?" "How many people have two pets?" (It may be necessary for children to come to the board and count the tally marks.) "Do more people have two pets or three pets?"

Activity 11.03   Lines

Begin the activity by leading the children in a discussion of different kinds of clothes people might wear. Direct the children's attention to different kinds of shirts that children in the class are wearing. Be sure that they notice that shirts either have buttons or do not.

Have the children wearing shirts with buttons line up. Then have those wearing shirts without buttons form a line beside the first line. Direct the students' attention to the length of each line. Ask what they can tell from the lengths of the lines. [If the line is longer, there are more with that kind of shirt.]

Data Analysis in the Second and Third Grades. In second and third grades, children continue to collect data in natural settings and gain more experience in conducting simple surveys in order to answer questions. They learn to use more formal language to describe these activities.

The children begin to use tables to organize data and use graphs to represent their data. They also learn to create a primitive bar graph by stacking squares to represent the number in each category. They learn to interpret, and later to create, bar graphs and pictographs. The students also conduct experiments and record and graph the outcomes.

The following sequence of activities illustrates how second- and third-grade teachers might continue to develop children's understanding of data analysis.

Activity 11.04 Data Stacking

Prepare a bulletin board for this activity in the following way: Cut a 1-inch by 4-inch strip of construction paper in each of these four colors: red, blue, yellow, and green. With a black marker, write the color name on each strip. Tack the four strips end to end parallel to the bottom of the bulletin board:

red	blue	yellow	green

Hand out to all the children a duplicated sheet showing four 1-inch squares. Have the children select a red crayon (check to see that everyone has the correct color).

Ask them to color the inside of one square red. Next, have them select a blue crayon and color another square blue. In the same way, have them color the third square yellow, and the last one green. Tell the children to pick their favorite color from those four and cut out the square that is their favorite color.

Have the children come to the bulletin board, one at a time, with the square showing their favorite color. Help them tack their squares to the board to create a simple "bar" graph.

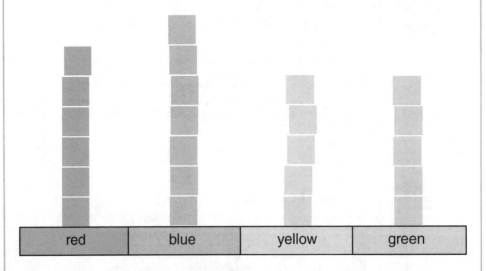

After the children have stacked their favorite colors, ask them to tell what they can see from the stacked colors.

Activity 11.05   Tally Marks

When the children are not watching, randomly place five red and seven yellow counting chips in the spaces of an egg carton. Explain to the children that some colored chips are in the carton and you are going to tell them what they are. Tell them the colors in the order that they happen to be placed in the carton. For example, you might say, "Red, red, yellow, yellow, yellow, red, yellow, yellow, red, yellow, red, yellow."

Ask how many red chips are in the carton and how many yellow chips are in the carton. Write their guesses on the board, then ask someone to count the chips to see who was right.

Explain that it is difficult to remember how many of each color was called. Tell the class that *tally marks* can be used to help keep track of how many of each color there are. Write the color names "Red" and "Yellow" on the board. Ask a child to take the egg carton and say the colors in the same order that they are in inside the carton. As the child says the colors, make tally marks next to the color names to show how many times each color has been called. When all the colors have been called, point to the marks and explain that these marks are called *tally marks*. Count the marks by "Red" and explain that since there are five tally marks here, there were five red chips. Count the marks next to "Yellow" and explain that since there are seven marks here, there were seven yellow chips.

Change the numbers of red chips and yellow chips in the egg carton, and repeat the activity, except have the children make tally marks to help them remember how many times each color was called.

Activity 11.06   Survey Tally

Tell the children that they can use tally marks when gathering information in a survey. Explain that you and the students are going to survey the class to see how many children in the class prefer baseball, football, or fishing.

Write the words "Baseball," "Football," and "Fishing" on the board. Have a child come to the board and use tally marks to record children's preferences. First, have the child who is recording place a mark by his or her own choice. Then, go around the room and have the other children indicate their choices, one by one. Go slowly to be sure that the tallies are made correctly.

Have another child come to the front and count the tallies. Ask the class to explain the results of the survey.

Activity 11.07 Frequency Tables

This activity is a follow-up to activity 11.06. After the children have used tallies to record their preference for baseball, football, or fishing, and after they have found the number who prefer each sport, create a table showing those numbers. Point out that the number who chose each sport is called the *frequency* of that choice. Explain that a table that shows the frequencies is called a *frequency table*.

Sport	Frequency
Baseball	6
Football	9
Fishing	5

Activity 11.08 Categories and Numbers

Draw a horizontal line on the board.

Explain that you and the children are going to make a *bar graph*. Have the children count to see how many students are in the class. Write "Boys" and "Girls" below the horizontal line. Next, draw a vertical line on the board and mark the inches where shown.

Cut two strips of colored paper about 2 inches wide and 20 inches long. Have children come to the board, hold the strips by the vertical line, and cut one so the length in inches matches the number of boys. The second strip should be cut so that the length matches the number of girls.

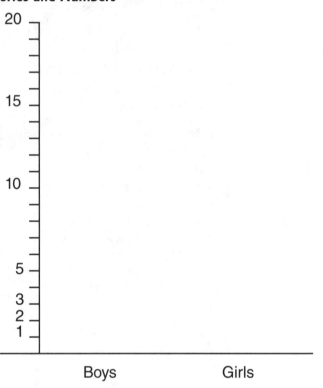

Show the children how to tape the strips onto the graph so the strips (the bars) show how many boys and how many girls are in the class. Explain that the length of the bars shows how many.

Activity 11.09 Tally Graph

Conduct a class survey of how many people have shoes with laces and how many have shoes without laces, using tally marks to record the data. Then lead the class to create a bar graph showing the results.

Activity 11.10   Stickers Can Show How Many

Completion of this activity requires three kinds of stickers that are readily available in most teachers' stores. You will also need a large sheet of poster board. In this example, suppose you have stickers picturing cats, flowers, and skunks.

Draw a vertical line on the poster board and print "Cat," "Flower," and "Skunk" to the left of the line as shown.

Tell the class that you have three kinds of stickers. Show them to the class. Explain that they are going to use the stickers to make a *pictograph*. Tell them that they will use the pictograph to show which kind of sticker the class prefers.

Have the children tell, one by one, which sticker they prefer, and place stickers on the graph to create a pictograph to show their preferences. Ask what the pictograph shows us about the class.

Data Analysis in Fourth Grade.   In fourth grade, students continue to collect data in natural settings and gain more experience in conducting surveys to answer questions. They may also begin to gather data from experiments and use their understanding of data organization to make sense of those results. The idea that organization of data makes the data easier to understand should be constantly reinforced. Students continue to learn to use more formal language to describe the data-gathering and -organizing activities.

In fourth grade, students will learn to interpret and construct broken-line graphs and circle graphs. As the children are introduced to these new kinds of graphs, they should develop a clear understanding that bar graphs and pictographs are used to show frequencies within categories, broken-line graphs are used to show change over time, and circle graphs are used to show the relative sizes of the parts when some quantity is divided into parts.

The children will learn to read and interpret line graphs that show how two variables are related. They will be exposed to box-and-whisker plots and stem-and-leaf plots, both of which provide visual imagery of the spread within data sets. They will use information from tables and graphs to solve problems and use the mean, median, and mode to describe sets of data.

The following sequence of activities illustrates how some of these concepts might be developed.

Activity 11.11   In the Box

This activity requires a small cardboard box that is less than 8.5 inches by 12 inches but larger than 5 inches by 7 inches. The box should have an open top.

Use masking tape to make a line on the floor about 8 feet from a wall. Place the box against the wall. Explain to the children that you are going to have everyone in the class stand behind the line and try to toss a cube into the box. Point out how many students are in the class. Ask them to guess how many will toss the cube into the box. Write down their guesses. Then ask, "How can we keep track of how many hit the box and how many miss the box?" [We can use tally marks to record each hit and each miss.]

Choose a student to tally the results. Have that person toss first, record the outcome, then continue to record the rest of the outcomes. When everyone has had a turn, count the tallies.

Finally, have each child create a bar graph showing the results of the experiment.

Activity 11.12   Predicting and Checking

This activity requires two cubes. Write the numbers 1, 1, 1, 1, 1, and 2 on the six faces of one cube. Write 4, 4, 4, 4, 5, and 6 on the faces of the other cube.

Show the class the numbers on each cube. Ask the children what would be the least possible outcome if you tossed the two cubes and added the two numbers showing. What would be the greatest possible outcome? What other outcomes would be possible? Write all the possibilities in a column on the board.

Explain that the two cubes will be tossed 30 times. Ask which outcome will occur most often. Choose a student to record each outcome by placing a tally mark next to that number on the board. When all the tosses have been recorded, count the tallies. Whose prediction was the best one?

Have each student create a bar graph showing the results of the experiment.

Activity 11.13   Showing the Ups and Downs

Have the students record the outdoor temperature at the same time every day for a week. At the end of the week, show the class how to construct a broken-line graph similar to this one.

Explain that a *broken-line graph* shows a change that takes place over time.

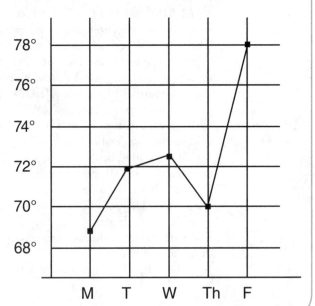

Activity 11.14   Another Week

Have the students record the outdoor temperature at the same time every day for a second week. At the end of the week, have the students work with partners to construct a broken-line graph showing the changes in the temperature for this week.

Activity 11.15   Selfish Sam

Tell the class this story:

A boy named Sam was very selfish. One day, when he had 12 pieces of candy, he decided to share it with three friends: Deb, Jo, and Al. Sam gave each of his friends 2 pieces of candy, but he kept 6 pieces for himself. Sam thought he was being fair with his friends because, after all, it was his candy. But, for some reason, his friends were upset.

Ask the class to tell why his friends were upset. Tell the class that they are going to make a different kind of graph that will show how the candy was divided. A graph like this might help Sam to see why the way he shared the candy upset his friends.

Draw a circle on the board. Ask what fraction of the candy Sam kept for himself. [One half] Draw a line separating the circle into two equal parts. Write "Sam" inside one of the two halves. Ask what part of the rest of the candy went to each of Sam's friends. [Each of them got one third of the remaining candy.] Divide the second half of the circle into three equal parts. Write "Al" in one part, "Jo" in one part, and "Deb" in the last part.

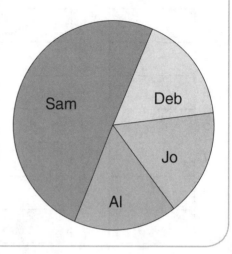

Explain that this is called a *circle graph*.

Adapting a Data Analysis Lesson

We will now examine a typical data analysis lesson that would probably appear early in a grade 2 textbook. Data are being gathered, analyzed, and graphed. However, to the child, the lesson appears to be about counting. We will begin by showing a lesson plan that is based on suggestions that you would likely find in the teacher's edition of the textbook.

LESSON OBJECTIVE

The student will solve problems by making a bar graph.

Lesson Opener

Place some (fewer than 10) objects on a table. Choose a child to come to the table, count the objects, write the number of objects on the board, and stand next to the number. Repeat the process with two other children. Ask who counted the most objects. Who counted the fewest objects?

Ask the children what kinds of shirts they like to wear. When a type of shirt is described, ask who else likes that kind of shirt.

Development

Direct the attention of the class to the picture on the first page of the lesson. Ask what is pictured. [Shirts on hangers] Ask how they are different. [The colors are different.]

Have the children count the red shirts. Ask how many red shirts there are. [Six] Direct the students to the columns of boxes below the picture. Have them use a red crayon to color the bottom six boxes in the first column—one for each red shirt. Ask them to do the same for shirts of each of the other colors pictured.

Monitoring Learning

Be sure that the children have counted correctly and have colored the correct number of boxes in each column:

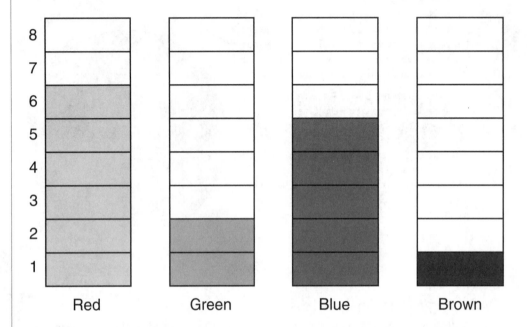

Direct their attention to the numbers next to the first column. Ask, "What do these numbers tell us?" [How many of each color] Explain that if they look at those numbers, they can tell how many without counting the boxes.

Practice

Have the children look at the picture on the second page of the lesson. Point out that this is another *graph*. Ask, "What has been counted?" [Different kinds of shoes] Ask, "How can we tell how many of each kind there were without counting?" [Look at the numbers beside the boxes.]

Explain that the graph shows what kinds of shoes the children in a class were wearing. The graph can help them answer questions. Tell the children that you are going to read some questions, and that they should look at the graph to figure out the answers.

Read the questions one at a time. Give the children time to find the answer. Then tell the children to write their answers in the answer boxes provided.

Closure

At the end of math time, remind the class that they have learned to use a graph to solve problems.

This is a good lesson. There is some development of the new ideas. There is some kinesthetic activity. There is visual representation of the ideas. There is communication from the children. And there are opportunities for the teacher to monitor the learning of the children.

However, we will revise the lesson plan to *increase* the amount of development. We will include *more* kinesthetic activity and more visual representations. We will plan for *even more* communication from and among the children. We will plan for *more continual* monitoring of learning.

LESSON OBJECTIVE

The student will solve problems by making a bar graph.

Lesson Opener

Scatter some (fewer than 10) counting chips on the floor at the front of the room. Choose a child to come pick up some, but not all, of the chips. Repeat the process with two other children. Ask the class who they think has picked up the most chips.

Have one of the children line up his or her chips in a row on the overhead projector:

Then have each of the other children line up their chips next to the first child's:

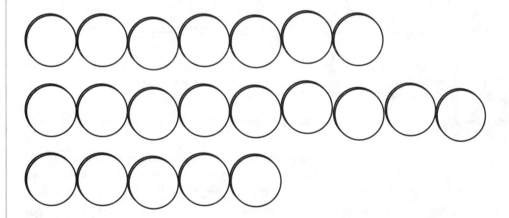

Monitor understanding. Watch the children's faces. At this point, most of the children will already see the answer. See if you can identify those who don't.

Ask the children if they can tell now who picked up the most chips. Who picked up the fewest?

Monitor understanding. Do the children whom you earlier identified as not yet seeing the answer now understand? Have someone count the chips to see how many each child picked up. Write the numbers on the board. Ask which number indicates the most chips and which number indicates the fewest chips. Ask if the students got the right answers when they looked at the rows.

Development

Ask the children if they like to wear shirts with buttons or shirts without buttons. When a child describes a type of shirt, ask who else likes that kind of shirt. Point out that some of the children are wearing shirts that have buttons and some are wearing shirts without buttons.

Have all the children who are wearing a shirt with buttons stand up; then have them sit down. Have all the children who are wearing a shirt without buttons stand up; then have them sit down. Ask how many have shirts with buttons. How many have shirts without buttons? Ask if there are more with buttons or more without buttons. If the children try to guess, accept their guesses, but then ask if they are absolutely sure their answers are correct.

Monitor understanding. Take note of children whose guesses indicate a lack of understanding.

Tell the children that they will look again to see who has buttons and who does not, but this time they will do it differently. Have all the children wearing shirts with buttons line up in a straight line. Then have those wearing shirts without buttons line up next to the first line. Be sure that the children are spread out evenly in both lines.

Ask which line has the most children. Ask what that tells us about the shirts. [The longest line tells us there are more shirts of that kind.]

Monitor understanding. At this point, nearly everyone should understand. Provide further explanation if it is needed.

Have children count to see how many there are of each kind of shirt.

Explain that instead of lining up people, we sometimes use objects to represent the people. Write "Buttons" on a card, and write "No buttons" on another card. Show the cards to the class and have someone read each of the cards. Place them on the table with one card directly above the other. Give everyone a square of paper. Have the children come forward one at a time and place their paper squares in line by the cards:

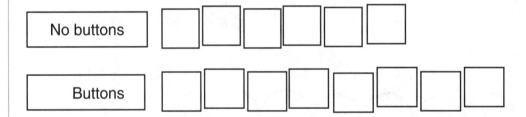

When all the squares are lined up in place, have the children gather around the table to see the result. Explain that what they have made is called a *graph*. Tell them that graphs like this help them see how many are in each group and help them to compare the groups to see which has more or which has fewer.

Monitor understanding. As before, observe the children's reactions to see who understands and who does not. Provide further explanations or additional examples as needed.

Tell the children that a graph makes it easier to see the answers to questions. Tell the children to suppose that they noticed that shirts come in many colors. Ask what questions they might have about the colors of shirts. Let the children suggest different questions, but lead them to questions about numbers of shirts in different colors.

Have the children look at the picture on the first lesson page. Ask what is pictured. [Shirts on hangers] Ask how they are different. [The colors are different.] Tell them that they are going to make a graph showing the numbers of shirts in the different colors.

Ask the children how many red shirts there are. [Six] Ask how they can find out. [Count them.] Have the children look at the columns of boxes below the picture. Ask how they can use those boxes to show how many red shirts there are. Have them use a red crayon to color the bottom six boxes in the first column—one for each red shirt. Have the children work with partners to figure out how many green shirts there are. When the partners are sure, have them color that many green boxes. Have the partners do the same for the blue shirts and the brown shirts.

Monitor understanding. Move around the class, observing to be sure that the shirts are being counted correctly and that the correct number of boxes are colored for each category:

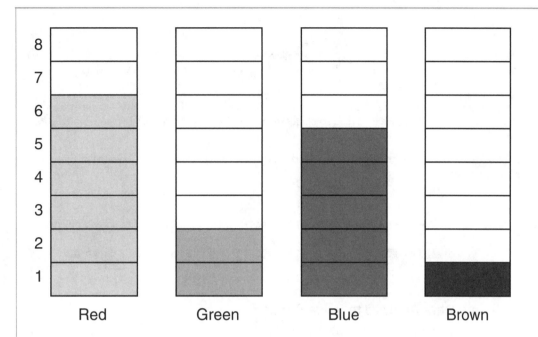

Ask the students what they can see from the graph. Which color has the most shirts? Which color has the fewest?

Direct their attention to the numbers next to the first column. Ask what those numbers tell us. [How many of each color] Explain that if they look at those numbers, they can tell how many without counting the boxes.

Show this graph with a paper covering the bottoms of the columns:

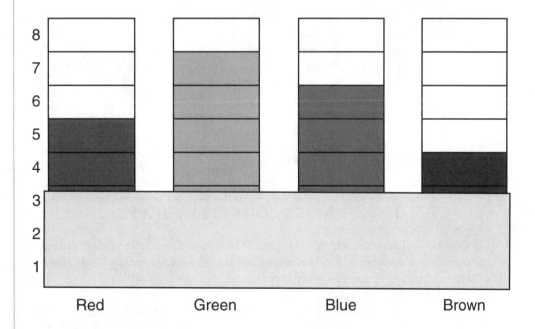

Ask how many red boxes there are. How many brown boxes? How many blue boxes? How many green boxes?

Monitor understanding. Pay attention to the students who do not volunteer answers. They may need more explanation.

Point out to the children that they are able to see how many without counting.

Using Data Analysis to Solve Problems

Data (information) are used to solve problems in all the grades. Sometimes the students will gather that data from the text of a book or website, but at other times, the data are provided in tables or graphs. In general, a problem is posed in the form of a question that is of interest to the students. The strategy used to solve the problem (answer the question) is to use or make a table or graph. And, of course, the strategy may also include gathering appropriate data. Older children may choose the questions that should be asked to produce the needed information, or they might even design a survey instrument to gather appropriate data.

By grades 2 or 3, students begin to be introduced to different kinds of graphs, each of which should be used with a particular type of data. The problem-solving process may then include the use of, or selection of, an appropriate graph. For younger children, the organization of the data or the representation of the data in an appropriate graph may make the solution obvious. Older children may be required to infer answers from the existing information, the tables, or the graphs.

Probability

Emphasizing the Big Ideas of Probability

As with data analysis, probability has several big ideas. They are big ideas because they are constantly recurring and because they form the basis for other probability concepts. The big ideas also provide a useful framework for the study of and the understanding of probability in the elementary grades.

One big idea of probability is the notion of *likelihood: Some events (things that happen) are more likely than other events. Some things are very likely to happen, and some may be sure to happen. Some events are very unlikely to happen, and some cannot happen—they are impossible.* The awareness of *likelihood* is the beginning of the understanding of probability.

Another big idea of probability is: *likelihood can be estimated.* Through observation of events that occur naturally and observation of the outcomes of experiments, we can estimate how likely particular events are to occur. *Estimates of likelihood* can be improved by such observation, particularly if the data gathered are well organized.

A third big idea of probability is: *likelihood (the probability that an event will occur) can be measured.* Measurement of probability requires a formal definition of probability. After students have learned to measure the probability of a particular event, the study of probability becomes more formal. The language and notation become more precise. The study of the probability of more-complex events becomes possible.

From Exploratory Experiences toward Conceptual Understanding: A Typical K–4 Development of Probability

Probability in Kindergarten through Second Grade.   In kindergarten through second grade, children begin to think about how likely things are to happen. They decide whether things will happen, might happen, or cannot happen. In kindergarten, children typically think about the likelihood of events in only natural, informal settings. By the end of grade 1, however, children will usually have considered events presented in textbook examples.

First-graders will be exposed to a fraction as part of a set. For example, if one of three animals is a dog, then one third of the animals are dogs. Although this is not considered to be probability, such thinking is the foundation of measurement of probability.

In second grade, children may begin using experimentation to determine how likely outcomes are. They may make predictions and then experiment to check those predictions. They may also consider the possibilities and identify the one that is most likely.

The following sequence of activities illustrates how a teacher might develop these probability concepts.

Activity 11.16   Who'll Come Out?

Tell the class that someone may be hiding behind your desk. Ask someone to look behind the desk to see if anyone is there. After he or she has indicated that no one is hiding there, have another of the children hide behind the desk. (For example, you might have Anna hide there.)

Then tell the class that you are going to have someone come out from behind the desk. Ask who they think it will be. [Anna] Ask why they are sure. [Anna is the only one behind the desk.] Tell them that they are right. It is sure to be Anna. That *will happen*. Say, "Come out from behind the desk!" [Anna will come out.]

Next, have two other children hide behind the desk. (For example, Juan and Emma might be chosen.) Tell the class that you are going to have someone come out from behind the desk. Ask who they think it will be. [It might be Juan, or it might be Emma.] Ask who thinks it might be Juan. Tell them that they are right. That *might happen*. Ask who thinks it might be Emma. Tell them that they are right. That also *might happen*.

Ask how many think it will be Superman. Ask why it could not be Superman. Tell them that they are right. Superman isn't real. That *can't happen*.

Repeat the activity with other examples that will happen, might happen, or can't happen.

Activity 11.17   Sure to Happen, May Happen, Impossible

For this activity, you will need a small box with a lid and counting chips in two different colors, such as red and blue.

Place a handful of red chips and a handful of blue chips on the table. Then hold up the box and ask the children what they think is in the box. Allow them to make guesses even if their guesses are not reasonable. Tell them that you are going to empty the box onto the table. Ask how many think it will be an elephant. Ask why it can't be an elephant. Tell them that they are right; it can't be an elephant. The box isn't big enough. That would be *impossible*.

Next, take the lid off and pretend to pour out its contents. Say, "Oh! The box was empty." Have the children watch while you place about 10 red chips in the box. Put on the lid and shake the box.

Tell the class that you are going to take something out of the box. Ask them what they think it will be. Ask why they think it will be a red chip. Ask if they are sure. Take out 1 chip. Tell them that they were right. It was a red chip. That was *sure to happen*.

Let the children see you place about 10 blue chips in the box with the red chips. Put on the lid and shake the box. Tell the students that you are going to take something out of the box. Ask them what they think it will be. Will it be a red chip? [It might be.] Tell them that they are right again. That *may happen*. Will it be a blue chip? That *may happen*.

Ask if it could be a yellow chip. No; that is *impossible*.

Activity 11.18 Best Guess, Worst Guess

For this activity, you will need a small box with a lid and counting chips in three different colors, such as yellow, red, and green.

Hold up the box so the class can see that it is empty. Write "20 yellow chips" on the board. Have a child come forward to count out that many yellow chips and place them in the box. Write "6 red chips" on the board. Have a child come forward to count out that many red chips and place them in the box. Write "1 green chip" on the board. Have a child come forward to place 1 green chip in the box.

Shake the box. Tell the children that 1 chip will be taken out of the box. Ask what color it might be. [Yellow, red, or green] Tell them that you want them to guess what color will be taken out of the box. Ask the children what they think would be the best guess. Why? Ask them what they think would be the worst guess. Why?

Write "Yellow," "Red," and "Green" on the board. Have a child come to the front and, without looking, take a chip from the box. Have that child make a tally mark by the color of chip that was drawn and place the chip back in the box. Have that same child stay at the board to record the rest of the outcomes. Move around the room, giving each child a chance to draw a chip from the box. Be sure that the chip is replaced and the box is shaken after each drawing.

When everyone has had a turn, have the children look at the results to see if they had picked the best guess and the worst guess. Point out that the *most likely outcome* is usually the best guess, and the *least likely outcome* is usually the worst guess.

Repeat the activity using other combinations of chips. Be sure that one color has many more chips than the other colors and that one color has a lot fewer chips than any other color.

Activity 11.19 Guess and Check

For this activity, you will need a small paper bag and 20 nickels. While the children are watching, use permanent markers to mark a red X on 12 nickels and a black X on 6 nickels. Leave the other 2 nickels unmarked.

Place the nickels in the bag.

Tell the children that everyone will have a chance to take a nickel out of the bag. Ask them to guess which kind of nickel will be drawn the most: red X, black X, or plain. Record how many children guess each kind.

Write "Red X," "Black X," and "Plain" on the board. Choose a child to be the recorder. Have the recorder come to the front and draw a nickel from the bag, and then use a tally mark to record the outcome. Place the nickel back in the bag and shake it.

Have the recorder make a tally mark for each outcome as the children come forward, one at a time, to draw a nickel. Be sure that the nickel is replaced after each drawing.

When everyone has had a turn, ask what guess turned out to be the best one. Remind the students that the best guess is usually the *most likely outcome*.

Activity 11.20 Good Guessing

Repeat activity 11.19 using different numbers of colored chips of different colors. Have the children discuss why some guesses are good ones and others are not good guesses. Ask how the number of chips of different colors is related to good guesses.

Have everyone write a short note to the teacher explaining how to make good guesses.

Probability in Third and Fourth Grades. In third and fourth grades, children will continue to consider likelihood informally. They will identify outcomes that are certain, possible, or impossible. The children will also choose from possible outcomes those that are more likely, less likely, most likely, and impossible. They will experiment to discover the most likely outcome.

In fourth grade, children will begin to think about likelihood more formally, by making estimates of likelihood by first considering all the possibilities. They will conduct experiments where the possibilities are obvious (for example, flip coins or spin spinners). Fourth-graders may formally define probability as *m* chances out of *n* possibilities. They will begin to consider pairs of events, like flipping a penny and flipping a quarter.

By grade 4, children will have formally defined *probability*. They will use the definition to determine the probability of events. They will also use experimentation to verify probabilities.

The following activities demonstrate how a teacher might develop some of these ideas of probability.

Activity 11.21 Possibilities I

For this activity, you will need a small paper bag and counting chips in four colors, such as red, blue, yellow, and green.

Show the students that the paper bag is empty by turning it upside down and shaking it. While they watch, place five red chips in the bag. Ask what is in the bag. [Some red chips] Place five blue chips in the bag. Ask what is in the bag. [Some red chips and some blue chips] Continue in the same way until there are five chips of each color in the bag.

Tell the class that you are going to take a chip out of the bag. Ask what color it will be. As each color is suggested, write that color on the board and ask if there are any other possibilities. Continue until all four possibilities have been named and they are listed on the board. Ask if it would be possible to get a white chip. [No.] Why not? [There are no white chips in the bag.]

Point out that all the possibilities have been listed. Any of those colors might be taken from the bag. Have the students come to the front, one at a time, to take a chip out of the bag. In each case, say, "Yes. That is one of the possibilities." Then replace the chip that was drawn. Continue until every color has been selected at least once. Ask why no one got a black chip. [That's not possible.] Ask why it is not possible to get a black chip. [No black chips are in the bag.]

Activity 11.22 Possibilities II

For this activity, you will need a cube with 1 written on two faces, 3 written on three faces, and 4 written on one face.

Pass the cube around so everyone can see what is on each face. Tell the class that the cube will be tossed, and we want to see what number will be on top. Ask what the possibilities are. [1, 3, or 4]

Have the children take turns tossing the cube. Record the outcomes. After each number has come up, point out that every possibility has happened. Ask why no one got a 2. [That's not possible.] Ask why it is not possible. [There are no 2s on the cube.]

Point out that some numbers came up more often than others. Ask why that happened. [There were more 3s and only one 4.]

Activity 11.23   Probabilities I

This activity is a follow-up to activity 11.22.

Have the children look at the cube and list the possibilities. [1, 3, and 4] Ask if these possibilities are equally likely. [No.] Why? [There are not the same number of 1s, 3s, and 4s.]

Ask how many faces a cube has. [Six] Ask if each of these faces could end up on top. [Yes.] Ask how many of the six faces have a 1 written on them. [Two] Write on the board "2 chances out of 6 possibilities will be 1." Ask how many faces have a 3 written on them. [Three] Write on the board "3 chances out of 6 possibilities will be 3." Ask how many faces have a 4 written on them. [Only one] Write on the board "1 chance out of 6 possibilities will be 4."

Explain that we would say that the *probability* that we will get a 1 is 2 out of 6. The probability that we will get a 3 is 3 out of 6. Ask what the probability that we will get a 4 is. [1 out of 6] What is the probability that we would get a 5? [0 out of 6]

Activity 11.24   Probabilities II

This activity is a follow-up to activity 11.23. You will need enough cubes for each set of partners. On all of the cubes, four faces will show a 2, one face will show a 5, and one face will show a 6.

Form groups of two or three partners. Give each group of partners a cube. Have them look at the cube, list the possibilities, and then write the probability for each possibility.

Discuss the results and check to be sure that everyone understands how to find the probabilities. Ask what the probability that you would get an 8 would be. [0 out of 6]

Activity 11.25   Predicting and Checking (variation 2)

Form groups of two or three partners. Give each group of partners a blank cube. Tell them that you want them to write either an 8 or a 10 on each face of the cube. They must decide how many of each number there will be.

After all the partner groups have finished writing a number on each face of their cubes, tell them to write the probability for each possibility.

Tell the class that you want each set of partners to think about the probabilities and predict how many times each possibility will happen if the cube is tossed 25 times. They should write down their predictions, then toss their cube 25 times and keep a record of the outcomes.

When everyone is finished, discuss the results. How accurate were the predictions? Why were they not exactly correct?

LESSON OBJECTIVE

The student will predict outcomes for probability experiments.

Lesson Opener

Show the class a small, empty paper bag. While the students are watching, place 3 red chips, 2 white chips, and 1 blue chip in the bag.

Tell the class that you are going to have a student draw one chip out of the bag. Ask the class to help you list all the possible outcomes.

Monitor understanding. Developing the concept of possible outcomes was the purpose of an earlier lesson. It is a basic concept, so it is important that you focus your attention on the children who are most likely to have misconceptions.

Ask the class if it is possible that the chip drawn will be blue. [Yes]
Is it possible that the chip drawn will be yellow? [No]
Is a black chip a possible outcome? [No]
Is a red chip possible? [Yes]
Is a white chip possible? [Yes]

Tell the class to suppose two chips would be drawn from the bag. Ask the children to list the possibilities. Have a child come to the board and record the possibilities. Continue until all the possibilities are listed.

Red Red	White White	Red White
Red blue	White blue	

Development

Remove the chips from the bag, and without the class watching, replace them with 15 yellow chips and 5 white chips.

Explain to the class that there are some white chips and some yellow chips in the bag. Tell them that someone will draw a chip, record the result, and then replace the chip in the bag. Repeat this pattern 10 times and record the results. Since there are only yellow chips and white chips in the bag, each outcome will be either yellow or white.

Ask the students to guess how many times the outcome will be white. Record their guesses.

Call on 10 students to come forward, one at a time, to draw a chip, record the color, and replace the chip in the bag. When the experiment is completed, compare the final result with the students' guesses.

Tell the class that you are going to repeat the experiment. Have the students guess, once again, how many times a white chip will be drawn. Record their guesses. Repeat the experiment. Compare the guesses with the results of the experiment.

Repeat the process again. Have students predict the results.

Monitor understanding. If a student's guesses are not improving, there is possibly a lack of understanding. Carry out the experiment again. Compare the student predictions with the outcome of the experiment.

Closure

Ask the class if they feel like the experiments made them better guessers.

Point out that gathering of experimental results can improve their ability to predict outcomes.

Using Probability to Solve Problems

In the elementary grades, problem solving using probability is focused on predicting future events. With younger children, that problem solving typically involves choosing a most likely future outcome. With younger children, the problem may be to determine whether a future outcome is impossible, possible, or sure to happen.

Exercises and Activities

1. Compare the original and revised versions of the *data analysis* lesson plan presented in this chapter. Identify:
   a. The additional development (if any)
   b. The additional visual representation of ideas (if any)
   c. The additional kinesthetic activity (if any)
   d. The additional student communication (if any)
   e. The additional monitoring of learning (if any)
   How can you revise the lesson to make it more effective?

2. Compare the original and revised versions of the *probability* plan presented in this chapter. Identify:
   a. The additional development (if any)
   b. The additional visual representation of ideas (if any)
   c. The additional kinesthetic activity (if any)
   d. The additional student communication (if any)
   e. The additional monitoring of learning (if any)
   How can you revise the lesson to make it more effective?

3. Find a lesson in a published K–4 mathematics textbook series that teaches students how to organize data.
   a. Follow the suggestions provided in the teacher's edition to prepare a lesson plan. Do not be creative. Follow the suggestions as exactly as you can.
   b. Revise the lesson plan by adding more development of the concepts, more visual representation of the ideas, more kinesthetic activity, more communication between and among the students, and suggestions for continual monitoring of learning.

4. Find a lesson in a published K–4 mathematics textbook series that teaches students how to make a bar graph.
   a. Follow the suggestions provided in the teacher's edition to prepare a lesson plan. Do not be creative. Follow the suggestions as exactly as you can.
   b. Revise the lesson plan by adding more development of the concepts, more visual representation of the ideas, more kinesthetic activity, more communication between and among students, and suggestions for continual monitoring of learning.

5. Find a lesson in a published K–4 mathematics textbook series that teaches students how to make a circle graph.
   a. Follow the suggestions provided in the teacher's edition to prepare a lesson plan. Do not be creative. Follow the suggestions as exactly as you can.
   b. Revise the lesson plan by adding more development of the concepts, more visual representation of the ideas, more kinesthetic activity, more communication between and among students, and suggestions for continual monitoring of learning.

6. Find a lesson in a published K–4 mathematics textbook series that teaches students how to use data gathered in an experiment to estimate the results if the experiment is repeated.
   a. Follow the suggestions provided in the teacher's edition to prepare a lesson plan. Do not be creative. Follow the suggestions as exactly as you can.

b. Revise the lesson plan by adding more development of the concepts, more visual representation of the ideas, more kinesthetic activity, more communication between and among students, and suggestions for continual monitoring of learning.

7. Describe an instructional/learning activity in which students toss a plastic cup to estimate the probability that it will fall right side up, the probability that it will fall upside down, and the probability that it will fall on its side.

References and Related Readings

National Council of Teachers of Mathematics. (2000). *Principles and standards for school mathematics*. Reston, VA: Author.

Tarr, J. E. (2002). Providing opportunities to learn probability concepts. *Teaching Children Mathematics, 8*, 482–487.

Websites

http://www.corestandards.org/the-standards/mathematics
The Common Core State Standards for Mathematics can be found at this site.

http://illuminations.nctm.org/
Data analysis and probability activities for pre-K through grade 4.

Activities to Take to Your Classroom

Index